Industries of Architecture

At a time when the technologies and techniques of producing the built environment are undergoing significant change, this book makes central architecture's relationship to industry. Contributors turn to historical and theoretical questions, as well as to key contemporary developments, taking a humanities approach to the *Industries of Architecture* that will be of interest to practitioners and industry professionals, as much as to academic researchers, teachers and students. How has modern architecture responded to mass production? How do we understand the necessarily social nature of production in the architectural office and on the building site? And how is architecture entwined within wider fields of production and reproduction – finance capital, the spaces of regulation, and management techniques? What are the particular effects of techniques and technologies (and above all their inter-relations) on those who labour in architecture, the buildings they produce, and the discursive frameworks we mobilise to understand them?

Katie Lloyd Thomas is a Senior Lecturer in Architecture at Newcastle University, UK, where she co-directs ARC, the Architecture Research Collaborative, and is an editor of the international journal *arq*. Her research is concerned with materiality in architecture and with feminist practice and theory. She is co-founder of the feminist collective 'taking place' (www.takingplace.org.uk) and edited *Material Matters* (Routledge, 2007). Her monograph *Preliminary Operations: Material theory and the architectural specification* is in preparation.

Tilo Amhoff is Senior Lecturer in Architectural Humanities at the University of Brighton, UK, and a Ph.D. candidate at the Bartlett School of Architecture (UCL). His research investigates the plan as a specific medium and cultural technique that established a particular way of administrating and governing various entities; such as the factory, the city, and the economy in late nineteenth- and early twentieth-century Germany. He is a founder member of *Netzwerk Architekturwissenschaft* (www.architekturwissenschaft.net).

Nick Beech is Lecturer in London's History at Queen Mary, University of London, UK. His research concerns the transformation of the construction industry and architectural professions during and immediately following the Second World War. Nick also researches British 'New Left' arguments of the mid-twentieth century relating to 'culture', 'the everyday' and state formation. He currently holds (2014–2016) an Andrew W. Mellon Foundation Fellowship with the Canadian Centre for Architecture.

Industries of Architecture invites us to rethink what constitutes the 'work' of architecture – in the past, the present, and in the future. In a reversal of the usual emphasis in the humanities on design as the exclusive field of architects' creative endeavors, *Industries of Architecture* offers an alternative view – one in which architects' engagement with labour, with legal systems, with manufacturing practices, and with business organisation are no longer treated as contingent, but as central to what architects do.

Adrian Forty, Professor Emeritus of Architectural History,
Bartlett School of Architecture, UCL, UK

Industries of Architecture offers intriguing new evidence of the breadth and depth of architecture's cultural diffusion. Its exploration of myriad aspects of architectural production supplies valuable historical documentation and useful theoretical strategies to shift the focus of architectural history away from the singular presence of architectural objects and toward the conditions and connections that make those objects possible.

Aggregate Architectural History Collaborative

CRITIQUES: Critical Studies in Architectural Humanities
A project of the Architectural Humanities Research Association

Series Editor: Jonathan Hale (University of Nottingham)

Editorial Board:

Sarah Chaplin

Mark Dorrian (Newcastle University)

Murray Fraser (University of Westminster)

Hilde Heynen (Catholic University of Leuven)

Andrew Leach (University of Queensland)

Thomas Mical (Carleton University)

Jane Rendell (University College London)

Adam Sharr (Newcastle University)

Igea Troiani (Oxford Brookes University)

This original series of edited books contains selected papers from the AHRA Annual International Conferences. Each year the event has its own thematic focus while sharing an interest in new and emerging critical research in the areas of architectural history, theory, culture, design and urbanism.

Volume 1: Critical Architecture

Edited by: Jane Rendell, Jonathan Hill, Murray Fraser and Mark Dorrian

AHRA provides an inclusive and comprehensive support network for humanities researchers in architecture across the UK and beyond. It promotes, supports, develops and disseminates high-quality research in all areas of architectural humanities.

www.ahra-architecture.org

Industries of Architecture

Edited by Katie Lloyd Thomas,
Tilo Amhoff and Nick Beech

Routledge
Taylor & Francis Group

LONDON AND NEW YORK

First published 2016
by Routledge
2 Park Square, Milton Park, Abingdon, Oxon OX14 4RN

and by Routledge
711 Third Avenue, New York, NY 10017

Routledge is an imprint of the Taylor & Francis Group, an informa business

British Library Cataloguing in Publication Data
A catalogue record for this book is available from the British Library

Library of Congress Cataloging in Publication Data
Industries of architecture / [edited by] Katie Lloyd Thomas, Tilo Amhoff
and Nick Beech.
    pages cm
  Includes bibliographical references and index.
  1. Architectural practice.   2. Architecture—Economic aspects.
  3. Industries—Social aspects.   I. Lloyd Thomas, Katie, editor.
  II. Amhoff, Tilo, editor.   III. Beech, Nick, editor.
  NA1995.I56 2016
  720.1—dc23   2015025829

ISBN: 978-1-138-94681-1 (hbk)
ISBN: 978-1-138-94682-8 (pbk)
ISBN: 978-1-315-67036-2 (ebk)

Typeset in Univers
by Keystroke, Station Road, Codsalll, Wolverhampton

Printed and bound in Great Britain by
TJ International Ltd, Padstow, Cornwall

Contents

Contents

Contents

Illustration credits

2.1 photograph courtesy the Estate of Allan Sekula
2.2 photograph courtesy the Estate of Allan Sekula
2.3 photograph courtesy the Estate of Allan Sekula
2.4 film still courtesy Doc.Eye Film
2.5 film still courtesy Doc.Eye Film

3.1 copyright Mary Banham, by permission of Reyner Banham/Architectural Association Photo Library
3.2 copyright DACS 2015, by courtesy of Bauhaus-Archiv Berlin
3.3 copyright DACS 2015, by courtesy of Bauhaus-Archiv Berlin
3.4 The Getty Research Institute, Los Angeles (910009), copyright Patricia Layman Bazelon, by courtesy of Lauren Tent
3.5 copyright 1986 Massachusetts Institute of Technology, by permission of MIT Press
3.6 copyright Mary Banham, by permission of Reyner Banham/Architectural Association Photo Library
3.7 photograph by Catalina Mejía Moreno, 2014

4.1 *Acier* (Journal of *OTUA*), no. 4 (1944), 14
4.2 *Acier* (Journal of *OTUA*), no. 4 (1944), 15
4.3 *L'Architecture d'Aujourd'hui*, no. 4 (January 1946), 12

5.1 copyright Chicago History Museum, HB-18679-C, Hedrich-Blessing, photographer
5.2 Mies van der Rohe Archive, the Museum of Modern Art, New York. MR5203.80, copyright DACS 2015
5.3 Mies van der Rohe Archive, the Museum of Modern Art, New York. IIT folder 114, copyright DACS 2015
5.4 Mies van der Rohe Archive, the Museum of Modern Art, New York. IIT folder 113, copyright DACS 2015

6.1 from the privately published *Modular Quarterly*, journal of the Modular Society
6.2 from the privately published *Modular Quarterly*, journal of the Modular Society

6.3   from the privately published *Modular Quarterly*, journal of the Modular Society
6.4   from the privately published *Modular Quarterly*, journal of the Modular Society
6.5   from the privately published *Modular Quarterly*, journal of the Modular Society

7.1   reprinted with permission by Arnoldo Mondadori Editore S.p.A., Milan
7.2   reprinted with permission by Arnoldo Mondadori Editore S.p.A., Milan
7.3   reprinted with permission by Arnoldo Mondadori Editore S.p.A., Milan
7.4   reprinted with permission by Editoriale Domus S.p.A., Milan
7.5   reprinted with permission by Editoriale Domus S.p.A., Milan

8.1   photo: Ilka Apocalypse, 2012
8.2   photo: Ana Paula Koury, 1998
8.3   drawing: produced by Ana Paula Koury for her book *Grupo Arquitetura Nova: Flávio Império, Rodrigo Lefèvre e Sérgio Ferro* (São Paulo: Romano Guerra/Edusp, 2003)
8.4   photo: Ana Paula Koury, 1998
8.5   drawing: produced by Ana Paula Koury for her book *Grupo Arquitetura Nova: Flávio Império, Rodrigo Lefèvre e Sérgio Ferro* (São Paulo: Romano Guerra/Edusp, 2003)
8.6   photo: Rodrigo Lefèvre Archive
8.7   cover, *O canteiro e o desenho*

11.1   drawing: Oshwal Association of the UK
11.2   schedule: Oshwal Association of the UK
11.3   photograph: Megha Chand Inglis
11.4   photograph: Megha Chand Inglis
11.5   photograph: Megha Chand Inglis
11.6   photograph: Megha Chand Inglis

12.1   courtesy Roberto Eustaáquio dos Santos, 2015
12.2   courtesy Roberto Eustaáquio dos Santos, 2015
12.3   courtesy Roberto Eustaáquio dos Santos, 2015

14.1   *Deutsche Architektur*, 2 (1957), 88
14.2   *Deutsche Architektur*, 4 (1963), 205
14.3   *Deutsche Architektur*, 1 (1972), 38–39
14.4   *Architektur der DDR*, 10 (1976), 555
14.5   *Form + Zweck*, 4 (1980), 7
14.6   *Form + Zweck*, 4 (1980), 8

15.1   reprinted from: Mate Baylon, *Upotrebna Vrednost Stana* [*The Flat's Use Value*] (Univerzitet u Beogradu, Arhitektonski Fakultet, 1975), p. 6, by courtesy of University of Belgrade, Faculty of Architecture
15.2   reprinted from: Mate Baylon, *Upotrebna Vrednost Stana* [*The Flat's Use Value*] (Univerzitet u Beogradu, Arhitektonski Fakultet, 1975), p. 5, by courtesy of University of Belgrade, Faculty of Architecture

15.3 reprinted from: *Blokovi 61–64 na Novom Beogradu, prva faza izgradnje* [*Blocks 61–64 in New Belgrade, the first phase of construction*] (Beograd: Gradjevinsko Preduzeće RAD, 1977)

15.4 reprinted from: *Blokovi 61–64 na Novom Beogradu, prva faza izgradnje* [*Blocks 61–64 in New Belgrade, the first phase of construction*] (Beograd: Gradjevinsko Preduzeće RAD, 1977)

15.5 reprinted from: *Izgradnja*, specijalno izdanje: Stan i Stanovanje [*Construction*, special issue: Flat and Housing], Beograd, 1984, 128, with permission of Association Izgradnja, Beograd

18.1 courtesy United States Geological Survey, *World Cement Production by Region 1930–2012*

19.1 original photograph: Mark Butt, annotation: Alexandra Kenyon
19.2 drawing: Matthew Soules and Cam Koroluk
19.3 drawing: Matthew Soules and Cam Koroluk
19.4 JDS Development Group
19.5 drawing: Matthew Soules and Cam Koroluk

21.1 Instituto da Habitação e da Reabilitação Urbana, Lisbon
21.2 Instituto da Habitação e da Reabilitação Urbana, Lisbon
21.3 Ricardo Agarez
21.4 Instituto da Habitação e da Reabilitação Urbana, Lisbon

22.1 drawing: Liam Ross
22.2 drawing: Liam Ross
22.3 drawing: Liam Ross
22.4 drawing: Liam Ross

23.1 drawing: Stefan White
23.2 drawing: Stefan White
23.3 table: Stefan White
23.4 drawing: Stefan White
23.5 drawing: Stefan White

24.1 Oskar Lasche, 'Die Elektrische Kraftverteilung in den Maschinebauwerkstaetten der Allgemeinen Elektricitaets-Gesellschaft, Berlin', *Z-VDI*, no. 5, 43 (1899), 115 (Textblatt 1)
24.2 Oskar Lasche, 'Die Elektrische Kraftverteilung in den Maschinebauwerkstaetten der Allgemeinen Elektricitaets-Gesellschaft, Berlin', *Z-VDI*, no. 5, 43 (1899), 115 (Textblatt 2)
24.3 Oskar Lasche, 'Elektrischer Einzelantrieb und seine Wirtschaftlichkeit', *Z-VDI*, no. 36, 44 (1900), 1193

24.4 Oskar Lasche, 'Die Elektrische Kraftverteilung in den Maschinebauwerkstaetten der Allgemeinen Elektricitaets-Gesellschaft, Berlin', *Z-VDI*, no. 6, 43 (1899), 143

24.5 Oskar Lasche, 'Die Turbinenfabrikation der AEG', *Z-VDI*, no. 29, 55 (1911), 1199

24.6 Oskar Lasche, 'Elektrischer Einzelantrieb und seine Wirtschaftlichkeit', *Z-VDI*, no. 36, 44 (1900), 1194

25.1 Archives of the Flemish Parliament, Brussels

25.2 1937 Camu report

25.3 University Archives, Leuven

25.4 *La technique des travaux* (May/June 1950)

25.5 Archives of the Flemish Parliament, Brussels

26.1 illustration: Sandra Kaji-O'Grady and Chris L. Smith

26.2 illustration: Sandra Kaji-O'Grady and Chris L. Smith

26.3 photograph: Sandra Kaji-O'Grady

26.4 photograph: Sandra Kaji-O'Grady

26.5 illustration: Sandra Kaji-O'Grady and Chris L. Smith

26.6 photograph: Sandra Kaji-O'Grady

28.1 photograph: Nick Beech

30.1 copyright ECD Architects. Photograph: Jake Fitzjones

30.2 copyright ECD Architects. Photograph: Jake Fitzjones

30.3 copyright Paul Davis & Partners

30.4 copyright ECD Architects. Photograph: Jake Fitzjones

30.5 copyright ECD Architects. Photograph: Jake Fitzjones

32.1 copyright Sarah Wigglesworth. Graphics by Fran Williams at Sarah Wigglesworth Architects

32.2 copyright Sarah Wigglesworth. Graphics by Fran Williams at Sarah Wigglesworth Architects

32.3 copyright Sarah Wigglesworth. Graphics by Fran Williams at Sarah Wigglesworth Architects

32.4 copyright Sarah Wigglesworth. Illustration by Adam Park, copyright DWELL project and the University of Sheffield. Graphics by Fran Williams at Sarah Wigglesworth Architects

32.5 copyright Sarah Wigglesworth. Illustration by Adam Park, copyright DWELL project and the University of Sheffield. Graphics by Fran Williams at Sarah Wigglesworth Architects

32.6 copyright Sarah Wigglesworth. Illustration by Adam Park, copyright DWELL project and the University of Sheffield. Graphics by Fran Williams at Sarah Wigglesworth Architects

Editors and contributors

Editors

Tilo Amhoff is Senior Lecturer in Architectural Humanities at the University of Brighton and a Ph.D. candidate at the Bartlett School of Architecture (UCL). His research investigates the plan as a specific medium and cultural technique that established a particular way of administrating and governing various entities, such as the factory, the city, and the economy, in late nineteenth- and early twentieth-century Germany. He is a founder member of *Netzwerk Architekturwissenschaft* (www.architektur wissenschaft.net).

Nick Beech is Lecturer in London's History at Queen Mary University of London. His research concerns the transformation of the construction industry and architectural professions during and immediately following the Second World War. Nick also researches European 'New Left' arguments of the mid-twentieth century relating to 'culture', the 'everyday' and state formation. He currently (2014–2016) holds an Andrew W. Mellon Foundation Fellowship with the Canadian Centre for Architecture.

Katie Lloyd Thomas is a Senior Lecturer in Architecture at Newcastle University, where she co-directs the Architecture Research Collaborative (ARC) and is an editor of the international journal *arq*. Her research is concerned with materiality in architecture and with feminist practice and theory. She is co-founder of the feminist collective 'taking place' (www.takingplace.org.uk) and edited *Material Matters* (Routledge, 2007). Her monograph *Preliminary Operations: Material Theory and the Architectural Specification* is in preparation.

Contributors

Ricardo Agarez is an architect (Dip. 1996) and architectural historian (M.Phil. 2004, Ph.D. 2013, RIBA President's Award for Research). He specialises in the history and theory of nineteenth- and twentieth-century architecture, having published specifically on national and regional identities, dissemination phenomena, housing and public architecture and the architectural culture in bureaucracy. He is currently FWO Pegasus Marie Curie Fellow at Ghent University.

João Marcos de Almeida Lopes graduated as an architect and urban planner from the Faculty of Architecture and Urbanism, University of São Paulo (USP) in 1982. He gained his Master's in Architecture in 1999 from the School of Engineering of São Carlos, USP and his Doctorate in the philosophy and methodology of science in 2006 from the Federal University of São Carlos (UFSCAR). Since 1999 he has been a professor at the Institute of Architecture and Urbanism, USP, acting as Associate Professor since 2011 and as Vice-Provost of Culture since 2014.

Karen Burns teaches in the Architecture program at the University of Melbourne. Her essays have been published in *Assemblage*, *Journal of Architectural Education*, *AD*, *Architectural Theory Review* and *Fabrications*. She is co-editing a forthcoming *Global Dictionary of Women Architects* with Lori Brown and was a chief investigator on the ARC-funded project 'Equity and Diversity in the Australian Architecture Profession'.

Robert Carvais, historian of law, is Director of Research at the CNRS, and professor of law at Paris architectural schools, President of the francophone association of construction history, and works on the interaction between history of law and history of science and technology. He tries to reconsider the birth of different branches of law through theoretical sources and practical norms. His works concern public health, labour and, especially, construction connected with law, justice and economy.

Megha Chand Inglis is a Teaching Fellow in History and Theory at the Bartlett School of Architecture, UCL and a doctoral candidate at the Welsh School of Architecture, Cardiff University. Her research is focused on the contemporary practices of hereditary temple builders from Gujarat, India. Megha received the RIBA President's Medal in 1999 and is interested in issues of cultural translation through the lens of postcolonial theory.

Justine Clark is an architectural editor, writer and researcher. She is founding editor of the website '*Parlour: women, equity, architecture*' and was a chief investigator on the ARC-funded project 'Equity and Diversity in the Australian Architecture Profession'. She was editor of *Architecture Australia*, the journal of record of Australian architecture (2003–2011) and is co-author of *Looking for the Local: Architecture and the New Zealand Modern* (Wellington: VUW, 2000).

Linda Clarke is co-Director of ProBE (Centre for the Study of the Production of the Built Environment), at the University of Westminster, and on the Board of the European Institute for Construction Labour Research (CLR). She has long experience of research on labour, labour history, vocational education and training, skills, employment and working conditions, and gender in the construction industry across Europe.

Felipe Contier is an architect. He graduated from the Faculty of Architecture and Urbanism at the University of São Paulo in 2009 and received a Ph.D. in the theory and history of architecture and urbanism at the Institute of Architecture and Urbanism at the University of São Paulo in 2015. In 2010 he organised Sérgio Ferro's book *A história da arquitetura vista do canteiro* (São Paulo: GFAU).

Gail Day's *Dialectical Passions: Negation in Postwar Art Theory* (Columbia University Press, 2011) was shortlisted for the Isaac and Tamara Deutscher Memorial Prize. She teaches in the School of Fine Art, History of Art and Cultural Studies at the University of Leeds.

Peggy Deamer is Professor of Architecture at Yale University. She received a B.Arch. from The Cooper Union and a Ph.D. from Princeton University. She is the editor of *Architecture and Capitalism: 1845 to the Present* and the forthcoming *The Architect as Worker: Immaterial Labor, the Creative Class, and the Politics of Design*. She is co-editor of *Building (in) the Future: Recasting Labor in Architecture* and *BIM in Academia*. She is a founding member of *The Architecture Lobby*.

Kevin Donovan has worked for award-winning Irish architecture practices. He teaches and lectures at both UCD Architecture and CCAE, Cork. He holds a Centennial Ph.D. Scholarship at UCD Architecture, where he is researching crossovers in cultures of making, writing and architecture in mid-century France. Forthcoming publications include book chapters in *Food and Architecture: At Table* (Berg, 2015) and *Infra Éireann – Making Ireland Modern 1914–2014* (Ashgate, 2015).

Claudia Dutson is completing a practice-based Ph.D. at the Royal College of Art on thermal control in architecture. Her work investigates 'smart architecture', through language games and performance and a feminist critique of techno-solutionism. She holds a BSc and MA in Architecture, and has written a book on artificial light. Before architecture she trained in media production, and worked in new media consultancy during the dotcom bubble (and burst).

Sérgio Ferro (b. 1938) was a professor of architectural and art history at the Faculdade de Arquitectura e Urbanismo of the Universidade de São Paulo (1962–1970) and then at the École d'architecture de Grenoble (1972–2003). He was also the director of the Laboratoire de Recherche Dessin/Chantier of the Ministry of Culture in France. His research is devoted to testing his Marxist-grounded theory through practical experimentation in architecture (in association with Flávio Império and Rodrigo Lefèvre) and in painting. Consequently, *Artes plásticas e trabalho livre* (*Fine Arts and Free Work*) is the counterpart to *Arquitetura e trabalho livre* (*Architecture and Free Work*, Cosacnaify, 2006, Jabuti Prize 2007). In 1992 he was made Chevalier de l'ordre des Arts et des Lettres by the French government.

Alice Fiuza is a Brazilian translator working with Portuguese, English and French, in fields such as Architecture, Anthropology, Social and Human Rights. She has a Certificate in Translation from McGill University and a BA in Translation from Université de Montréal, Canada, as well as a Degree in Architecture from Universidade Federal de

Chris L. Smith is Associate Professor in Architecture at the University of Sydney. Smith and Sandra Kaji-O'Grady have a current project funded by the Australian Research Council titled 'From Alchemist's Den to Science City: Architecture and the Expression of Experimental Science'. He has published widely and is currently working on a monograph, *Bare Architecture: A Schizoanalysis*.

Matthew Soules is Assistant Professor of architecture at the University of British Columbia. His work explores the relationship between socio-political ideology and contemporary architecture and urbanism. Soules pursues this work through a range of activities, from research and writing to the design of objects, spaces, and buildings. His writing has been widely published, including in *Praxis*, *Harvard Design Magazine*, *Topos*, and *306090*.

Tijana Stevanović is an architect pursuing a Ph.D. in Architectural Theory and Criticism at Newcastle University, where she also teaches. Tijana's thesis explores Yugoslav self-management's conditioning of architectural practice in New Belgrade. Her texts have appeared in journals: *arq*, *An Architektur;* edited volumes: *Pedagogies of Disaster*, *Critical Cities vol. 3*. and *Rethinking the Social in Architecture* (forthcoming). She was OSI/Chevening scholar at SSEES, University College London 2009–2010, and also holds its MA in Identity, Culture and Power.

Christine Wall is Reader in the Faculty of Architecture and the Built Environment, and Co-Director of the research institute, ProBE, at the University of Westminster. She was Principal Investigator for the Leverhulme Trust-funded project 'Constructing Post-War Britain: Building workers' stories 1950–1970' and recently published *An Architecture of Parts: Architects, Building Workers and Industrialisation in Britain* (Routledge, 2013).

Stefan White is a Senior Enterprise Fellow at the Manchester School of Architecture directing the centre for Spatial Inclusion Design-research (cSIDr), a community-engaged research and design partnership between Manchester's City Council, Architecture School and Universities. Operating alongside the MArch Projects atelier, they focus on the spatial inclusion of multiply-excluded populations (emphasising experiences across the life-course) to develop innovative cross-sector projects working to make cities and neighbourhoods more inclusive.

Sarah Wigglesworth heads a London-based architectural practice, which is interested in working with clients and users to explore meaningful and sustainable places for everyday activities. Sarah is Professor of Architecture at the University of Sheffield where she heads the DWELL (Designing for Wellbeing in Environments for Later Life) research project that aims to design exemplary places for older people.

Chapter 1

Industries of architecture

Tilo Amhoff, Nick Beech and Katie Lloyd Thomas

> Since 1945, perhaps under American influence, **industry** has again been general-
> ized, along the line from effort, to organized effort, to an institution. It is common
> now to hear of the **holiday industry**, the **leisure industry**, the **entertainment
> industry** and, in a reversal of what was once a distinction, the **agricultural indus-
> try**. This reflects the increasing capitalization, organization and mechanization of
> what were formerly thought of as **non-industrial** kinds of service and work.[1]

'Industry', Raymond Williams tells us in his 1976 introduction to *Keywords*, was one of
five words that, along with class, art, democracy and culture, he could 'feel' connected
together 'as a kind of structure' of his immediate world.[2] His account of the changing
meanings of the word 'industry' and its uses by authors from Adam Smith to Friedrich
Engels is revelatory. According to Williams, the meaning of 'industry' was once simply
the human quality of diligence or effort (its first application was to distinguish 'cultivated'
fruits from 'natural'), before it gradually came to mean the 'organised effort' of industrial
production, and finally extended to include a much wider arena of work activity.

It is Williams's expansive sense of 'industry' – specific, yet polyvalent,
historically contingent, and ambivalent – that we follow in our own selection of the
term for the title of this collection and emphasise through its pluralisation. Williams
destabilises any singular a-historical meaning of the term and indicates directions that
are central to the aims of this book. First, 'industry' should not be understood simply in
terms of mechanisation or limited to the 'factory mode of production'. In early political
economy the shift to modern industry was characterised by the organisation of

machinery into a system, but also by the cooperation of wage-labourers towards a common aim under the leadership of an entrepreneur. It was the organisation of machines in the factory system *together with* the labour process that was identified as transforming manufacture into industrial production. 'Industry' is never just a matter of technology, but always also a matter of social organisation and social relations.

Second, we cannot assume that 'industry' identifies any one particular form of technical and social organisation. For example, whilst industry and the 'industrial revolution' emerged under capitalism, Williams reminds us that industrialisation was also central to twentieth-century socialist projects. And, as Michael Ball has insisted, the formations of capitalism vary according to specific contexts, and hence also 'industry' is always already localised.[3]

Third, industry is understood as dynamic – what constitutes industry has undergone enormous change. At least in our own local context in the UK we might characterise this as a transition from a factory mode of production (identified by the entrepreneurial, *laissez-faire* model of the nineteenth century) to a corporate and state mode of production (supported by state institutional bureaucratic and technocratic planning), and now to a mode of production that is global, decentralised and responsive to financial capital requirements, when 'industry' is no longer concentrated in specific building typologies or processes of production but has to be considered as more spatially dispersed across institutions and techniques.

The shift towards a corporate mode is tacit in Williams's definition – in so far as he identifies the increasing 'industrialisation' and interconnection of activities previously considered non-industrial (such as knowledge or education). While we recognise that architects and historians responded to the factory mode in the first half of the twentieth century, and also to the state and corporate modes of the mid-twentieth century, it is the need to better understand architecture in the mode of production today and to identify key questions and appropriate methods of enquiry by returning to earlier formulations, transforming them and proposing new frameworks of understanding, that drives the presentation of essays here.

The scale and nature of contemporary transformation has only proliferated since the publication of *Keywords*, and these changes are particularly significant in the sphere of architectural production. They include the now-ubiquitous adoption of 'building information modelling' (BIM), new techniques of digital fabrication and materials' design, the performance-led design and evaluation of buildings as well as the ever-extending frameworks of regulation that are themselves performance-based and as such increasingly shift responsibility from the state to industry. Moreover, these changes have implications for the planning, realisation, and occupation of buildings. They necessarily alter the ways in which architects design and the kinds of parameters that inform their approaches. They may – and it is our contention for this volume that they do – also influence the conceptual frameworks through which architects understand and approach design.

A fourth aim of this volume, then, is to bring issues from 'professional practice', 'project management', or the 'merely technical' realms, where debates are usually more to do with pragmatics and efficiency, into the architectural humanities – to history and theory, and to design – for the possibility of a more critical engagement. For example, digital design and fabrication has profoundly altered the day-to-day practices of architects and their relationship to production processes, and at the same time, informed architectural theory. Following Jon McKenzie's argument with respect to performance studies, we would also ask to what extent the embracing of 'performativity' in architectural discourse is in fact informed by the very conditions of production that the use of the concept seeks to undermine.[4] To what extent is the re-conception of the design of objects in terms of actors (human and non-human), goals and relations, no less informed by the new performance paradigm in corporate and contractual organisation, materials specification and regulation? The theoretical tools – the basic concepts, categories and procedures of knowledge formation – that are deployed in this volume and elsewhere are, we argue, not just *productive* of our subject, but are *produced* by that subject.

Researching the industries of architecture

Our own intellectual positions are varied but our common concern is that the industries of architecture are too often passed over in silence or, when confronted, treated as if external to the architectural humanities. The collaborative project that has become this book (and also a companion publication)[5] began with our shared interest in architecture's technical literatures. In Tilo Amhoff's case, these were eighteenth- and nineteenth-century specifications in London, and also a wide range of plans for the building of the city, for the factory (see Amhoff, Chapter 24), and for the economy, towards historical projects that aim to understand exchanges between architecture and other practices and institutions. Nick Beech examined building contracts of the 1940s for demolition work at the South Bank that demonstrate how relationships between public and private institutions, technologies and wider social relations were transforming in the post-war period in Britain. Katie Lloyd Thomas looked at architectural specifications from the seventeenth century to the present day, which exhibited profound differences in their modes of description of building materials. She argued that they should be understood as concepts emerging from industry with significant theoretical purchase. We convened a first very lively symposium, 'Further Reading Required: Building specifications, contracts and technical literature' (UCL, 2011), with a small group of researchers and practitioners also concerned with these texts from as diverse disciplines as literature and law, and it resulted in a special issue of *Architectural Research Quarterly* on the topic.[6] This book includes new contributions to this field: some authors make use of technical literatures for the development of their research (see Mhairi McVicar, Chapter 5; Tijana Stevanović, Chapter 15; Stefan White, Chapter 23; and Amhoff, Chapter 24) while others argue they need to be considered as subjects in their own right (see Robert Carvais, Chapter 20; Ricardo Agarez, Chapter 21; Liam Ross, Chapter 22; and Sarah Wigglesworth, Chapter 32).

 The ostensibly narrow focus of this first project necessarily implies a much broader engagement with the industries of architecture. The forms that technical literatures take, and the profound effects they have on what is built and how building is constituted, executed and evaluated, can only be understood by taking into account developments in the industry and in practice. Our concerns developed alongside a

Architecture as industry: labour and work

There have been many histories of what Howard Davis so aptly calls 'the culture of buil-ding', and of these Linda Clarke's *Building Capitalism* is a tour-de-force.[14] The shift from artisanal to industrial building (which, at least in the UK, began in the late eighteenth century) cannot be separated from changes in social relations and relations of production in building. Architecture was integral to scientific management before and beyond the avant-garde's projection of an idealised machine aesthetic. Therefore to investigate archi-tecture today *as* an industry is inevitably to consider the division of labour, to consider the labour of those involved in building, as we do in Part III, and also to recognise that archi-tects are not just 'authors' but also 'workers', as we do in Part IV. To acknowledge this within the discipline demands that we critically question the position and relation of the profession of the architect to other elements in the division of labour, and to accept the possibility of what Manfredo Tafuri described as 'the proletarianization of the architect, and his [or her] insertion . . . within the planning programs of production'.[15]

Industrialisation brought on a radical split between 'intellectual' and 'manual' labour. This split inspired searing critiques in the nineteenth century, still reflected upon today, that sought not improvement of the 'product' of production but emancipation within the production process itself – both as imagined in the ideal (see Kapp, Chapter 12) or in the critique of the present (see Wall, Chapter 6; and de Almeida Lopes, Chapter 10). Mid-twentieth-century socialist societies also struggled to resolve the problem of exploitation through the division of labour in production. Those architects who attempted to engage directly with production as the key site of liberation found themselves frustrated (see Torsten Lange, Chapter 14) or caught in the complexities of wider socio-economic, political, and cultural structures – particularly the necessarily hierarchical professional structure of architecture itself (see Stevanović, Chapter 15).

Whether taking a historical approach as suggested above, or accepting an ontological distinction between 'labour' and 'work' – as famously provided by Kenneth Frampton following Hannah Arendt[16] (the former designating the never complete, habitual, inescapable and ever-repeated brute act of living, the latter the singular, creative, *non-natural* autonomous act) – architectural discourse largely has accepted the division of labour as relatively straightforward. The 'architect' is, almost by definition, distinct from the construction site, and therefore not 'of labour'.

Other recent critiques of architecture have increasingly drawn upon the more radical charge – latent within Marx's commentaries on the most advanced forms of industrial capitalism – developed within Italian *autonomia* critiques, that the key location for capitalist exploitation, class formation and struggle, and social reproduction is not in the 'factory' or the material production site itself – but in 'immaterial labour'.[17] Consciousness of the exploitation that occurs within immaterial/knowledge production (see White, Chapter 23) has the potential to radically shift architectural debates from considerations of the figure of the architect as 'outside' of, or 'autonomous' from capitalist exploitation (whether as puppet or puppet-master) and instead understand that figure as protagonist in class struggle. As Peggy Deamer asserts in Chapter 13: 'If we [architects] cannot identify as workers, we fail to politically position ourselves to combat capitalism's neoliberal turn.'

Further, the binary distinction between intellectual and manual labour is open to critique. Considering labour, knowledge and technique as mutually co-productive offers new possibilities for action and agency in architecture (see de Almeida Lopes, Chapter 10). The stripping out of agency and knowledge, so frequently ascribed to mechanisation and factory production, can be shown to rest on Eurocentric assumptions (see Megha Chand Inglis, Chapter 11). And the division of labour and exploitation may cut along other lines – such as gender (see Karen Burns and Justine Clark, Chapter 16). Within architectural discourse then, 'labour' necessarily raises questions of social material needs, autonomy (or its counter – exploitation) and knowledge, and as such remains a key problematic when attending to the industries of architecture today.

Architecture for industry: from economy to technology and techniques

In the most general sense, architecture can be understood as serving the market, and we also want to consider it in so far as it is mobilised *for* industry. Contemporary design increasingly resembles a technology employed to capture global capital (see Matthew Soules, Chapter 19), responding to the needs of the financial industry. Alternatively, we might consider the shifting professional position of the architect (through 'Design and Build' contracts for example) in a macro-economic context that privileges the manufacturer over the client (see Andrew Rabeneck, Chapter 18). If others would insist on a different dynamic, prioritising the division of labour over circulation and exchange as the principal horizon of historical change (see Janssen, Chapter 17), this still appears to directly confront architecture's significance. Design, as a practice, discourse or 'product' (as considered in Parts I and II), is relegated to symptom. The vicissitudes of design and the building as aesthetic object appear as merely instrumental or frankly irrelevant. We might also ask to what extent architectural criticism and its growing interest in the industries of architecture is itself a product of contemporary economic crises?

At the same time, architecture serves other industries in so far as it is a conduit for the sale of manufactured goods and services – building products and tools, drawing and design technologies and software, office goods and so on (see Dutson, Chapter 27; and John Gelder, Chapter 29). There are close relationships between the development of architectural technologies and design and the insurance industry and the degree to which risk is distributed to the state or taken on by private enterprise (see Ross, Chapter 31). Architecture generates building typologies that facilitate specific forms of work – such as the office (see Jens van de Maele, Chapter 25), the laboratory (see Sandra Kaji-O'Grady and Chris L. Smith, Chapter 26), or the factory (see Amhoff, Chapter 24). While the factory has long been the model for other building types, which had to be 'like the factory', the workspaces of the 'knowledge economy' today encourage the social nature of collaborative work, while blurring the boundary between life and work. In that respect we understand architecture as an agent *for* industry; its techniques are both informed by the requirements of other industries, and in turn they are mobilised in the organisation of social relations.

Notes

We would like to thank the participants at the 11th International AHRA Conference, 'Industries of Architecture: Relations, Process, Production', especially our important keynote contributors not represented in this volume – Aggregate Architectural History Collaborative and Adrian Forty – and our advisory team. Their contributions to debates and discussions before, during, and after the conference have also shaped our ideas. We extend our warmest thanks to Kim McCartney, for her outstanding administrative support throughout, and to our sponsors and volunteers. (For full details of the event see www.industriesof architecture.org.)

1   Raymond Williams, *Keywords* (London: Croom Helm, 1976), p. 11.
2   See Raymond Williams, *Culture and Society 1780–1950* (Harmondsworth: Penguin, 1963), pp. 13–19.
3   Michael Ball, *Rebuilding Construction* (London: Routledge, 1988), p. 37.
4   Jon McKenzie, *Perform or Else: From discipline to performance* (London: Routledge, 2001).
5   See Katie Lloyd Thomas, Nick Beech and Adam Sharr (eds), 'Into the Hidden Abode', a special issue of *Architecture and Culture*, 3, 3 (2015).
6   *Architectural Research Quarterly*, 3, 16 (2012).
7   See proceedings and conference programmes of the European Architectural History Network Fourth International Meeting, Turin, 2014; and the Society of Architectural Historians Sixty-Eighth Annual Conference, Chicago, 2015.
8   See for example, Aggregate Architectural History Collaborative, *Governing by Design: Architecture, economy and politics in the twentieth century* (Pittsburgh, PA: University of Pittsburgh Press, 2012); Mathew Aitchison (ed.), *The Architecture of Industry: Changing paradigms in industrial building and planning* (Farnham: Ashgate, 2014); Peggy Deamer (ed.), *The Architect as Worker: Immaterial labour, the creative class, and the politics of design* (London: Bloomsbury Academic, 2015); Rob Imrie and Emma Street, *Architectural Design and Regulation* (Oxford: Wiley-Blackwell, 2011); Christine Wall, *An Architecture of Parts* (London: Routledge, 2013).
9   See James Andrachuk, Christo C. Bolos, Avi Forman and Marcus A. Hooks (eds), *Money*, a special issue of *Perspecta*, 47 (2014); Nisa Ari and Christianna Bonin (eds), *Workspace*, a special issue of *Thresholds*, 44 (2016); and Brendan Cornier and Arjen Oosterman (eds), *The Shape of the Law*, a special issue of *Volume*, 38 (2014).
10 David Gartman, *From Autos to Architecture: Fordism and architectural aesthetics in the twentieth century* (New York: Princeton Architectural Press, 2009).
11 Mauro F. Guillén, *The Taylorized Beauty of the Mechanical: Scientific management and the rise of modernist architecture* (Princeton, NJ: Princeton University Press, 2006).
12 Mary McLeod, '"Architecture or Revolution": Taylorism, technocracy, and social change', *Art Journal*, 2, 43 (1983), 132–147.
13 See for example, Reyner Banham, *Concrete Atlantis: US industrial building and European modern architecture 1900–1925* (Cambridge, MA: MIT Press, 1986); Sigfried Giedion, *Mechanization Takes Command: A contribution to anonymous history* (New York: Oxford University Press, 1948); Michael Farr and Nikolaus Pevsner, *Design in British Industry: A mid-century survey* (Cambridge: Cambridge University Press, 1955).
14 See Linda Clarke, *Building Capitalism: Historical change and the building process in the production of the built environment* (London: Routledge, 1991); Howard Davis, *The Culture of Building* (New York: Oxford University Press, 2006); Akira Satoh, *Building in Britain: The origins of a modern industry* (Leicester: Scolar Press, 1995); John Summerson, *The London Building World of the Eighteen-Sixties (Walter Neurath Memorial Lecture)* (London: Thames & Hudson, 1974).
15 Manfredo Tafuri, 'Toward a Critique of Architectural Ideology', in *Architecture, Theory, Since 1968*, ed. by K. Michael Hays (Cambridge, MA: MIT Press, 1998), p. 31.
16 Kenneth Frampton, 'Industrialization and the Crises in Architecture', *Oppositions*, 1 (1973), 57–81.
17 See Maurizio Lazzarato, 'Immaterial Labour', in *Radical Thought in Italy*, ed. by Paolo Virno and Michael Hardt (Minneapolis, MN: University of Minnesota Press, 1996), pp. 133–147.
18 Sigfried Giedion, *Walter Gropius: Work and teamwork* (London: Architectural Press, 1954), p.14.
19 Andrew Leach, 'The Conditional Autonomy of Tafuri's Historian', *OASE*, 69 (2006), 14–31 (at p. 16).
20 Katherine Shonfield, 'Why Does Your Flat Leak?' in *Walls Have Feelings: Architecture, film and the city* (London: Routledge, 2000), pp. 32–52.

Part I

Architecture and the representation of industry

Chapter 2

Allan Sekula's industries of architecture and architectures of industry

Gail Day

Think of Allan Sekula and what comes to mind is his close and sustained attention to the maritime economy – the focus for a number of his projects: *Fish Story, TITANIC's wake, Deep Six/Passer au bleu, Freeway to China, Black Tide/Marea negra (fragments for an opera), Tsukiji, Lottery of the Sea, The Forgotten Space*, and *Ship of Fools/The Dockers' Museum*.[1] The built environment is often present in his photographs, inescapably part of the scene; however, it appears – at least at first glance – that its role is contingent rather than active. We readily recall the container and bulk-cargo ships, barges, and freight trains; the gantry cranes associated with intermodal trans-shipment; oil spills in Galicia, a pilot arriving to guide a large vessel into harbour on the Basque coast; or a boy grasping the viewing binoculars on the Staten Island Ferry. Above all, Sekula seems to be an artist concerned with logistics, the transportation and transit of commodities and people, someone more interested in flows and processes than in the static structures of architecture. Yet, these opposite qualities connect. As Sekula and his collaborator Noël Burch argue: 'As ships become more like buildings – the giant floating warehouses of the "just-in-time" system of distribution – factories begin to resemble ships, stealing away stealthily in the night, restlessly searching for ever cheaper labour.'[2] The latter half of this chiasmus is captured by a memorable sequence in Sekula's major photo-text project *Fish Story* (1995): the dismantling of Fontana's giant Kaiser steelworks in 1993, and its preparation for shipment from California to China on the *Atlantic Queen*.[3]

There remains, however, an intractable problem facing any artist committed to a critical-realist epistemology: the materiality of capitalism's social relations exceeds empirical detectability. As Marx intimated: the value-form is not comprised of matter, but of social substance.[4] In its classic articulation, this problem has centred on the very motif of industrial architecture. Sekula has repeatedly returned to Bertolt Brecht's comment (one reiterated by Walter Benjamin, and derived from Fritz Sternberg): a photograph of a factory reveals little of the social relations of capitalism.[5] The point here is not so much that we do not see the working activities inside the building (although, as many radical documentarians have experienced, corporate control increasingly determines how work-place interiors may appear). The question of the seen and the unseen, of what enters or fails to enter into photographic representation – be that inside the factory, or down-stream at the new container terminals – is not *only* a matter of where photographers and filmmakers choose (or are allowed) to point their cameras. Faced with reified social rela-tions, it is inadequate to rely on a naïvely conceived or 'naturalistic' approach to docu-mentary. Instead, using allegorical ruses, 'something must be constructed'. For Sekula, the technique of montage – allied to a critically reflexive conception of documentary – could help pierce capitalism's 'double veil of appearances and abstractions'.[6]

Furthermore, it is important to modify this chapter's opening point. It is not entirely accurate to describe Sekula's project as an exploration of commodity circulation and the maritime economy, although, of course, it involves that topic. More precisely, we should say that he uses this theme to advance the *critique* of political economy – one modelled on Marx's, but posed via visual and verbal, discursive and lyrical means, and infused with personal history. His is a critical concern with 'dismal science' (Thomas Carlyle) and the 'lottery of the sea' (Adam Smith).[7] Such critique demands a perspectival shift away from the 'standpoint of capital'; it requires that we conduct a workers' enquiry, as militant partisans 'from below'.

Structures, for Sekula, are often metonyms for labour. Indeed, there is an image in *Fish Story* of a memorial to construction workers – who were killed building a motorway from Seoul to Pusan – where a double metonymy is in play: Sekula's camera displaces us to the very outer edge of a monument that itself indexes the connection to the risks of the labour process.[8] Another photograph in *Fish Story* shows a chair in the Los Angeles County Museum of Art (LACMA): an object not only dislodged into a museum, but relegated to its storage facilities.[9] The chair was designed by Richard Neutra for the Channel Heights estate in San Pedro, a wartime project commissioned by the Federal Works Agency to house the employees of the Los Angeles harbour and shipyards. An earlier chapter of *Fish Story* evidences the relocation of yet another San Pedro house.[10] The chair and the house in transit remind us of a Los Angeles that is very different to today's city, belonging to an era when – provoked by the exigencies of war – there was a politics of public housing. Such social schemes later fell victim to policies of privatisation, closely allied to McCarthyism, and were denounced by lobbies of developers and right-wing Republicans as evidence of 'creeping socialism'.[11] These metonyms for the historical repression of labour, its organisations and impact on public policy are notable for also taking us to the sites of social reproduction: the invisible underpinning to the supply of labour-power (which has been an interest of Sekula's since his *Aerospace Folktales*).

Sekula's most direct engagement with architecture has centred on Frank Gehry, whose buildings seem to figure capital's ideology of the eternal present.

Figure 2.1
**Allan Sekula, Fish,
Saché, *TITANIC's wake*
(1998/2000), 74cm x
102cm. Permission to
reproduce original
colour photograph by
Allan Sekula courtesy
the Estate of Allan
Sekula.**

The architect's work features in a number of Sekula's projects and Sekula participated in a number of symposia related to Gehry's role in urban redevelopments. In *Fish Story*, we encounter Gehry's *Lead Fish* – an image taken in 1988 and, like the Neutra chair, located in the LACMA.[12] The architect's Samsung Museum in Seoul figures in one of the essays to *Fish Story* (linked to Pusan by the motorway where construction workers lost their lives); his Kobe 'Fish Dance' restaurant forms a vector of *Project for Yokohama* (2001). The Bilbao Guggenheim features in *TITANIC's wake* (2003), as well as in its associated essays. Sekula's essay 'Between the Net and the Deep Blue Sea', which was published in *October*, prompted a public stand-off with Juan Ignacio Vidarte, Director General of Bilbao's Guggenheim.[13] The Walt Disney Concert Hall is the primary topic of *Facing the Music* (a group exhibition curated by Sekula in 2005), and of Sekula's own short film *Gala*.[14] With *The Forgotten Space*, he again returns to the Bilbao museum. It would be all too easy to be sucked into the vortex of the debates about Frank Gehry; however, the point I wish to draw out is the rhetorical dimension to Sekula's intervention.[15] His counter arguments are conceived dialectically; analysing existing rhetorical ploys, these tropes are redeployed both to target and to turn the dominant narrative against itself.[16] Major urban redevelopments, with their signature architectural projects, figure the 'visible' counterpoint to the 'invisibility' of relocated ports.[17] However, the contrast is not just spatially dispersed. As we will see, this high visibility is itself a function within a complex social occlusion. The built environment therefore plays an active (rather than merely contingent) role for Sekula, one tightly entwined with the restructuring of maritime industries and global supply chains.

Referring to his photo-project *TITANIC's wake*, Sekula hinted that we should understand Gehry as one of the 'characters' in an 'historical novel'.[18] From an assemblage of modest 'diaristic' photographs, Sekula sought to summon an 'epic resonance' that could provide insights into modern capital. In *TITANIC's wake*, 'Gehry' appears in a

panoramic diptych of Bilbao, set in the middle distance against the district of Abando. Our prospect is from across the river, high on the Artxanda hillside. Looking out across the city, we see how Bilbao is penned into the plains of the Nervión by Artxanda and the range to the south – as Sekula and Burch remind us, a critical issue for the spatial demands of container ports. To the left of the Guggenheim, the 'La Salve' bridge, built in the early 1970s, is shown before the embellishment of Daniel Buren's *L'arc rouge.* Sekula stands on the promontory that once marked Bilbao's historical boundary on the right bank, separating it from the neighbourhood of Deusto. In *The Forgotten Space*, Artxanda's slopes – although a little further to the east – are used for an interview with Arantxa Rodríguez, an expert in planning and urban economics, and a critic of the rhetoric and premises of the 'Bilbao effect'. As she notes, the vista presents an urban archaeology. This spatial arc – both in the diptych of *TITANIC's wake* and in the film-pan of *The Forgotten Space* – is temporally layered, offering an epic sweep of history. Appropriately, in the diptych, Sekula stands close to the spot where a structure called Olimpo once stood, which – in addition to its allusion to the prospect of the gods (and perhaps also to cameras and optical technology) – was once the studio of sculptor Joaquín Lucarini, whose works adorn the city's post-Civil War buildings.

Highly conscious of the history of the panorama, Sekula does not try to create a seamless continuity across the two panels.[19] Marked by a postwar apartment block sited on our side of the river, a rupture registers Bilbao's two aspects: the spectacularly

Figure 2.2
Allan Sekula, Bilbao (diptych), *TITANIC's wake* (1998/2000), 74cm x 173cm. Permission to reproduce original colour photograph by Allan Sekula courtesy the Estate of Allan Sekula.

visible and temporally assertive 'now-ness' of the Guggenheim and the contrasting regress of a 'disappearing' port. Sekula further emphasises the inherent internal dislocation within the diptych by altering the angle of his camera. In the right-hand panel, our view tips down, thereby expanding the foreground to show a steep-sided wooded clough, two pylons, a tiny plot of domestic-scale cultivation, and workshop structures built into the hillside. In May 1999, just months after Sekula took these images, this area was blasted to form part of the looping slip roads for the motorway and tunnel complex that cuts through the mountain northwards, connecting city to airport, and westwards to the areas of the modern port. Looking over the clough and deeper into the distance, we glimpse the industrial zones – Deusto, Zorrozaurre and Zorroza – the last now housing the easternmost terminals of the Port of Bilbao, the closest it now comes to the city centre.[20] Two bridges punctuate the river's seaward trajectory. Based on Chicago's lifting bridge, the older Puente de Deusto was originally built in 1936, but reconstructed following the bombardments of the Civil War; the defeat of Republican Bilbao was emphasised by the bridge's formal renaming in reference to the Spanish dictator. Further still, we see the Puente Euskalduna, erected in 1997, and named after the shipyard at the western end of Abandoibarra that closed in the late 1980s. The Astilleros Euskalduna had been a centre of socialism and militant trade unionism, and the resistance to the plant's closure persisted through three years of demonstrations and occupations. Dramatic images taken by photojournalists of the Battle of Euskalduna on the Puente de Deusto contrast with the non-spectacular visual strategies preferred by Sekula. The confrontation between riot police and workers defending a future for their families emerges in a discussion Sekula reports with Miren del Olmo, a daughter of a Bilbao shipyard worker. Del Olmo – a crew member of the *Global Mariner*, the campaign ship of the International Transport Workers' Federation, which Sekula memorialised in his work *Ship of Fools* – recalls how in her youth and on her way to an English class, cries prompted her to look back, to see the bridge she had just crossed disappear in a 'fog of tear gas'.[21]

The view in the diptych echoes that in an old postcard – notably, it bills itself as a *vista parcial* – of the brewery 'La Salve', which was located below Olimpo in the adjacent clough, just behind our position around the promontory. The establishment supplied the riverside pavilions and beer gardens of the Campo de La Salve. The name for bridge, beer and popular rendezvous captures multiple senses: the custom of singing a salutation to the Virgin Mary, the *Salve Marinera*, as ships leaving Bilbao passed this spot, seeking protection for a safe return; the theme of danger, captured by the connection to nautical salvage and rescue; the traditional allusion to the healing of the spirit; and the material soothing of labouring bodies, the quenching of thirst and relaxing of tired muscles. Although he questions the claims being made, Sekula offers us a further inflection: the efforts of modern planners to find an economic balm. Thus, the seemingly casual document of Gehry's Guggenheim presented by Sekula's diptych is, in fact, a rebus: the (failed) command of an Olympian panorama interplays with partial views and a disjunctive vision; a momentary snapshot incorporates multiple times, where archaeologies of the past collide with those of the future.

The Bilbao diptych is embedded among a number of photographs from Saché, a locality (in the region of the Loire) that introduces further characters: modernist sculptor Alexander Calder (in whose former atelier Sekula had a residency); and Honoré de Balzac, who occasionally resided in a local chateau, and whose series of novels forming *La Comédie humaine* is renowned for drawing the social physiognomy of emergent French capitalism.[22] The Saché images mostly occupy the opening sequence, although several appear in the middle section and derive from nearby Tours (from the SNCF factory and the workshop where Calder's metal sculptures were manufactured).[23] *TITANIC's wake* is often enigmatic precisely because of the photographs' disarming 'everydayness'. There is only scope here to indicate how, by using visual similes, Sekula inserts 'Gehry' both before we arrive in and after we leave Bilbao. The Guggenheim is prefigured by the opening image: set against an out-of-focus landscape of water and bare trees, an arm stretches horizontally, its hand grasping a fish around the gills. The piscine form, of course, alludes to the museum. Sekula also reads Gehry's buildings as akin to Lazlo Moholy-Nagy's 'light modulators', and the fish's silvery scales catch the weak winter rays in a manner that is echoed by Gehry's titanium-clad structure. The Bilbao diptych is followed by a photograph of a fisherman's hut, again set in Saché's chilly low light. The cabin provides another iteration of the museum's metal cladding, but more directly picks up the corrugated roofs of the old workshops in the clough. The containers in the rail goods terminal, glimpsed to the right of the museum, also shared the form. Arguably, there are also echoes of the 'vernacular' of corrugation famously deployed by Gehry himself for his residence in Santa Monica, while the metal frame to the left of the fisherman's hut seems to parallel the architect's use of chain-link fencing. The subsequent diptych – two views of the Touraine landscape, with pornographic adverts pasted to the rear of road signs – alludes to Balzac's eroticisation of the local geography in his *Le Lys dans la vallée*. A little later in the sequence, a Russian factory ship in Seattle harbour initiates the theme of rust, to which we will return.

Specifically, 'Gehry' concentrates Sekula's critique of the vitalist rhetoric that accompanies the accounts of a post-industrial society. The rhetoric is vitalist in its very form: in its hyperbole. And it combines two levels of vitalistic content: at the economic level, a boosterist obsession with the 'propulsive' 'miracle' of the 'Bilbao effect'; and, at the symbolic level, a vitalism of biomorphic forms (fishes, whales, sails, aeroplanes). Deploying an 'excess' of imagistic language – a pumped-up 'symbolic hypertrophy' – this official discourse sets the city as a contrasting backdrop of 'functional atrophy' against which the museum appears to glow all the more brightly, bringing 'life' and 'revitalisation' to ailing areas.[24] Gehry makes much of his interest in the baroque – especially Bernini's handling of emotional drama. Sekula re-situates Bernini historically, emphasising his role as manipulator of light and overwrought spectacles: all in the service of resurgent papal authority. Gehry, then, is cast as artist-architect for a modern counter-reformation: of, as Sekula once put it, the 'absolute and unalloyed dominion of capital'.[25]

Sekula focuses on Gehry's use of titanium. As a substance, titanium was a 'strategic metal' in the Cold War, important in military applications, believed to elude the ravages of time and seawater. When he was in Bilbao, not long after the Guggenheim and Puente Euskalduna had opened, Sekula spotted dirt accumulating on the building's surface, and he read this as 'a tarnishing of the myth'. The conflict between Sekula and the museum's director turns on the valences of the word 'corrosion'. Insisting that titanium cannot corrode, Vidarte engaged solely at the literal level, failing to recognise how Sekula's use of the motif was an allegorical deployment and 'metaphoric play'.[26] In turn, Sekula retorted: pointing out the obvious (the confusion of literal and figured speech) and objecting to Vidarte's repetition of 'the myth of the immortal metal that never rusts'; 'titanium has come to stand for the illusion of eternal imperviousness to the elements, and thus suits well the immortalist fantasies of contemporary elites'.[27]

Figure 2.3
Allan Sekula, Fisherman's hut, Saché, *TITANIC's wake* (1998/2000), 66cm x 173cm. Permission to reproduce original colour photograph by Allan Sekula courtesy the Estate of Allan Sekula.

Sekula, then, allows the trope to reverberate, so that the physical properties associated with the building's metal carapace acquire social characteristics. This time-transcendent imaginary of capitalism as 'eternal present' conforms, of course, to the classic definition of ideology.

This vitalist rhetoric has an obscuring function. As sheathing, Gehry's deployment of titanium symbolically evokes sea creatures, the full sails of early merchant vessels and modern streamlined bodywork. Yet like so many baroque creations, the building's structure is veiled; literally concealed, it also metaphorically elides the materiality of time and labour. Out of view is the transition from design to execution: the mediating labour of engineers; the translation of plans into building schedules; and the truing-and-fairing done onsite by construction workers. In Bilbao, following an earlier experiment in Barcelona, Gehry used the computer-aided design software CATIA. Invented by Dassault Systèmes with IBM for automotive and aerospace producers, CATIA, as Andrew Friedman explains, 'is a means for deskilling the ornery building trades', reducing labour time and labour costs, transforming the internal labour relations of the construction industry, and submitting contractors to IBM.[28] Gehry's work, Sekula argues, serves as a 'monument to the absolute hegemony of intellectual labour afforded by computer-based manufacturing'.[29]

There will always be a negation of capital's claimed immortality. This apparent supremacy of capital and intellectual labour is ironised by a moment in Sekula's film *Gala*. The film opens in Spring 2003 amidst the construction of Gehry's Walt Disney Concert Hall in downtown Los Angeles, where a light display, designed by Light America, is being tested in preparation for the lavish opening night in October. The post-Soviet supply of cheap titanium having dried up, the metal cladding is here stainless steel. It is a reflector for dancing lights and a screen on which to project further spectacular layers: film clips of actor Ed Harris playing artist Jackson Pollock and conductor Esa-Pekka Salonen celebrate the flourishing gestures of vital creativity.[30] At one point, however, the computer controlling the projections defaults to its instruction screen, revealing the labour

Figure 2.4
Allan Sekula and Noël Burch, *The Forgotten Space* **(Doc.Eye Film in co-production with WILDArt FILM, 2010). Film still, courtesy Doc.Eye Film.**

underpinning this relative newcomer to the architectural industries – as well as alluding to the devices of the filmmaker himself.

Sekula develops a critique of the longstanding fantasies of capital's political economists, the utopia of self-propulsive value-creation, of capital without labour (capital as 'unalloyed'), and the absenting or flattening of time. Recalling his first trip to Bilbao, Sekula has remarked on the irony of finding, adjacent to the newly built museum, tanks of hydrofluoric acid (which can oxidise titanium). The RENFE rail goods terminal where this acid was located is visible in the diptych from *TITANIC's wake*; and drawing on footage shot in 2002, this same yard – and the containers of acid – feature prominently in *The Forgotten Space* (2010), the award-winning film that Sekula made with Noël Burch.

Interestingly, back in 2005, five years before the release of *The Forgotten Space*, Sekula envisaged that the film would begin and end 'with questions about [Gehry's] maritime imaginary'.[31] The intention was to explore 'the connection, or disconnection, between this sci-fi neo-baroque space of architecture and the space of the cargo container, linchpin of the global factory system'.[32] The comment confirms how the architectural theme is entangled with that of the port. In the end, however, instead of framing the entire project, 'Gehry' was reduced to a brief chapter, entitled *Rust*, towards the film's close. The opening to this section underscores Sekula's concern with rhetoric, and, following the scenes set in East Asia, Bilbao is offered as an opportunity to 'rethink'. In their 'Notes for a Film', Sekula and Burch describe the Guggenheim as 'a delirium of neo-baroque maritime nostalgia wedded to the equally delirious promise of the "new economy"'.[33] The metaphor of delirium is an established motif in architectural discourse, from Rem Koolhaas's account of New York to Fredric Jameson's analysis of architecture and land speculation. Burch and Sekula take up and turn around the vitalism associated with the Guggenheim, literalising the metaphor in order to present it as a type of epistemological disorder.

Shooting the Guggenheim from the site of the RENFE terminal, a filmic dissolve marks the shift from 2002, with the yards still in action, to 2009, when the

Figure 2.5
Allan Sekula and Noël Burch, *The Forgotten Space* (Doc.Eye Film in co-production with WILDArt FILM, 2010). Film still, courtesy Doc.Eye Film.

terminal had given way to the landscaping of Abandoibarra. This device – known as the 'iris wipe' – is itself regarded as somewhat dated. Although it is actually accompanied by a dissonant score, its insertion almost invites us to hear a harp's accompanying glissando. In addition to merely signifying a simple transition in time, Burch and Sekula use this technique to signal the entry into capital's dreamworld: winter gives way to summer; industry to the service economy; the world of work to one of leisure; forklift truck drivers working on a chilly wet day pass over to tourists, feet up, resting in a sapling's shade.

Nevertheless, although he charts the removal of industry from the heart of Bilbao, Sekula avoids the popular photographic genre of industrial ruins, with its picturesque rustbelts. Nostalgia for abandoned mercantilist structures is ideologically laden, and not easily usable by those who want to resist the neoliberal agenda, prone to melancholic quietism and left-pessimism. Neoliberal rhetoric typically adopts a 'presentist' register, while narrating a historicist logic that both sentimentalises the past and projects its own specific vision of the future. Urban boosterists assert their template for a 'better world' with a hyperbolic rhetoric that Sekula describes as 'redemptive'. Yet, he has also criticised those opponents of boosterism who counter this 'redemptive' version with another hyperbolic form: one of 'apocalyptic foreboding'.[34]

The theme of 'rust' does not figure 'de-industrialisation'. We are reminded of this just seconds before the transition to the Bilbao chapter, when, through the testimony of an experienced seaman, we learn of the difference between 'good' and 'bad' ships; working on the latter entails a constant labour to paint over the corrosion. We are reminded again in the Bilbao chain-yard that is about to be relocated downstream; the heaps of rusty chains are not residues of a past, but basic requirements of the contemporary shipping industry. 'Rust', then, is a type of materialist *vanitas*, a challenge to capital's dreamworld and its perpetual rhetorical labour of elision and displacement. Against the claims to limitless 'vitality', abundant 'life' and to a state of organic permanence, Sekula reminds us that – like fish and ships – this social formation is perishable.

Notes

1   Allan Sekula, *Fish Story* (Rotterdam: Witte de With and Düsseldorf: Richter Verlag, 1995); *TITANIC's wake* (Graz: Edition Camera Austria, 2003); *Deep Six/Passer au bleu* (Calais: Musée des beaux-arts et de la dentelle, 1996); *Freeway to China (Version 2, for Liverpool), 1998–99* and *Black Tide/Marea negra*, 2002/03 in *Performance under Working Conditions* (Vienna: Generali Foundation, 2003); *Ship of Fools/The Dockers' Museum*, ed. Hilde Van Gelder (Leuven: Leuven University Press, 2015). Sekula's films and film essays: *Tsukiji* (2001; 44 mins); *Lottery of the Sea* (2006; 179 mins); *The Forgotten Space* (with Noël Burch, 2010; 112 mins; Doc.Eye Film).

2   Allan Sekula and Noël Burch, '*The Forgotten Space*: Notes for a Film', *New Left Review*, 69 (May/June 2011), 78.

3   Sekula, *Fish Story*, Plates 85–90.

4   Karl Marx, *Capital*, vol. 1 (Chapter 1:3), *Marx Engels Collected Works*, vol. 35 (London: Lawrence & Wishart, 1996), p. 57.

5   Bertolt Brecht, 'No Insight Through Photography' (c.1930) and 'The *Threepenny* Lawsuit' (1931–2), in *Bertolt Brecht on Film and Radio*, ed. by Marc Silberman (London: Methuen, 2000), p. 144 and pp. 147–199 (at p. 164).

6   Allan Sekula, 'On *Fish Story*: The Coffin Learns to Dance', *Camera Austria*, 59/60 (1997), 49–59 (at p. 49).

7   Allan Sekula, 'Dismal Science', in *Fish Story* (Rotterdam: Witte de With and Düsseldorf: Richter Verlag, 1995), pp. 41–54 (Part 1) and pp. 105–137 (Part 2); *Dismal Science: Photoworks 1972–1996* (Normal, IL: University Galleries of Illinois State University, 1999).

8   *Fish Story*, Plate 61.
9   *Fish Story*, Plate 94.
10 *Fish Story*, Plates 12–13.
11 Ehrhard Bahr, *Weimar on the Pacific: German exile culture and the crisis of modernism* (Berkeley and Los Angeles: University of California Press, 2007), p. 165.
12 *Fish Story*, Plate 9.
13 Juan Ignacio Vidarte, 'Letters and Responses', *October*, 104 (Spring 2003), 157–159. Since 2008, Vidarte has also been the Solomon R. Guggenheim Foundation's Deputy Director and Chief Officer of Global Strategies.
14 See Edward Dimendberg (ed.), *Facing the Music: Documenting Walt Disney Concert Hall and the Redevelopment of Downtown Los Angeles: A project by Allan Sekula* (Valencia, CA: East of Borneo Books, 2015).
15 There is a local dimension to Sekula's interest in Gehry, with Sekula's San Pedro (the area where he grew up) contrasting with Gehry's Santa Monica. The example of Gehry is at the fore of key discourses concerning the city: from Fredric Jameson's account in 'Spatial Equivalents in the World System' to Mike Davis's book *City of Quartz*. Against the genre of hyperbolic and fantasied representations of Los Angeles, Sekula emphasises instead the alternative tradition of socialist and realist writers and filmmakers – the approaches to which Thom Anderson also turns at the end of his film *Los Angeles Plays Itself* (2003) (see Dimendberg interview). Sekula was also critical of Reyner Banham's fantasy of the city's 'post-urban utopia' in *Los Angeles: The Architecture of Four Ecologies* (Allan Sekula, *Photography Against the Grain: Essays and Photoworks, 1973–1983*, p. x).
16 Allan Sekula in Ed Dimendberg, 'Interview: Allan Sekula', *BOMB Magazine* (Summer 2005), http://bombmagazine.org/article/2754/allan-sekula (accessed 24 May 2015).
17 This motif of hyper-visibility-and-occlusion runs through Sekula's works. His *Geography Lesson: Canadian notes* (1988) considers the nickel-mining town of Sudbury, Ontario, and the federal capital, Ottawa, exploring the way the Canadian landscape has been figured aesthetically and officially, while its 'non-landscapes' fall below the threshold of recognition. Here, Arthur Erickson's 1979 glass-walled Bank of Canada is set against Sudbury, helping Sekula to underscore the material symbiosis of banking capital, industrial capital and state administration, and to show the contradictions underpinning the figurations of hegemonic discourse, Allan Sekula, *Geography Lesson: Canadian notes* (Cambridge, MA: MIT Press, 1997). We see this again in his film *Lottery of the Sea*, which includes chapters addressing Barcelona's development of the Forum in Diagonal Mar.
18 Allan Sekula, 'Im Kielwasser schwimmen', *TITANIC's wake* (Graz: Edition Camera Austria, 2003), pp. 105–116 (at p. 107).
19 In 'Dismal Science', Sekula explores the panorama's history. The staticity and unity of Dutch maritime tableaux are contrasted with the implicit mobility of nineteenth-century representations of the sea (*Fish Story*, p. 106). The turn to the detail in the twentieth century indicates how the panoramic became inadequate to the new world of submarines (p. 110). Despite its clear association with military history, the panorama's vision was paradoxical and unstable (p. 43): an interplay of command and mastery (military, imperial), on the one hand, with, on the other, a perpetual anxiety about what might lie outside the encompassing vision. The panorama was always 'haunted by the threat of collapse or counter-expansion' (p. 47).
20 Zorrozaurre is a peninsula formed from Deusto's old shoreline by the failure to complete the Canal de Deusto in the 1960s. At the time of writing, it is currently earmarked for gentrification, with a signature project by Zaha Hadid.
21 Allan Sekula, 'Between the Net and the Deep Blue Sea (Rethinking the Traffic in Photographs)', *October*, 102 (Autumn 2002), 3–34 (at p. 34).
22 Sekula, *TITANIC's wake*, p. 42.
23 Comprised of 31 photographs (several of which are diptychs), *TITANIC's wake* also includes images from Istanbul, Seattle, Lisbon, Turin, Limassol, Novorossijsk, and a location off the Albanian coast.
24 Sekula and Burch, 'Notes for a Film', p. 79. The argument about the play of discourse around the 'Bilbao effect' can be found advanced in: Arantxa Rodríguez, Elena Martínez and Galder Guenaga, 'Uneven Redevelopment: New urban policies and socio-spatial fragmentation in metropolitan Bilbao', *European Urban and Regional Studies*, 8.2 (2001), 161–178; and in Rodríguez and Martínez, 'Restructuring Cities: Miracles and mirages in urban revitalization in Bilbao', in *The Globalized City: Economic restructuring and social polarization in European cities*, ed. by Frank Moulaert, Arantxa Rodríguez and Erik Swyngedouw (Oxford: Oxford University Press, 2005), pp. 181–207. See also Joseba Zulaika, *Crónica de una seducción: El museo Guggenheim Bilbao* (Madrid: Editorial Nerea, 1997); *Guggenheim Bilbao Museoa: Museums, architecture and city renewal* (Reno: University of Nevada, 2003). It is instructive to compare Sekula's argument to Hal Foster's in 'Why All the Hoopla?', *London Review of Books*, 23 August 2001, pp. 24–6; developed for *Design and Crime (And Other Diatribes)* (London: Verso, 2002), pp. 27–42. The critique of vitalism was prompted by Sekula's irritation with the celebratory treatment of the architect by Kurt Forster in 'The Museum as Civic Catalyst', *Frank O. Gehry: Museo Guggenheim Bilbao* (Stuttgart: Edition Axel Menges, 1998). See Sekula, 'Between the Net and the Deep Blue Sea', pp. 10–20; and 'Project for Yokohama, 2001' in *Performance under Working Conditions*, pp. 314–319.

25   Allan Sekula in Katarzyna Ruchel-Stockmans, 'Interview with Allan Sekula', in *Critical Realism in Contemporary Art: Around Allan Sekula's photography*, ed. by Jan Baetens and Hilde Van Gelder (Leuven: Leuven University Press, 2006), pp. 136–151 (at p. 147). Note Sekula's play on the word 'unalloyed'.

26   Allan Sekula, 'Letters and Responses', *October*, 104 (Spring 2003), 160–161 (at p. 160).

27   Sekula, 'Letters and Responses', p. 160.

28   Andrew Friedman, 'Build It and They Will Pay: A primer on Guggenomics', *The Baffler*, 15 (November 2002), www.thebaffler.com/salvos/build-it-and-they-will-pay (accessed 24 May 2015).

29   Sekula, 'Between the Net', p. 20.

30   Sekula in Dimendberg, 'Interview', p. 6.

31   Sekula in Dimendberg, 'Interview', p. 10.

32   Sekula in Dimendberg, "Interview', p. 10.

33   Sekula and Burch, 'Notes for a Film', p. 79.

34   Sekula in Dimendberg, 'Interview', p. 9.

Chapter 3

Walter Gropius's silos and Reyner Banham's grain elevators as art-objects

Catalina Mejía Moreno

In Reyner Banham's slide collection are numerous photographs of his visits during the 1970s and 1980s to grain elevators in the USA and Canada. They are archived and catalogued alongside his own photographs of others from the early twentieth century, including the image Walter Gropius used to first introduce the now iconic North and

Figure 3.1
Reyner Banham Slide Collection. Some photographs of elevators taken by R. Banham in his various trips between the 1970s and late 1980s. Copyright Mary Banham. By permission of Reyner Banham/ Architectural Association Photo Library

South American silos into architectural discourse in his 1911 lecture 'Monumentale Kunst und Industriebau' (Monumental Art and Industrial Building). Together these images provide an account through photography of Banham's return to these canonical buildings (Figure 3.1). They allow us to question Gropius's and Banham's deliberate choice of photographic representations, and to explore their (apparently) different use of photography as a vehicle to introduce ordinary and vernacular industrial buildings as art-objects worthy of architectural attention.

The buildings appear in lectures and publications as structures with explicit connections to modern architecture, either as precursors of 'a new monumentality'[1] or as 'a form of allegory'.[2] Gropius's and Banham's approach is arguably distinct, and indeed they use different terms ('silo' for Gropius, 'elevator' for Banham), but the original site from where the relationship between modern architecture and industrial buildings emerged was to be the same: the buildings' iconic photographs.

My aim is twofold. First, I want to demonstrate that while the buildings were originally introduced as industrial *structures* by nineteenth-century engineering journals, their transition to industrial *architecture* was prompted by Gropius's interpretation of the silos as art-objects based on the buildings' 'corporeality'. A second transition was prompted by Banham's later reading of the grain elevators as 'architectural objects', whose significance lay (as Canadian artist Melvin Charney had argued in 1967) in their industrial nature and in their embodied mechanical 'processes'. Second, although Gropius's and Banham's starting points are different – and despite Banham's emphasis on the elevators as 'process' – both Banham and Charney appear to abandon this idea to return finally to the silo instead of the elevator, thus to the same reading of industrial building as art-object.

Walter Gropius's silos

In 1911 Walter Gropius addressed his first-ever public lecture, 'Monumental Art and Industrial Building', to the exclusive audience of the Folkwang Museum in Hagen. The lecture's subject was the rigorous study of the purpose and design of contemporary industrial buildings and, accompanying his voice, Gropius showed images of the North and South American silos, two years before they were first fixed in printed media in the Werkbund's yearbook as illustrations for his article 'Development of Modern Industrial Architecture' in 1913.[3] Thereafter they were repeatedly published: by Le Corbusier (1923), Erich Mendelsohn (1926), Walter Curt Behrendt (1927), Bruno Taut (1929) and more recently by Jean Louis Cohen (1995), Anne Marie Jaeggi (2000) and Hadas Steiner (2006–2013), amongst many others.

Due to the slide lecture's ephemeral nature, only a few glass slides (*Lichtbilder*) and Gropius's original manuscript remain. The manuscript's layout and materiality suggest the divided structure of the lecture. The first part comprises seventeen imageless typewritten pages, and the second part the so-called 'illustrations' to Gropius's argument – a series of sixty-nine thumbnail photographs and their corresponding descriptions (see Figure 3.2). As the title of the lecture suggests, the imageless part is itself divided

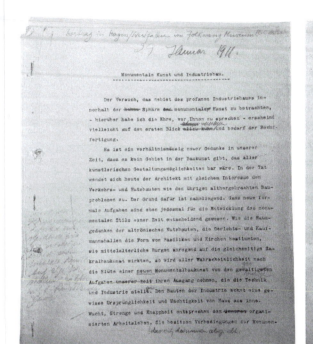

Figure 3.2
Pages 1 and 18 of
Monumentale Kunst
und Industriebau
lecture manuscript that
evidence the lecture's
divided structure.
Copyright DACS 2015.
By courtesy of Bauhaus-
Archiv Berlin

in two: first 'On Monumental Art' followed by 'On Industrial Buildings'. 'On Industrial Buildings' establishes the relationship between industrial design and production by touching upon proposed reforms in factory design and the enhancement of the social performance of architecture. 'On Monumental Art' frames the discussion of industrial buildings as precursors of a coming 'new monumental style' and is my focus here.

Corporeality

Gropius's 1911 lecture stands out for his appeal to monumentality as a necessary precondition of the 'new industrial building's monumental art'. It was, he claimed, made manifest either in the buildings' embedded 'spirit of labour' or in their 'corporeality'. While the 'spirit of labour' related mainly to factory buildings and belonged to a wider discussion at the time,[4] the notion of 'corporeality' clearly related to the silos as material objects, as well as to other industrial building typologies such as zeppelin halls and torpedo pontoons.

For Gropius the concept of 'corporeality' was a prerequisite for understanding industrial buildings *as* art. In this he followed concepts formulated by art historians Alois Riegl and Wilhelm Worringer whose quest for monumentality, derived from empathy theory, involved abstracting and psychologising historical styles into simple, massive and geometric forms capable of evoking powerful emotions. According to late nineteenth-century aesthetic discourses, 'corporeality' (*Körperlichkeit*) necessarily implied

no need. The argument was being aided by the agency of the projector and its projected *Lichtbilder* whose shadows embodied the 'corporeal' (or volumes in black) and the light rays the 'invisible' (or absence of solid material).

The projected photograph as *Lichtbild* enabled the audience to visualise Gropius's interpretation of the silo. As a visual part of his performance the light-images underscored an argument that the silos as vernacular industrial buildings could nevertheless enter architectural discourse as representative art-objects of the *new industrial building's monumental art*. Similarly, decades later, when Banham revisits the grain elevators, another set of photographs play a determining role in his own construction of industrial buildings as art-objects.

Reyner Banham's grain elevators

Before their well-known appearance in *A Concrete Atlantis: US Industrial Building and European Modern Architecture 1900–1925*, Reyner Banham first returned to the grain elevators in his discussion of megastructures in relation to the 1967 Montreal Expo, which took place in the shadow of a series of obsolete elevators that sat on the riverfront of the St Lawrence River and across the exhibition grounds. Banham initially defined them as megastructures *trouvées* due to their 'impressive size' and their 'purely functional enormity'.[10] Interest in the elevators' physicality and also their industrial and mechanical nature first surfaced then.

Process

In his lectures and publications Banham was overtly critical of Gropius's use of photographic images of the silos as material and sculptural 'objects of awe' as in traditional aesthetics and, unquestionably, as an object of aesthetic experience as informed by contemporary empathy theory discourses. Conversely, and as a critical response to Gropius's understanding, Banham attempted to return attention to their industrial nature and embedded mechanised processes. Originally he saw them as 'architectural objects' insofar as they were both 'structures' and 'mechanical services'[11] and instead opted to call them grain elevators, thus emphasising their mechanical nature.

In his 1980 article 'Catacombs of the Modern Movement: Grain elevators in myth and reality', Banham turned to the ruined interiors of the elevators where some of their mechanisms are housed – conveyors, spouts and bin-bottoms.[12] Alongside these images Banham wrote that:

> An elevator is not a monument, it is a *process*. What makes it an elevator rather than a simple silo is the mechanical device which raises the grain to the top of the bins, and the other mechanical installations that move the grain from bin to bin or dump it out into ships, trucks, barges or rail cars.[13]

The term 'process' is used here deliberately, and although it is not used as explicitly again, Banham nevertheless elaborated on the elevator as a mechanical process and typological evolution. Canadian architect and artist Melvin Charney had made a similar argument in 1967, and Banham's reading is present in 'Catacombs of the Modern Movement' and in two other publications: 'Buffalo Archaeological'[14] and his 1986 book *A Concrete Atlantis*. In all cases the starting point is the tension between the modern imagery and the elevators' physical existence. In response, the grain elevator is presented as a mechanised process for the handling and commercial exchange of grain (as introduced by Joseph Dart in the late nineteenth century), and as a typology of process through the evolution of the elevators' subsidiary architectural parts.[15]

Banham's reading of the elevators as *process* and not simply as the modernists' image is initially addressed in his 1980 articles, most explicitly in 'Catacombs'. 'Buffalo Archaeological' is Banham's first printed publication on the subject. It addresses the physical existence of the elevators as invaluable witnesses to industrial history and as 'heroic fragments of former civilizations' and 'magnificent ruins'.[16] His own photographic depictions of the elevators in a state of disrepair appear alongside extensive informative, factual and personal captions that describe the elevators as existing material evidence of typological developments and mechanisation processes.

'Catacombs' is not only concerned with the obsolescence of the structures. There, Banham's choice of personal photographs acts as counterpart to the argument he is introducing: the grain elevators should be understood in terms of their industrial processes – as *process*. For instance, when criticising modern imagery and in order to demonstrate that Gropius misread the elevators simply as monumental containers, Banham chooses an image of the Patterson elevator in California and, through words, he underlines the difference between cylindrical containers and the interstitials amongst them. To introduce his point about mechanical process, he uses a photograph of the circular rooms and segmental interstitials that housed the elevators' conveyors and spouts, as well as detailed captions describing the function of Buffalo Electric's elevators' marine towers or pioneering legs.[17]

Nevertheless, in both articles Banham makes clear that this understanding of the elevator as process stems from his *return* to these canonical buildings. This return, evidently embedded in the postmodern tradition of revisiting the past, turns to the *ruin* as the motivation to elaborate on the elevators as a mechanical process and to the *monument* and the *monumental* to describe their ruinous physical existence and typological evolution through photographs and words.

However, after more than six years of research, visits, lectures and surveys almost none of the images that Banham collected and produced which refer to the elevators' mechanical processes appeared in *A Concrete Atlantis*. Most of the photographs he used either replicate or reproduce those used by others so often before. Nevertheless and despite Banham's un-archival stance[18] and the fragmented nature of his papers housed at the Getty Research Institute, there is important material that offers detailed visual accounts of *A Concrete Atlantis*'s textual descriptions of the elevators' mechanical processes and typological developments. For instance: there is an undated survey map of the Geological Survey of the US Department of Interior that locates all of

Buffalo's terminal elevators. It evidences the geographical particularity of the terminal elevators (those on which Banham concentrates) in contrast to the transfer elevators. There is also a series of undated images from Joseph Dart's mechanical elevator and Oliver Evans's flourmill that graphically describe the mechanical particularities that led to Dart's description of the elevators as a 'labour saving device' or Banham's interpretation of the elevators as an 'assembly of mechanisms'. There is a series of detailed photographs of the elevators' bucket conveyor-belts and of the plansifters as well as of the human labour involved in the sack-filling operation in a number of Peavey Company and Hennepin County Historical Society catalogues. Moreover, there is a series of photographic proofs from Patricia Layman Bazelon, Banham's commissioned photographer for *A Concrete Atlantis*, that document in detail the moment of the arrival of the barge, and the process of scooping out the grain by the elevators' 'legs' and the scoopers (Figure 3.4).[19] Others portray the free disposition of the legs in relation to the bins (thus the advantages of the introduction of electricity) and the sliding or rolling power pick-ups that allow the legs to move on rails (thus 'allowing a greater number of legs to simultaneously service the same number of bins and/or boats').[20] Evidently, Banham had collected visual material that could have supported the arguments about process that he made in *A Concrete Atlantis* but instead he mostly selected iconic photographs, or those that at least mimicked them.

Figure 3.4
Contact sheet taken by Patricia Layman Bazelon from 1985 that shows the sequence of the scooping of the grain in one of Buffalo's grain elevators. The Getty Research Institute, Los Angeles (910009). Copyright Patricia Layman Bazelon. By courtesy of Lauren Tent

The return to the art-object

The case of the building's typological development proves to be different. Most of the typological transformations of the elevators can be validated from the elevators' exterior, hence through the historical and personal sets of poorly reproduced photographs that Banham selected for *A Concrete Atlantis*. In Banham's words, what those photographs as documents, 'recorded of the transformations of the structure even before the *Jahrbuch* photograph was taken, and those that had been wrought upon it since, proved to be a capsule history of the industry and the building type'.[21]

For instance, photographs of the exterior of the General Mills (formerly Washburn Crosby) elevator from different time periods[22] proved useful to illustrate that the:

> sensational advances in both construction technique and conceptual attitudes [evident in] what had formerly been a strictly cylindrical form of construction of both limited and limiting capability became a far more flexible and adaptable instrument of spatial enclosure. Further evidence of this can be seen by examining the rest of this 'façade'.[23]

Banham's persuasive use of exterior shots may show the elevators' typological developments but, more importantly, it underlines his method of contrasting historical material with personal photographs. Architectural historian Hadas Steiner proposes that this recurring method has traditionally 'illustrated' Banham's arguments, but I want to suggest instead that in the case of the elevators and most noticeably in *A Concrete Atlantis*, this method creates a new, parallel and almost contradictory argument: the return to the elevators as art-objects.

Figure 3.5
Reyner Banham, *A Concrete Atlantis: US Industrial Building and European Modern Architecture*, page spread 162/163. Copyright 1986 Massachusetts Institute of Technology, by permission of MIT Press

Chapter 4

The collaborations of Jean Prouvé and Marcel Lods

An open or closed case?

Kevin Donovan

In 1939 the French Technical Bureau for the Use of Steel organised a building exhibition where twelve teams of architects and builders each presented a design.[1] One piece distinguished itself in its complexity and evidence of collaboration: Model No. 3, the work of Marcel Lods and Jean Prouvé.[2] It was made mostly of one material – steel in sheet form – industrially worked. Other pieces in the exhibition used a variety of pre-existing, separate, prefabricated materials and elements, clearly ordered in their assembly by the architect. No. 3 advocated instead what appeared to be a single, bespoke, industrialised construction, attempting to synthesise the efforts of architect and fabricator (Figure 4.1).

  This joint work, however, is complexified by the relatively antipathetic positions of its collaborators. The predominant conceptualisation of industrialised building in mid-century France was one that has come to be described as 'open', that is to say made of prefabricated, systematised and serialised building elements, designed to be combined in various ways by an architect. The architect of Model No. 3, Marcel Lods, was a proponent of this so-called 'open' industrialisation, encapsulating its most salient principle in his maxim: 'houses are not made in factories; elements which allow architectural composition are'.[3] The position of the architect was secured by his role as composer; 'we will compose with prefabricated elements', he maintained.[4] Such was the method he employed for the Cité de la Muette at Drancy. Constructed between 1932 and 1934, this was the first of the *grands ensembles* mass-housing projects in France, and its use of efficiently made, factory-produced and serialised concrete elements was to become the model for the country's post-war housing reconstruction.[5] The favour in which this preconditions the model, confining experimentation to that which is already partially understood.[26] It is not so much a case of the serial departing from the model, but the inverse. The serial leads the model.

If, for Lods, serialisation was the corollary to prefabrication, Prouvé was ambivalent about this. Though a number of his projects – particularly furniture and metal partitions – entered repetitive production, this was largely to feed the experimental side of his business, rather than to be its main goal. Once the designed object ceased to be a vehicle of research, his interest waned.[27]

Workers' thresholds

If Prouvé was interested in material objects in development, he was also interested in the development of those who made them. He characterised his workers as '*compagnons*'. The word signifies more than camaraderie, but implies '*compagnonnage*', a term used to designate members of a guild-like, sworn group of journeymen and craftsmen of the kind associated with the raising of the cathedrals. The *union compagnonnique*, however, in its reformed state is a mid-nineteenth-century recasting by a group known as the *Société des amis de l'industrie*. The term '*compagnon*', therefore, must be understood within the complex enfolding of craft into industry in late nineteenth-century France. The Eiffel Tower, for Deborah Silverman, demonstrative of 'a "*new world*" made possible by advanced technology and scientific rationalism',[28] was constructed by members of the *compagnons forgerons serruriers*.[29]

Where traditional *compagnnonage* required the worker to follow a single object from beginning to end of production, Prouvé's workers instead followed what he termed the 'constructive idea'.[30] Thus, they were not bound to move with the object, nor were they confined to a station, as was becoming increasingly common in industry, but constantly re-negotiated the relationship with their environment, materials and fellows. Workers were relatively free to shuttle between mobile groups ever-forming and dissolving in the atelier. The schedule of work, fees and the distribution of benefits were all arranged cooperatively. The results of such entwining of attention are visible in the design and construction of the Flying Club project, where elements often manifested a complex double-functioning. The void in the structure of the roof, for example, designed ostensibly for lightness, was also a conduit for warm air to heat the building, relying on the secondary capacity of the metal planes to radiate. Meanwhile, the void of the folded panel stiffeners also drained rainwater from the building's surface, and the hollow columns contained pipes to conduct the services: water, electricity and air. This synergetic convergence of function arising out of a collective attendance to technical process on site arose from the free and continual re-establishment of connections and concerns (material, technical and social) throughout the workshop, operating across the thresholds of the project, rather than between them.[31]

This synergy is also apparent in correspondences across scales. The elasticity of the thin sheet, its capacity to assume a curved form from which it can return, is a characteristic of this material apparent to those who continually work it. A hint of this principle ran through the entire building from the small clips holding elements together, to the curved partitioning strips in the roof, the structural elements of the large globe in the map room, as well as the slightly concave metal roof and the bowed façade panels. The building's springing aesthetic, shared with the other collaborative work of Lods and Prouvé, resulted directly from the exigencies and experience of making work as a unit (Figure 4.2).

If Prouvé encouraged lively quasi-independent working toward the constructive idea, Lods advocated a stricter hand. The trajectory he envisaged from factory to

Figure 4.2
The folded metal details of the *Aeroclub Roland Garros* translated for the OUTA exhibition, *Acier* (Journal of *OTUA*), no. 4 (1944), 15

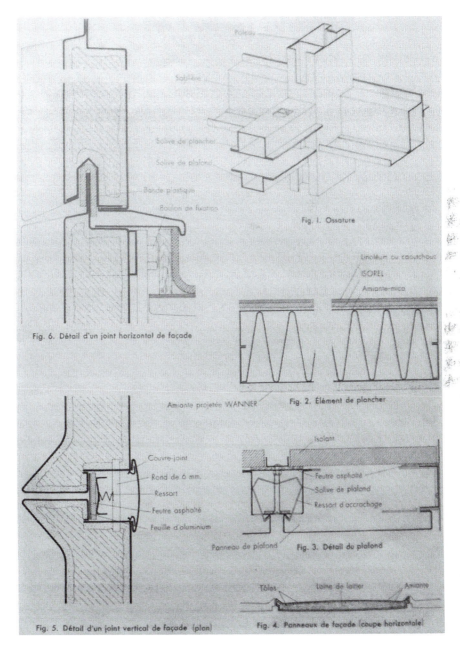

Fig. 1. Ossature

Fig. 6. Détail d'un joint horizontal de façade

Fig. 2. Élément de plancher

Fig. 3. Détail de plafond

Fig. 5. Détail d'un joint vertical de façade (plan)

Fig. 4. Panneaux de façade (coupe horizontale)

built product required the intervening labour to be closely managed. He pressed for the 'control of the workforce' and 'the scientific organisation of the site' with a view to suppressing the happenstance of a worker's labour within production.[32] He photographed the sequences in which his buildings should be erected.[33] This attitude to site reveals the advantage for Lods of the atelier as a separate place of research. The atelier served to usefully contain the fluidity of experimentation within a phase preceding production. Again, the image of the threshold arises; once production begins on the industrialised site, the space and period of the atelier are superseded.

Deleuze and Guattari insist that the motility of metal engenders a mobile spirit in its worker, who produces light, portable objects and is obliged to 'follow the mineral flow of the earth . . . a flow necessarily confluent with nomadism'.[34] This is the spirit of Prouvé, designer of furniture-like building – *immobilier* as *mobilier*.[35] 'Nothing is more mobile than industry', he maintained.[36] Furthermore, he did not conceive of the atelier as confined in place and time, but as a mobile unit of people, dispatched with the building elements not only to install them but also to make alterations on site. This occurred at Buc: the building was erected first in the atelier, bringing the site to the workshop, then erected again, to the delight of Lods, in just four days on site by the same atelier team. They also, however, remade the building's vertical joints on site when these failed on installation. Whereas Lods described the developing façade in terms of 'mistakes' to be 'corrected', Prouvé used the term 'practice', embracing change as development. Lods admitted to being 'panic-stricken' by hand-made joints, avowing in a conversation with Prouvé that 'all types revisions or bricolage should [be] severely proscribed' (Figure 4.3).[37]

Figure 4.3
Raising the *Aeroclub Roland Garros*, 1935. *L'Architecture d'Aujourd'hui*, no. 4 (January 1946), 12

Prouvé's bricolage extended to the use of machinery. If Lods welcomed the machine partly because 'it is not paid', Prouvé saw it is as an essential complement to creative work.[38] Oxy-acetylene torches and steel presses were not commonly used in metal construction in the early 1930s, and their integration by Prouvé stretched the transformative resources of the atelier workers. His machines broke down frequently, either because they were doing work for which they were not designed or because they had been remade in the atelier from other machines, and it was in their repair or reconfiguration that new possibilities for making emerged.[39] At the Flying Club, for example, the structural frame for the map room globe was formed using a press for making shoes, recycled from a neighbouring workshop.[40] Attendances here, then, entailed human and non-human elements, and the machine worker, though industrialised, was not considered a serial operative.

My discussion began with Model No. 3. The competition brief required participants to 'use modern industrial methods to the maximum . . . [to employ] standardised elements . . . to do away with on-site bricolage, to suppress all imperfections'.[41] This work, then, should be an example of 'open' industrialisation, in the sense meant by Lods, and does, indeed, appear to be composed of perfectly interconnecting modular pieces. The model is, however, a synecdoche, not just as a single bay of a projected building, but as a partial representation of a continuing practice spread across several collaborations. While the whole building might easily be imagined as a repeated version of these building elements, we must acknowledge that any recombination will require negotiation, between the collaborators themselves, the materials, the elements, the machines and the atelier workers. The sprung wall panels will require calibration, the sheet metal of the beams will be folded differently depending on the loads to be carried. Sometimes the sheet-metal press will begin to lead the process, only to break down. Opportunities for double functioning will be taken where they present themselves, both in the atelier and on site. Errors will ensue, but so will innovations. We can, to put it in the terms used within this chapter, expect Prouvé's atelier to carry the project, back and forth over material and workers' thresholds in any further iterations it sustains. And yet, for all the innovative promise of 'closed' industrialisation, the model in its current form could not stand without the two standardised tubular-steel lengths, products of 'open' industrialisation, rather poignantly in evidence at the corners.[42] This ambiguity in the model is compounded by the description of the assembly in the accompanying publication; it is 'bolted or soldered depending on requirement'. If it is not entirely open, neither is it entirely closed. The ultimate value of the model, then, is its demonstration, not of a unified position, but of the creative potential apparent in the tension between these two approaches to building industrialisation.

Notes

1   *L'Office pour la technique de l'utilisation de l'acier* (*OTUA*) was founded in 1928 to promote the French steel industry.
2   Here, I use the name of Lods as shorthand for his practice with Eugène Beaudoin. Of the two, Lods had the closer collaboration with Prouvé.
3   Radio interview with Lods by Jacques Chancel, *Radioscopie*, France Inter, 1976.

4   Marcel Lods, 'L'Industrialisation du bâtiment', *L'Architecture d'aujourd'hui* (1945), 29–30 (at p. 30).

5   The system at Drancy is an intensification of the famous panel-factory model employed by Ernst May five years earlier, cited by Lods in the above-mentioned article.

6   The *Plan Construction*, a national plan to promote construction research, is discussed in Dominique Clayssen, *Jean Prouvé: l'idée constructive* (Paris: Dunod, 1983), p. 114.

7   Prouvé made, for example, the steel moulds for the concrete panels.

8   Armelle Lavalou, *Jean Prouvé par lui-même* (Paris: Editions du Linteau, 2001), p. 58.

9   Catherine Prouvé, 'Trajectories', in *Jean Prouvé: The Poetics of the Technical Object*, ed. by Alexander von Vegesack, Catherine Dumond d'Ayot, and Bruno Reichlin (Weil am Rhein: Vitra, 2006), pp. 366–371 (at p. 371).

10 Gilles Deleuze and Félix Guattari, *A Thousand Plateaus: Capitalism and Schizophrenia* (Minneapolis, MN: University of Minnesota Press, 1980), p. 410.

11 Ibid., p. 411.

12 Ibid., p. 451.

13 Marcel Lods, *La cité de la Muette à Drancy* 1933, cited in Pieter Uyttenhove, *Marcel Lods: Action, Architecture, Histoire* (Paris: Verdier, 2009), p. 129.

14 The building, destroyed in the Second World War, is discussed in detail in Peter Sulzer, *Jean Prouvé Œuvre complète*, 4 vols (Basel: Birkhauser, 2000), 2: 1934–1944, pp. 116–126.

15 Béatrice Simonot, *La Maison du Peuple: un bijou mécanique* (Blou: Monografik, 2010), p. 29.

16 Lavalou, *Prouvé*, p. 42.

17 Jean Prouvé, *Les constructions métallliques en tôles pliées assemblées par soudure*, a paper delivered to the *Société des ingénieurs soudeurs*, January 1950.

18 Clayssen, *Idée*, p. 73.

19 Gaston Bachelard, *La Terre et les rêveries de la volonté: essai sur l'imagination de la matière* (Paris: José Corti, 1947), p. 226.

20 Gaston Bachelard, *L'Air et les songes: essai sur l'imagination du mouvement* (Paris: José Corti, 1943).

21 Bachelard, *Terre*, p. 213.

22 Ibid., p. 46.

23 Deleuze and Guattari, *A Thousand Plateaus*, pp. 450–451.

24 The term appears throughout his lectures at the CNAM in the 1950s, and in interviews from the period.

25 Marcel Lods, 'Vers un domaine bâti réalisé industriellement', *Bulletin de l'Académie d'architecture* (1970), 30–41 (at p. 36).

26 The model, Baudrillard maintains, does not give birth to the series – 'this conception . . . is completely at loggerheads with lived experience, which implies a continual inductive movement from the series into the model'. Jean Baudrillard, *The System of Objects*, trans. by James Benedict (London: Verso, 1996), p. 154.

27 Jean Boutemain, an employee of Prouvé, attested to this in an interview of 1988: 'the main reason (for the production of "ordinary" partitions and metal joinery) was to feed the atelier. It had to keep going: Prouvé was bored by these.' See Jean-Claude Bignon and Catherine Coley, *Jean Prouvé – entre artisanat et industrie*, 2 vols. (Nancy: École d'architecture de Nancy, 1990), 1: 1923–1939.

28 Deborah Silverman, *Art Nouveau in fin-de-siècle France: Politics, Psychology and Style* (Berkeley, CA: University of California Press, 1989), p. 4.

29 J.K. Birksted, *Le Corbusier and the Occult* (Cambridge, MA: MIT Press, 2009), p. 281.

30 See Clayssen, *Idée, passim*.

31 Lods visited Prouvé's atelier on numerous occasions during the project and most of the drawings for the project were made there.

32 Marcel Lods, *La cité*, cited in Uyttenhove, *Lods*, p. 129.

33 Uyttenhove, *Lods*, p. 122.

34 Deleuze and Guattari, *A Thousand Plateaus*, pp. 412–418 (at p. 416).

35 (Immobile) building as (mobile) furniture.

36 Lavalou, *Prouvé*, p. 60.

37 Sulzer, *Œuvre complète*: 2, pp. 122–123.

38 Marcel Lods, 'La Reconstruction immobilière', *Mémoires de La Société des ingénieurs civils de France*, 98 (1945), p. 149.

39 Bignon and Coley, *Jean Prouvé – entre artisanat et industrie*, p. 45.

40 Ibid., p. 47.

41 Anon., *Acier*, no. 1 (1944), 6.

42 Prouvé ordinarily railed against the use of tubular steel of continuous section, particularly in otherwise folded structures, as it exemplified for him the unthinking approach to material use in construction prevalent among many Modernist designers.

Chapter 5

The production of
the Commons

Mies van der Rohe and the art
of industrial standardisation

Mhairi McVicar

In a 1924 article applauding but rejecting traditional handwork, Mies van der Rohe declared a vision of elevating industrial methods to an art. Industrial methods promised to override what Mies termed the 'irresponsibility' of the individual by producing architectural components within standardised systems. Employing a precisely controlled materials palette and detailing system developed at the Illinois Institute of Technology (IIT) campus over the preceding twelve years, the Commons Building[1] by the Office of Mies van der Rohe should have exemplified this promise. The correspondence, sketches, drawings, and shop drawings, however, of even one detail – a pressed steel window frame – reveal that this component alone required over a year of negotiations between numerous individuals. No matter how standardised the components or precise the instructions, the processes of architecture are inevitability shaped by the individual personalities who draw, write and build the work, a fact which continues to challenge expectations of absolute certainty and control in architectural production.

The perfection of 'industrial methods'

'As I was born into an old family of stonemasons', the architect Mies van der Rohe wrote in his 1924 article 'Building Art and the Will of the Epoch!', published in *Der Querschnitt*, 'I am very familiar with hand craftsmanship and not only as an aesthetic onlooker. My receptiveness to the beauty of handwork does not prevent me from recognizing that handcrafts as a form of economic production are lost.' Our needs, Mies continued,

Figure 5.1
**The Commons, IIT,
Office of Mies van der
Rohe, 1955, Chicago
History Museum,
HB-18679-C; Hedrich-
Blessing, photographer**

have assumed such proportions that they can no longer be met with the methods of craftsmanship. This spells the end of the crafts: we cannot save them anymore, but we can perfect the industrial methods to the point where we obtain results comparable to mediaeval craftsmanship.[2]

Referencing Henry Ford's publication *My Life and Times* as presenting 'mechanization in dizzying perfection',[3] Mies proposed in the same year that industrialisation could solve the 'social, economic, technical and even artistic questions'[4] through a fundamental reorganisation of the building trades and the wholesale adoption of industrial materials and processes. The industrial production of all parts, Mies wrote,

> can only be carried out systematically by factory processes, and the work on the building site will then be exclusively of an assembly type, bringing about an incredible reduction of building time. This will bring with it a significant reduction of building costs. The new architectural endeavours, too, will then find their real challenge.[5]

In his early writings, Mies variously defined 'the new architectural endeavours' as the search for honesty,[6] clarity, order, and economy, accessible through the adoption of industrial materials and methods which enforced precise planning and discipline from all involved, from architect to builder.[7] In a 1923 publication describing the benefits of 'ferroconcrete' Mies had warned against the perils of letting construction crews 'loose in the house'.[8] Mies's 1938 proposals as incoming Director for an architectural curriculum at the IIT in Chicago similarly sought to 'leave no room for deviation'.[9] Applied to all aspects of architectural production – from education, through design, to construction – industrialisation offered the allure of streamlined, efficient, predictable, repeatable and controllable processes, free from the uncertainties of individual input, or, as Mies put it, of the 'irresponsibility of opinion'.[10]

The Commons, IIT, Chicago

As the fourteenth constructed building on the IIT campus, Mies's Commons Building[11] – a one-storey plus basement pavilion comprising shopping and student centre facilities – might reasonably be expected to manifest such ideals. Design on the Commons began in December 1952,[12] thirteen years after Mies first began proposals for a campus on a 32' x 24' grid, composed throughout with a strictly repetitive materials palette. From their first constructed project at IIT (the 1943 Metals and Minerals building) Mies's office had repeatedly scrutinised precise detailing solutions for junctions between exposed wide flange steel columns, buff-coloured brick infill panels, and glass set in a steel frame.[13] Speculative unbuilt projects, and constructed prototypes of pavilion, classroom building and high-rises had iteratively tested typological variations of corners, roof junctions, and column expressions, exhaustively investigating the potential of raising standardised industrial components to an art.

The professional context within which the IIT campus was developed was one resolutely focused on efficiency, economy, and rationalisation. Following an 1871 fire, the City of Chicago had entered a boom period of rapid and ambitious rebuilding, enabling developers to push for larger, faster, and more efficient and predictable building processes.[14] As the structural and environmental engineering requirements of increasingly complex buildings moved beyond the scope of a single author, the emergence of specialist professions had encouraged the systematic organisation of both the building industry and the architectural profession.[15] By the 1880s, most Chicago practices had at least one partner with an engineering background.[16] As professional journals published articles advising architects on 'how to arrange their office spaces to maximise efficiency and productivity',[17] the systematic organisation of architectural production was supported by a wealth of prefabricated elements, which promised to simplify, speed up and rationalise all aspects of architectural production.

The value of prefabrication

The archives of the Office of Mies van der Rohe reveal a snapshot of architectural practice in mid-twentieth-century Chicago. Manufacturers' advertisements highlighted the efficiencies of systematisation and prefabrication: Speed-way Manufacturing Company's product literature for a Speed-Way Floor Clip;[18] Materials Service Corporation Redi-Mix Concrete promising 'Scientific Controls Guarantee: production governed by a scientific system of equipment and control';[19] thousands of prefabricated products systematically organised within Sweets Catalogue.[20] The emphasis on the container in Mies's European work, William Jordy has suggested, became an emphasis on the component in US projects.[21] In a 1959 BBC interview, Mies spoke directly of the benefits of prefabrication, noting that

> the value of prefabrication is the value of getting elements which we can use freely as we have doors and bathtubs . . . Now in our steel buildings we have about 3,000 windows and only two shapes. I think that is the best way of prefabrication.[22]

Dismissing the prefabrication of an entire building as too complicated, Mies stated instead that 'it is much better to deliver elements which we can use in a free way. Otherwise it can be terribly boring.'

The possibilities of prefabricated elements appear obvious at the Commons. Here was a building that could repeat the systems tested at numerous completed buildings constructed in the same materials, using the same structural grid, located on the same urban campus. A wider range of conceptual and constructed US typologies – including Farnsworth House and 860–880 Lake Shore Drive – offered an extensive archive of detailing solutions. In a 23 January 1953 letter to IIT housing manager Jack Guard,[23] Mies emphasised the repetitive nature of the commission, submitting, at the earliest stages of design, detailed unit prices based first on 'a comparison with the unit process of other campus buildings and second by a rough material break down on the building'.[24] At the Commons, the possibility of using identical, prefabricated elements, in a standardised, pre-tested system – of mechanisation in dizzying perfection, of factory processes and assembly-type work on the building site – could not, perhaps, have been more feasible.

'Our standard screen frame could be used'

On 17 June 1953, a letter from Hope's Windows to the attention of Mr [Myron] Goldsmith referenced a quote of $5,395.00 for sash and screens delivered 'in accordance with your detail and specification with the understanding that sash would be built into bar stock frames with the ornamental iron contractor'. As cost of job must be reduced, Hope's Windows explained, 'we submit the following alternate for your consideration'. The letter described four alternate details, including one alternate that suggested that '[i]f sash are made as per our detail our standard screen frame could be used in lieu of the tubular frame.'[25] Written seven months into the project development, the letter proposed alternates to achieve value engineering, including this suggestion that the supplier's own standard details be used in lieu of custom profiles proposed by Mies's office.

When design on the Commons began in December 1952, Mies's office was active in the design or construction of thirty projects, located in six US states and two countries – an office dealing with numerous, diverse, and physically dispersed

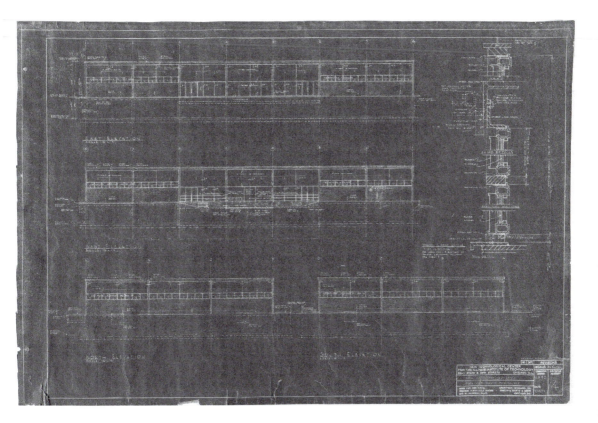

Figure 5.2
**The Commons, IIT.
Blueprint drawing,
Elevations (East, West,
North, and South) and
window sections,
28 May 1953. Mies van
der Rohe, Architect/
Friedman, Alschuler &
Sincere, Associate
Architects and
Engineers. Mies van der
Rohe Archive, the
Museum of Modern Art,
New York. MR5203.80,
copyright DACS 2015**

commissions. Mies was absent for seven weeks during the pre-bidding stage of the Commons – a stage in which negotiations with suppliers such as Hope's Windows over detailing and associated costs were underway. The project also passed through the hands of five architects in Mies's office over an eighteen-month period – from Mies himself, to Myron Goldsmith, Gene Summers, Joseph Fujikawa, and intern David Haid. The project correspondence reveals a decidedly complex process of decision-making regarding revisions which were not always initiated by Mies's office, and which were often in response to the practicalities of material availabilities, costs, time pressures, and legal frameworks – and a multitude of individual opinions.[26]

One component, multiple hands

Project correspondence for the Commons gives detailed insights into the impact of time and cost pressures on the project. The detailing of a steel window frame alone required input, over a period of fourteen months, from five organisations: numerous architects within Mies's office; architects and structural engineers at Friedman, Alschuler & Sincere; Hope's Windows; Gerber Ornamental Iron; and other unlisted suppliers of the glass itself. Hope's Windows' proposal excluded glass, glazing, screen application, and field painting: the design, construction and 'punch-list' involved numerous negotiations between customised elements and is repeated elsewhere in the project. A study by Thomas Beeby highlighted idiosyncrasies within the column and roof detailing, revealing

Chapter 6

Modular men

Architects, labour and standardisation in mid-twentieth-century Britain

Christine Wall

> It was British architects above all others who, in the post-war years, threw themselves into the 'industrialization of building', and by their enthusiasm carried the process further than architects had ever done before.[1]

Reyner Banham's statement provides a good starting point for an examination of the immediate post-war years and a closer look at what he terms architects' 'enthusiasm', which might also be interpreted as a vigorous attempt to maintain professional control of the building process in the face of encroachment by civil engineers and contractors.[2] Within the construction industry the term industrialisation was not precisely defined. Construction always included an element of factory production, either on site or off site, but the manner in which this was carried out depended on scale, materials organisation and a host of other issues, with one factor largely ignored by the architectural profession: the role of labour.

When factory manufacture was still in its infancy in the early nineteenth century there were passionate debates on whether working with machinery under regimented conditions was beneficial or detrimental to the welfare of the working classes, with many discussions focused on the effect of machinery on skilled artisanal labour. Adam Smith had already, in *The Wealth of Nations* (1776), proposed that the division of labour increased productivity and profit, and Charles Babbage, later, added the observation in 1832 that within a factory the distribution of skilled and semi-skilled labour to particular tasks saved on wages, and also on training. But it was Andrew Ure in *The Philosophy of Manufactures* (1835), who imagined a future in which 'self-acting' machines superseded human labour altogether. For Ure, labour must be subordinate to the 'vast automaton' of a centrally powered factory, and he explicitly argued for mechanical systems as a means to break the autonomy of the skilled worker as, 'the more skillful the workman, the more self-willed and intractable he is apt to become'.[3] Ure was deeply antagonistic to the idea of workers' combinations because stoppages and walk-outs were hugely disruptive to the running of the early, unwieldy, steam- or water-powered mills he described, and he proposed the factory system itself as a means to control the working class.

In Britain it was John Ruskin who provided a counter-narrative to Ure. The earliest formulation of Ruskin's writings on the production of architecture are found in *The Seven Lamps of Architecture* (1849), later elaborated in the famous passages in *The Stones of Venice* (1851–1853), in the chapter entitled 'On the Nature of Gothic Architecture', an influential tract not only for the Arts and Crafts movement but also for the building craft unions.[4] Ruskin's forceful arguments against repetitive machine-based tasks, the separation of intellectual from manual labour, and his arguments for a close relationship between architect and craftsmen, preferably with the architect gaining hands-on experience of the practicalities of building, appealed directly to architects. The following account of 'light and dry' component building reveals that these nineteenth-century views on labour in relation to industrialisation were still very evident in mid-twentieth-century architectural approaches to industrialised building.[5]

Despite the problematic application of the term industrialisation to the fragmented site-based process of building it became widely used within architecture as part of the rhetoric of modernism and associated with the notion of progress. The foundations were laid early in the twentieth century in Britain: a particularly fertile period for experimentation in prefabrication and standardisation. This period saw the publication of a number of reports. For example, the Committee on New Methods of House Construction established by the Ministry of Health published four reports in 1924–1925 on the relative merits of housing in steel, timber, concrete and pre-cast concrete blocks. It is notable that the members of this committee included two representatives of organised labour, Richard Coppock of the National Federation of Building Trade Operatives (NFBTO) and George Hicks of the Amalgamated Union of Building Trade Workers (AUBTW), neither of whom raised any objections to the new materials and methods recommended.[6] Research into industrialised methods continued throughout the inter-war period at the Building Research Station.[7]

As well as this British research, the American industrialist Alfred Farwell Bemis's *Rational House Building* (1936) became a key text for architects committed to standardisation and prefabrication, and is notable for being the first to argue that a standardised module was a requirement for industrialisation and that the size of this module should be four inches, derived from the size of a timber stud.[8] Less well known is Alfred Bossom's account of skyscraper building published in 1934, where he set out an early manifesto for industrialisation which, as well as standardisation and prefabrica-tion, argued for efficient site organisation.[9] Based on his experience in the USA, Bossom recommended that architect and contractor cooperate from the outset of a contract, setting up long-term agreements with operatives' organisations and materials suppliers.

Bossom regarded building as a cooperative enterprise best entered into as teamwork but recognised that in Britain, with its rigid class structure, this ideal was going to be difficult to achieve.

In 1945, a team of architect investigators headed by Mark Hartland Thomas and including Richard Llewelyn-Davies, travelled to Germany to assess its building industry, where they interviewed Ernst Neufert, the former Bauhaus student who became Commissioner for Building Standardisation under Albert Speer. All wartime building in Germany had been regulated by dimensional standardisation set down in the German Industrial Standard (DIN) No. 4171. The system was compulsory during the war years, and it continued in use even after the ordinances had been abolished, suggesting that it had become to a certain extent standard practice. Hartland Thomas returned with a copy of Neufert's book, *Bauordnungslehre* (1936), which he had removed for careful scrutiny before making 'recommendations for adoption in Britain and America'.[10] It is quite likely he had access to all of Neufert's design work and he praised the German construction industry in his own small book on modern architecture for the layman *Building is Your Business* (1947).[11]

With the challenge of post-war reconstruction ahead, industrialisation was considered the solution to increase efficiency and production in a British building industry widely perceived as in desperate need of modernisation.[12] During the war Coppock (NFBTO) and Luke Fawcett (AUBTW) had represented the interests of organised labour in the coalition government and were preparing for some form of nationalisation of the building industry in the post-war period. This did not materialise under the first post-war Labour government when Aneurin Bevan, Minister responsible for housing, gave in to pressure from private-sector building contractors and shelved plans for a National Building Corporation. Organised building labour no longer had a voice at government level. In 1951, when the first of three successive Conservative governments came to power, housing provision was a key election issue and the construction industry became the focus of unusual attention with a number of government reports pointing to low efficiency and productivity. Hartland Thomas and (now Lord) Bossom responded to these by inaugurating the Modular Society in 1953, with the aim of promoting industrialisation through campaigning for 'co-ordinating [of] dimensions of materials, components and fittings on a modular basis'.[13] Although it supposedly comprised 'all those concerned with building from clients to craftsmen' there was a noticeable and significant absence of any representatives of the operative workforce, and membership was heavily weighted towards architects, many of them well-known establishment figures.[14]

The Society's journal *The Modular Quarterly* published debates and arguments on the key determinants of industrialisation,[15] the size of a module, joints and jointing methods and tolerances, and also provided advertising space for manufacturers' products. Its regular meetings, dinners and site visits also provided excellent networking opportunities between manufacturers, contractors and architects. The Society argued that modular coordination would reduce the wastage involved in traditional building, as modular structures would be built to order and fitted together on site. In turn this would transform the construction process, from muddy chaos to clean and rational orderliness through using a unified system of components, chosen by the architect from a catalogue

Figure 6.1
The *Modular Quarterly*,
Autumn 1958

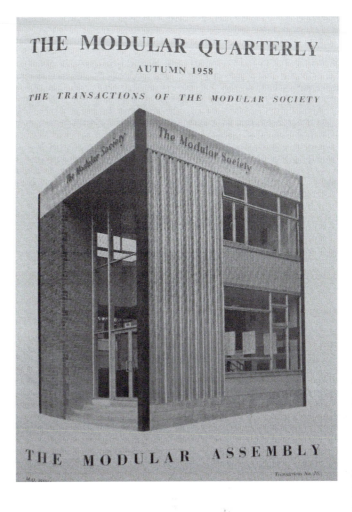

and fitted, ideally without any adjustment, on site. As such, modular coordination was promoted in Britain and internationally as a system which would give total control over the building process to the architect, and which

> Places at the disposal of the individual creator accurate and universally understood definitions which make it possible both to reduce the diversity of the product used in building – and to manufacture them on an industrial scale – and to reconcentrate in the hands of the designer the power to define *in toto* the object to be achieved.[16]

The Modular Society quickly adopted four inches as a basic module size in May 1954, and compiled and published the first edition of a *Modular Catalogue* of compatible components available from manufacturers. They followed this with a well-documented public relations exercise in constructing a 'Modular Assembly', promoted as the first building to be designed entirely on the basis of the four-inch module, erected on the South Bank in 1958.

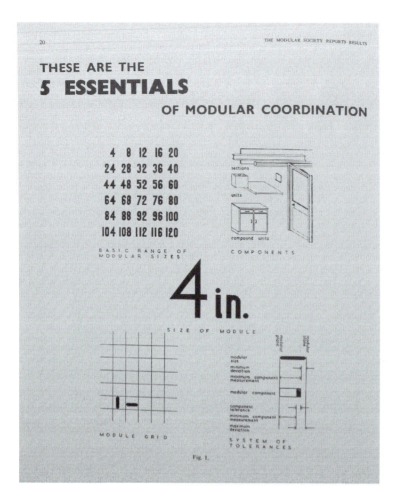

Figure 6.2
**The five essentials of
modular coordination.**
Modular Quarterly,
Summer 1958

The first, outline drawings for the proposed Modular Assembly appeared in the *Modular Quarterly* of Autumn 1956, drawn-up by Hartland Thomas who was eager to experiment with the idea of designing to strictly applied modular rules.[17] The structure, a twenty-foot cube, incorporated as many changes of material as possible while still maintaining 'unity of idea' through strict adherence to three design rules:

1. Every component, even structural framework, must 'keep its station' on the assembly-grid.
2. Modular components must have appropriate external dimensions in whole multiples of the module measured to centres of joints.
3. A modular joint must only occur within the clearance between two components.

The third rule is followed by the caveat that the actual size of clearance in modular design was, as yet, undecided. Hartland Thomas went on to emphasise the distinction between the modular coordination of components – the 'manufacturer's business' – and the design of modular buildings – the 'architect's business'. He used naval terminology

Figure 6.3
Presentation drawings for the first Modular Assembly. *Modular Quarterly*, 1958

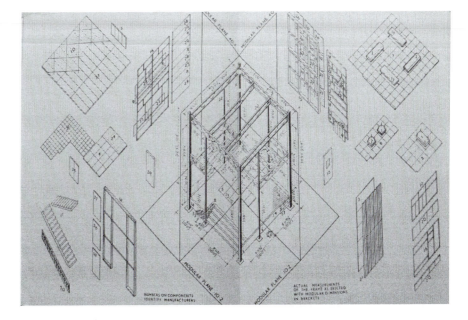

(it would seem without any irony) to describe the role of the architect, as being akin to 'the commodore of a convoy'.[18]

Amended plans and details, confusingly dispensing with dimensions in favour of modular notation, appeared in the *Modular Quarterly*, together with an invitation to members to participate in the erection of the Assembly on the basis of 'provide and fix'.[19] The response was 'electric', with twenty-six firms expressing interest, including Pilkington Brothers, Hills, Holoplast, Gardiner, E.C. Gransdon, Howard Farrow, Crittalls and a roll-call of firms involved with the school-building program in Hertfordshire, which later developed into CLASP.[20] The next stage was the onsite assembly of the small building, although the Technical Committee carefully pointed out that it was not to be judged as a building but as an experimental 'demonstration of the possibilities of building with modular components'.[21]

The object was to use as many modular components as possible that could be bought 'off the shelf' to demonstrate the possibilities of an open approach to dimensional coordination rather than closed systems, like CLASP, that depended on manufacturers supplying specific components for each respective scheme. Final drawings were published as a double-page exploded axonometric, a drawing form usually associated with engineering drawings, thus assuming a factory-based manufacturing process, and conveying the fitting together of all the various components. The completed Modular Assembly officially opened on 1 October 1958, with the Modular Society employing a uniformed commissionaire to man the door.[22] It existed for only ten weeks before being dismantled, but succeeded in attracting visits from Hugh Molson, Minister of Works and HRH Prince Philip and it was widely reported in the trade press.

A series of post-mortem public meetings were arranged following the dismantling of the Assembly to analyse the experiment. The reports of these meetings were published in the *Modular Quarterly* and reveal a number of criticisms from the contractors. Introducing engineering tolerances on site was 'going too far, particularly in view of the shortage of skilled craftsmen in the industry after the war'.[23] It was revealed that there were problems with all the close-fitting components such as wall tiles and floor tiles, which did not line up with the modular grid. But the most fundamental problem, and the one with the most consequences, was the inaccuracy of the structural framework. Here it was found that not only were the dimensions of the components inaccurate but the reinforced concrete columns had also been positioned out of their 'stations' on the modular grid, leading to further cumulative problems in fitting adjacent components. Mr Pryor of Howard Farrow commented on the reality of site work:

> It was one thing for the purist designer to pinpoint exactly the position of the column but another to do it in practice when handling a 20-foot-long column in a high wind with a large crane. In fact about 1½ inches tolerance was allowed on the base plate bolts for adjustments, but it was impossible to pull or push a column weighing a couple of tons to within an eighth of an inch.[24]

Michael Hatchett, a Modular Society member and site foreman, was responsible for the supervising of the construction of the Assembly and he remembers the site as being chaotic and poorly organised, with a number of changes of site agent during the construction process.[25] He also recalled that actual construction tolerances were quite different to the design tolerances, and that as the contractors were delivering their services for nothing – in fact they were paying for the privilege of being involved – the project was understood by them purely as a publicity exercise.

Although these problems with site construction had been conscientiously noted and were reported back to the technical committee, they were completely dismissed at a special meeting held on 1 December 1958 to assess the experiment. On the general question of accuracy of construction carried out by the building operatives it was stated that:

> Whilst we should not demand greater accuracy in assembly than is reasonable for current practice, the adoption of modular co-ordination was likely to produce an automatic and progressive improvement in accuracy. This had been the experience in mechanical engineering over the last 150 years.[26]

This extraordinary statement revealed that the sentiments of Ure were still current: 'automatic improvement' implying that the labour force were subservient to and integrated with technological progress and that there was no human agency involved in the process of building. Issues of skill, the need for training in the new occupations associated with industrialised building and the building labour force itself did not concern the Modular Society's Technical Committee. Despite the considerable problems with the building process, Hartland Thomas and the other members announced the experiment an unqualified success, stating that 'modular buildings should now be designed in full confidence that modular components will be forthcoming and with tolerances settled by their manufacturers according to the method that we have shown'.[27]

Not all architect members of the Modular Society had a complete lack of interest in the skills required for industrialised building. In 1956, well before the site work on the Modular Assembly began, William Tatton Brown addressed a meeting of fifty Society members and drew on his experience of school building in Hertfordshire to explain the new problems arising from building with standardised, prefabricated components:

> It is often supposed that insofar as mechanisation eliminates manpower, it reduces the need for human skill. In fact, of course, the reverse is the case. Prefabrication calls for a greater and not a lesser degree of skill at all levels . . . the craftsman has to exercise a higher degree of care in handling costly components of far higher quality and finish than those normally delivered on to a building site. A far higher degree of precision in fixing is also required as the slightest bodge or botch will be immediately apparent.[28]

Tatton Brown concluded that, as far as site skills were concerned, a new trade of 'Assembler and Jointer' was needed, who would be 'equipped with hand-powered tools, toggles and rivet guns and all sorts of mechanical devices which enable industrial products of high precision to be assembled quickly and accurately'.[29] These prescient remarks anticipated the construction practice of the future. Tatton Brown, reprising the sentiments of Ruskin, Morris and Lethaby, considered labour an integral part of building and in embracing industrialisation represented many architects, working mainly in local authority and government departments, who pioneered CLASP and similar light and dry systems.[30]

The Modular Society built two further structures. Alan Diprose designed a structure in the GRID system of pre-cast concrete framework for the NFBTE-organised

Figure 6.4
Modular Assembly at IBSAC 1964. *Modular Quarterly,* **Autumn 1964**

IBSAC 1964 Exhibition for the promotion of various housing systems to local authority clients. There were no post-mortems as, according to Diprose, 'the Modular Society Pavilion at IBSAC 1964 demonstrated that the theory of modular co-ordination is proved beyond doubt in practical application'.[31]

The third and final Assembly was designed by Bruce Martin for the 1966 IBSAC Exhibition, using the newly introduced metric 100mm module and the A75 structural timber system designed by three members of Farmer & Dark Architects in the 1950s. Martin's design allowed for the names of the manufacturer to appear on all the components they contributed so that the whole structure acted as a two-storey advertising stand for the participating firms.[32]

By the mid-1960s industrialised building was promoted under Harold Wilson's government by the Ministry of Housing and Local Government (MHLG) as essential in enabling construction to work 'more like a factory industry'.[33] This was part of an MHLG directive to support the Labour government's decision to increase

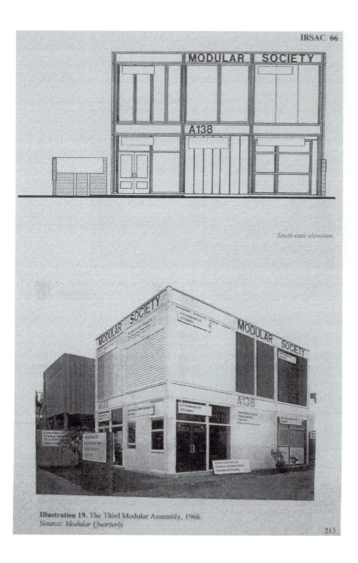

Illustration 19. The Third Modular Assembly, 1966.
Source: *Modular Quarterly*

213

Figure 6.5
Bruce Martin's Modular Assembly. *Modular Quarterly,* **Autumn 1966**

industrialised house building in the public sector and, for the first time, the operative workforce were included in a definition of industrialisation:[34]

> Not least, industrialised building entails training teams to work in an organised fashion on long runs of repetitive work, whether the men are using new skills or old.[35]

This statement clearly assumes a Taylorist organisation of the building site and state endorsement of factory methods in the building industry. But by 1968 sections of the architectural press were expressing growing cynicism with the whole field of industrialised building. The tongue-in-cheek comments of the editor of *Architectural Design*, Monica Pidgeon, were typical:

> Component systems for industrialized building seldom go further than a good joint, a universal cladding panel or a well worked out planning grid. Like nesting tables they seem to have boundless possibilities but their usefulness is strictly for the special occasion.[36]

There were more serious criticisms from the Building Research Station, succinctly expressed in an article by Joe Eden, pointing out that inter-changeability of components had already been achieved in mechanical engineering, after a hundred years of careful research, without the need for a module and that a greater exchange of experience between engineering and building would be beneficial.[37] He was particularly critical of the concept of a modular grid:

> Imaginary components can be fitted into imaginary holes, real components will fit or not fit into real holes, but fitting real components into imaginary holes may be a mental exercise but is metrological nonsense.[38]

The Modular Society was most successful in its long-term connection with the British Standards Institute (BSI) after Martin, a founder member of the Society, took up a post as Head of Modular Co-ordination Studies and co-opted members onto various BSI committees to promote the Society's particular version of modularity. Although prolific in its campaigning, educational initiatives, publications and public lectures, the Modular Society never addressed the fundamental relationships between labour, skill, tolerances and component building, even though these had been forensically examined in great detail in the first Modular Assembly. This blindness to labour concerns by the bow-tie-wearing architects of the Modular Society was fairly typical of the wider architectural profession.

Arguments for factory-based systems building, or offsite manufacturing, which only require semi-skilled workers to assemble a structure on site were prevalent throughout the twentieth century, and still persist. This notion, erroneously based on Adam Smith and resting on the assumption that the process of building can be split into a series of simple, separate tasks with a consequent reduction in time spent on workforce training, has greatly contributed to the enormous gulf between design and implementation which now characterises the British construction industry. Coppock's comment, made at the NFBTO's conference in 1950, is an accurate description of the role a considerable number of architects played in late-twentieth-century industrialisation in Britain and a counterpoint to Banham's praise:

> We would like to, if we possibly could, get [architects] down away from the wonder place in the skies to the realities of life . . .

Notes

1   Reyner Banham, 'Revenge of the Picturesque: English architectural polemics 1945–65', in *Concerning Architecture: Essays on architectural writing presented to Nicholas Pevsner*, ed. by John Summerson (London: Allen Lane, 1968), pp. 265–274 (at p. 271).
2   T.P. Bennett, 'The Architect and the Organisation of Post-War Building', *RIBA Journal* (January 1943), 63–74.
3   Andrew Ure, *The Philosophy of Manufactures* (London: Charles Knight, 1835), p. 20.
4   John Ruskin, *The Works of John Ruskin*, ed. by E.T. Cook and A. Wedderburn, 39 vols (London: George Allen, 1903–1912), X: *The Stones of Venice, Vol. 2* (1903), pp. 151–230.
5   The author is very grateful to Routledge for permission to use material previously published in Chapter 5 of *An Architecture of Parts: Architects, building workers and industrialisation in Britain* (London: Routledge, 2013). This has been considerably reworked for the purposes of this chapter.
6   Department of Health, *New Methods of House Construction Interim Report* (London: HMSO, 1924).
7   See Mariam Bowley, *The British Building Industry: Four studies in response to resistance and change* (Cambridge: Cambridge University Press, 1966); and R.B. White, Building Research Station, *Prefabrication: A history of its development in Britain* (London: HMSO, 1965).
8   Albert Farwell Bemis, *The Evolving House*, 3 vols (Cambridge, MA: Technology Press, 1933–1936), III: *Rational Design* (1936).
9   Alfred. C. Bossom, *Building to the Skies: The romance of the skyscraper* (London: Studio, 1934).
10 British Intelligence Objectives Sub-Committee Trip No. 1289, *The German Building Industry* (1946), p. 26. (Photocopy of the report held at the Institute of Civil Engineers Library, London.)
11 Mark Hartland Thomas, *Building is Your Business* (London: Allan Wingate, 1947).
12 See, for example: Ministry of Works, *Working Party Report on Building* (London: HMSO, 1950); Committee on the Cost of House-Building, *The Cost of House-Building* (London: HMSO, 1948); Anglo-American Council on Productivity, *Report on Building* (1950) (Cornell University Library); Ministry of Works, *Further Uses of Standards in Building: Second progress report of the standards committee* (London: HMSO, 1946); Ministry of Works, *Quicker Completion of House Interiors. Report of the Bailey Committee* (London: HMSO, 1953); and OEEC, *Cost Savings through Standardization, Simplification, Specialisation in the Building Industry* (Paris: OEEC, 1954).
13 Bruce Martin's papers. Statement to the Press.
14 This description appeared in the inside front cover of every edition of the *Modular Quarterly*.
15 In addition to the published output of the Modular Society this chapter also draws on material deposited with the RIBA Archive by Eric Corker in 1987. The author also interviewed Sir Roger Walters and Bruce Martin. Martin kindly made available his personal papers and records of the Technical Committee of the Modular Society and his correspondence with Mark Hartland Thomas.
16 *Proceedings of the Ad Hoc Meeting on Standardisation and Modular Co-ordination in Building* (Geneva: UN, 1959), Para. 15.
17 *Modular Quarterly*, 4 (1956), 27–29; A.L. Osborne and R.A. Sefton Jenkins, 'Joints and Tolerances in Modular Structures', *Modular Quarterly*, 3 (1955), 50; Bruce Martin, 'The Size of a Modular Component', *Modular Quarterly*, 4 (1956), 16–23.
18 *Modular Quarterly*, 1 (1959), 18.
19 R.A. Sefton Jenkins, 'Design for a Modular Assembly of Modular and Non-Modular Components', *Modular Quarterly*, 1 (1956/7), 22–23.
20 *Modular Quarterly*, 2 (1957), 24; and *Modular Quarterly*, 2 (1958), 17–18.
21 Ibid., p. 17.
22 RIBA Archives, Modular Society, Box 3, Technical Committee Minutes, 1957.
23 '1st Public Forum on the Modular Assembly', *Modular Quarterly*, 1 (1958/9), 14–17.
24 Ibid., p. 23.
25 Author's personal communication, 4 March 2000.

26   RIBA Archives, Modular Society, Box 3, Technical Committee Minutes, 1 December 1958.
27   RIBA Archives, Modular Society, Box 3, Technical Committee Minutes, January 1959.
28   *Modular Quarterly*, 1 (1956), 16.
29   Ibid.
30   A detailed account is found in Andrew Saint, *Towards a Social Architecture: The role of school building in post-war England* (New Haven, CT: Yale University Press, 1987); and, with a specific focus on these architects' relationship with labour, Christine Wall, *An Architecture of Parts: Architects, building workers and industrialisation in Britain, 1940–1970* (London: Routledge, 2013).
31   Ibid.
32   A full set of photographs and drawings appeared in *Modular Quarterly*, 3 (1966), 6–13, including a photograph of an inscrutable, but probably bored, Princess Margaret visiting the stand and 'inspecting' an exhibition of modular plumbing pipework.
33   Ministry of Housing and Local Government (MHLG), Circular No. 76/65, *Industrialised Housebuilding*.
34   Cmnd. 2838 (1965) *Housing Programme 1965–1970*.
35   MHLG, Circular No. 76/65.
36   Monica Pidgeon, *Architectural Design*, 38 (January 1968), 3.
37   Joe Eden, *Metrology and the Module*, Building Research Station Current Papers, 68 (1968), 148–150.
38   Ibid., p. 150.

Chapter 7

Post-1965 Italy

The 'Metaprogetto sì e no'

Alicia Imperiale

The twenty years after the end of the Second World War in Italy were marked by an urgent need to provide adequate housing for a rapidly growing population. Architects held the conviction that architecture, which utilised advanced industrialised techniques, could improve the quality of life for all citizens. Modular building systems were explored for their capacity to allow for the rapid construction of housing and other civic structures. This was the beginning of a period of startling changes in post-war Italy. Population growth and mass migration from the countryside and small towns to large cities caused crises and reactions. By the early 1960s, responses to the population boom and the need for housing at a mass scale were met with architectural innovations intended to deal with the issue of housing the *grande numero* (greater number). The need for a comprehensive planning program soon became clear, and the first national set of urban planning guidelines were established in 1962 in order to address these transformations. The *metaprogetto* (metaproject) was an overarching conceptual framework that sought to coordinate industrialised building processes with: prefabricated building components, the industries that would produce these architectural components, and the architects that would build new housing projects within the new urban planning initiatives. This was seen as a necessity in order to move from traditional and local production of housing to building at a large scale. The metaproject was an approach towards building that presented solutions to the housing problem by leveraging scientific developments such as systems theory, Umberto Eco's philosophical concept of the 'open work', and advances in the prefabrication of architectural components. The architectural application is *fabbricazione aperta* (open fabrication) through which prefabricated building components were to become interchangeable among different manufacturers. Hence, the basis of the metaproject is the development of an open system of prefabricated building components combined with a national organisation of labour and distribution.

The metaproject in theory

The Italian architect Alessandro Mendini in his 1969 article, 'Metaprogetto sì e no' (The metaproject yes and no) provides a critical lens with which to understand this period and offers the metaproject as a solution to the problem.[1] Mendini, better known as the editor of *Casabella* after 1970 and for his role in the promotion of 'radical architecture', had thought deeply in his earlier writings about the role of technology in architecture. Through the metaproject, Mendini countered the need for industrially produced architecture with his critique of the underlying capitalist system. The metaproject, conceived of and developed by Mendini, G. Mario Oliveri and other collaborators associated with Nizzoli Associati architects, was an idea based on the coordination of industrially produced building components used to produce large-scale prefabricated projects or mega-structures. Their concept of the metaproject is most clearly shown in their collaborative project for the CECA competition of 1965, and through a series of essays published in *Casabella* and brought together in Oliveri's book *Prefabbricazione o metaprogetto edilizio* (Prefabrication or the building metaproject) of 1968 (Figure 7.1).[2] The metaproject was not thought of simply as a concrete solution, but as both a call to unify the field of prefabrication dispersed amongst many individual manufacturers, and a political agenda, searching to enact large-scale policy changes in the entire building industry. An intended result was summarised by Mendini as the:

> demythicisation of the planner, because his role is integrated with those of all the others taking part in the 'integrated plan' (politicians, industrialists, etc.). A fundamental socio-political-philosophical objective should be that of 'superseding the models of all contemporary civilisations based on the primacy of economic values and on the principle of authoritarianism', with a view to recovering the pre-eminence of primal values long since lost.[3]

Mendini identified the metaproject as a planning scheme, an organised approach to design, harnessing industry, distribution, and a coordinated building system that would assure individual expression. He believed that a centralised system that was based on industrialised processes was necessary to provide fair access to housing for all citizens. Mendini saw the dangers of centralised state control of industry and labour, and his concern is expressed in the equivocal title of his essay, the 'yes' and 'no' of the metaproject. Mendini's concerns echoed a similar critique by the architectural historian Manfredo Tafuri, an active participant in the early 1960s on large-scale planning schemes as a solution to the crisis of the population boom. In his seminal essay 'Per una critica dell'ideologia architettonica', published in the journal *Contropiano* in 1969, Tafuri discusses the close connection that architecture has with larger economic and political

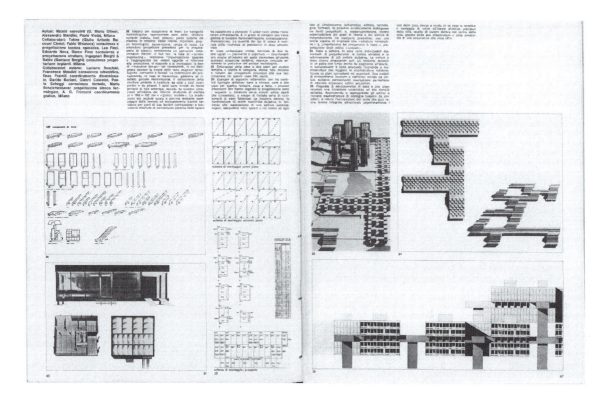

processes. The planning processes proposed through urban and architectural theories point, beyond themselves, to larger issues of the restructuring of production and consumption – to 'the plan of capital'. In Tafuri's analysis of Ludwig Hilberseimer he sees the individual building element or 'cell' as the first part of the larger economic structure. The individual building, an idea that Mendini calls the *unicum*, is, according to Tafuri:

> no longer an 'object' now. It is only the place in which the individual cells, through elementary assembly assume physical form. As infinitely reproducible elements, these units conceptually embody the primary structures of a production line that dispenses with the ancient concepts of 'place' and 'space'.[4]

He continues:

> In the rigid articulation of the production plan, the specific dimension of architecture, in the traditional sense of the term, disappears. As an 'exception' to the homogeneity of the city, the architectural object has completely dissolved.[5]

It is in this overall context that the idea of the metaproject is situated. Mendini, ever curious about its theoretical and linguistic aspect, summarised the metaproject as:

> a kind of logical analysis of architecture, for which the true and correct building language is prefaced by a sort of metalanguage . . . separating the metaproject

Figure 7.1
Alessandro Mendini, Paolo Viola, with collaborators Tekne as technical consultants and Ingegneri Borghi & Baldo, as engineering consultants. From Enrico D. Bona, 'Possibilità per la fabbricazione aperta: Le indicazioni che si possono trarre dai risultati del concorso indetto dalla Ceca', *Casabella*, 325 (April–June, 1968), 46–47. Reprinted with permission by Arnoldo Mondadori Editore S.p.A., Milan

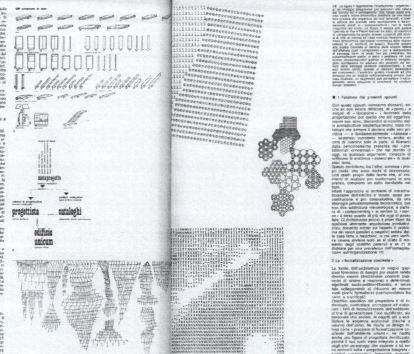

Figure 7.2
From Alessandro Mendini, 'Metaprogetto sì e no' (The problem of building metadesign), *Casabella*, 333 (Feb. 1969), 5–6. Reprinted with permission by Arnoldo Mondadori Editore S.p.A., Milan

from the architectural project and thinking of the metaproject as a principle of latent relationships and as a generative strategy that operates through such vehicles as modular coordination.[6]

The building metaproject, then, is a kind of overall framework in which industrialised building could be utilised to design a wide range of different architectural projects. Mendini's essay is highly theoretical, highlighting the linguistic basis of the building metaproject together with other formal structuralist compositions (Figure 7.2). He described these as *reproductive structures*, illustrating his essay with design studies from the HfG Ulm, Paul Klee's drawings, diagrams of concrete poetry, modular sculptures by William Tucker, and a volumetric study of a fugue by J.S. Bach by Heinrich Neugeboren. Mendini's examples parallel the combinatorial and serial work discussed by Eco in his essay on the 'open work'. Mendini, apparently conscious of publishing this study in an architectural magazine, redirects the discussion of the metaproject to bear more specifically on the issues of building. He states:

> Without overly intellectualising the discussion, a fundamental question regarding housing is this: how can one design a product-dwelling that is high quality but produced in extremely large numbers?[7]

In the Appendix to Oliveri's book, Paolo Viola provides a concrete description of the metaproject by discussing the five-year plan established in 1962 by the Milan public housing department (*L'Istituto Autonoma per le Case Popolari di Milano*).[8] Already several years into the period of economic boom, rational methods of production and organised forms of labour were considered to meet the demand for housing and other public buildings, which reflected a new scale of government-sponsored building. The proposal to industrialise building systems and labour practices was radical in a country whose building programs were principally based on local workmanship, utilising onsite masonry techniques with the use of only a few standardised parts. Viola claims that the metaproject will provide a new dimension to the issue of housing, one that linked the various economic, professional, social, cultural, and technical aspects of building.

Following other earlier studies, such as the 1946 *Manuale dell'Architetto* or *Il Problema Sociale Costruttivo ed Economico dell'Abitazione con Particolari Costruttivi di Architettura*, building manuals were developed and introduced to Italian architects and the building trades to provide a series of rules and standards for construction. These rules and norms were established for construction elements and building procedures. Tables of components, for example, provided a menu of parts that could be combined in various ways, thus generating form and producing a singular building, which Mendini called the *unicum*.[9] However, the most radical aspect of the metaproject idea is that the singular architectural component would be the generative principle of design. In this scenario, it is as if the industrially produced component itself has agency to generate projects by establishing a part-to-part relationship and creating larger architectural compositions from the bottom up, destabilising the idea of monumental architecture. According to Mendini, the most interesting aspect of this approach is that after the designer establishes the generative rules and component elements, the building *organism* may grow in an organised manner, which at the same time is open and relatively free.[10] These conceptual avenues, Mendini acknowledged, opened up the possibility of architecture cultivating new approaches in relation to traditional building techniques and artisan practices. In his words, the 'moment that one thinks beyond only designing and constructing the individual house, the metaproject undoubtedly provokes an evolutionary break and a complexity in the genetics of housing'.[11] Viola echoes this sentiment and believes that in the idea of the metaproject the modular coordination and production of building elements would increase productivity and capacity to meet increased market demand without limiting design expressiveness and would support innovative procedures, materials, form, and technology.[12] Moreover, Viola claims, the metaproject was a social project guided by a novel approach to building systems that must begin as a political desire to create, through programming, a more efficient political administration and opportunities for projects to be bid through national design competitions. In short, the metaproject was conceived of as a reform of the national economy. It asked the state to provide guidelines over production in a coordinated way that would provide a high quality product (housing) to all citizens through systematic building techniques, categories of products, and standardisation of quality. By adopting standardised building components to design various types of buildings a great variety of architectural solutions could be generated that could be responsive to the individual occupants and to the context in which they would be placed.[13]

The metaproject in practice

Central to the post-war recovery and to the future building programs in Italy were inter-European programs such as the Shuman Plan, a treaty ratified in 1951, which coordinated the steel and coal industries in its European member nations. Known as the CECA (*Comunità Europea del Carbone e dell'Acciaio*) or the European Coal and Steel Community, this plan was formed as an alliance of European industrialised countries, notably bringing ex-combatant Germany into an alliance with Italy, France, and the Benelux countries. Coal and other energy sources for instance were monitored by a centralised agency.[14] Such extra-Italian agencies spurred the industrial development of the peninsula, and encouraged proliferation of large-scale competition calls. This was similar to the complex combination of theoretical concepts and industrially produced architecture that was presented by the metaproject. Competitions for housing, infrastructure, and industrial facilities were the logical extensions of the complex interplay of international economics and national production. One could postulate that sponsored competitions at the national and international levels which had, until recently, operated only at regional levels were fuelled by a kind of meta-level of funding (Figure 7.3).

In 1965, the CECA sponsored an international competition that asked European designers to use industrially produced steel in a prototypical housing scheme for a family unit of five people – specifically two parents, two children and one other adult. The guidelines were quite open. The requirement was that minimally, the structure, the ceiling, the windows, and doors were to be designed in steel for a minimum of 10,000 units produced annually. The competitors had to design a light structure made of prefabricated elements to arrive at an apartment unit that, when combined with variations of certain elements such as roofs of different shapes, balconies, and loggias, would lead to the following housing types: a free-standing single family house, single family row houses, a two-storey building for four families, and a multi-family building. All parts of the building were to be factory made, and consideration had to be given towards transportation to the site.

The goal was to satisfy the requirements by combining the various base elements and the accessory elements to be able to offer housing on the commercial market. All the materials for construction needed to be produced in large factories; the use of any singular artisan-made elements was explicitly forbidden. Using the idea of combinations of the base components, the design solutions were required to demonstrate the maximum flexibility and variety possible by the standardised elements.[15] In his 1968 essay 'Possibilità per la fabbricazione aperta' for which Mendini wrote the introduction, Enrico D. Bona described the competition requirements and published the winning schemes. In addition he discussed the theoretical aspects inherent in the competition, including that of producing industrial building-products that would be interchangeable within the European countries. Competitors were required to ensure that housing elements would be developed so that various sizes and scales of housing could be constructed, a requirement that is also in line with the concept of the metaproject. Another inherent aspect of the idea of an interchangeable, open set of

ARTE PROGRAMMATA
E PREFABBRICAZIONE

una proposta di Bruno Morassutti e di Enzo Mari

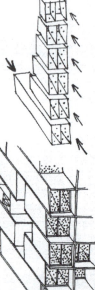

Figure 7.4
Enzo Mari and Bruno Morassutti, Programmed architecture, details of the axonometric view of the shifting of the various apartment units. Lara Vinca Masini, 'Arte Programmata e prefabbricazione', *Domus* 428 (July, 1965), 13. Reprinted with permission by Editoriale Domus S.p.A., Milan

change in regard to a dramatic increase in goods and materials in post-war Europe. In *Future Shock*, published in 1970, Alvin Toffler posits that the proliferation of modularity and the principle of indeterminacy, which encouraged the infinite ways in which elements could be brought together, were symptomatic of a new 'ephemeralisation of man's links with things that surround him'.[20] Elémire Zolla in *Eclissi dell'intellettuale* (The Eclipse of the Intellectual) explored the relationship between man and machine more than a decade earlier, questioning the paradoxical condition of what he termed 'mass man' in the

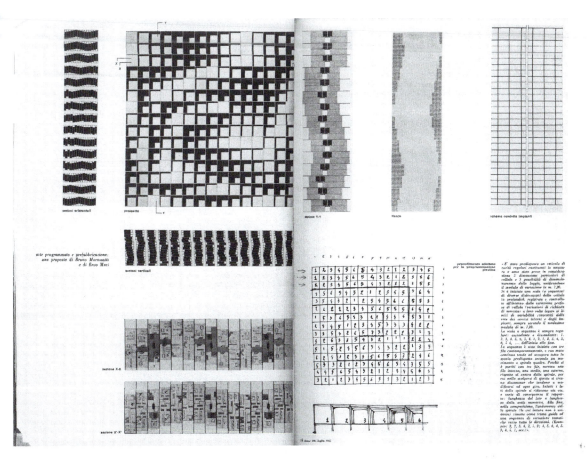

Figure 7.5
**Enzo Mari and
Bruno Morassutti,
Programmed
architecture. The
numeric diagram is
the procedure for
the programmed
development of the
simple apartment
elements that are
designed to fit into
an overall gridded,
reinforced concrete
structure. Lara Vinca
Masini, 'Arte
Programmata e
prefabbricazione',
Domus 428 (July 1965),
13–15. Reprinted with
permission by Editoriale
Domus S.p.A., Milan**

decline in the intellectual, cultural, social, and artistic creations of humankind under the impact of scientific advances.[21] The economic, social, political, and formal implications of the culture of indeterminacy in architecture in relation to rapidly expanding urban agglomerations is what Mendini allows to oscillate as the 'yes' and 'no' of the metaproject.

Conclusion

Mendini advanced the discussion from the practical to the theoretical aspects of the metaproject in his essay 'Metaprogetto sì e no'. He understood the metaproject as a dynamic system, one that could improve the environment, if understood as in holistic relationship with the natural environment. He believed that this could be accomplished by conceiving the prefabricated elements that constitute architecture and infrastructure as being coordinated and able to adapt to any new site or circumstance. Cybernetics, system theory, and similar scientific approaches were extended to enable humanity to be viewed as nested within a living system. This lens was useful and necessary when seen in light of a worldview of massive population growth, and as a way to deal with the idea of large numbers of people in a socially responsible, humane, and engaged manner.[22]

The issues of occupant-driven design, growth and change, and the industrialisation of building components were part of the leitmotif of post-war prosperity. The crisis in housing – framed by the idea of the open work and facilitated by new techniques of fabrication – was explored in earnest, but there was a decisive turn away from this towards the end of the decade, and towards a new mistrust of systems of control. By the late 1960s, issues of ineffective housing and urban planning had come to a head, and changed Italy irrevocably. While Mendini, as late as 1969, called for the necessity of industrialised processes of production for building, he was already critical of an overly technocratic approach. In the metaproject essay he refers to a report by the Rome-based FAO (Food and Agriculture Organisation of the United Nations), which presented quantitative data on growing populations around the world.[23] To take on this enormous task, Mendini believed that architects must be prepared to investigate construction on an industrial scale, arguing that the metaproject would permit housing to be manufactured through components and that 'freely joining the components in time and space guarantees the basic possibilities for a completely open construction system: distributional, productive, and expressive freedom'.[24] Most importantly, a project was no longer conceived of as a *unicum*, a singular building, but as a kind of growing organism that would develop in a responsive and responsible relationship with the environment. He also thought that the metaproject was a generative concept, meaning that the structure could germinate in an indirect manner, and create infinite morphological solutions that would be diverse, while still being homogeneous.[25]

The idea of organic growth and the city as a continuously growing organism of built structures is a concept that challenges static ideas of the city. Mendini went further, and claimed that this kind of growth was a step in the 'complexity of building genetics', a concept that holds significant traction in contemporary architectural discourse.[26] Thus, urban growth and the buildings that facilitate it were seen as a continuum, blurring the distinction between the building and the urban fabric, in a way that, as Mendini states, 'the "growing" organism must respond to resolve inter-agent problems, render the growth in different parts homogeneously, yet is tied together by the idea of the metaproject'.[27]

The need for, yet ambivalence towards, modern technology and the industrialisation of the building industry is indicated in the idea of the metaproject as 'yes' *and* 'no'. It was necessary to adopt advanced industrial techniques to be able to build housing, but there was a danger in uncritically embracing a technological and bureaucratic model. Overall, one can see in this period the problem that was hiding in plain sight – that of conceiving of the building process as fully rationalised while still being flexible enough to adapt to various situations. These questions still remain today. The comprehensive discussion regarding the philosophical, political, social, and aesthetic issues that surrounded the *metaprogetto*, its positive aspects and its problems, provides a set of interrogative tools to view our current condition.

Notes

1   Alessandro Mendini, 'Metaprogetto sì e no' (The problem of building metadesign), *Casabella*, 333 (February 1969), 4. The first page of the essay is in English and the quotations are in the original text. The remainder of the essay is in Italian. I do not believe that the English translation of the title in

     Casabella accurately conveys Mendini's consideration of both the positive and negative aspects of the metaproject and hence use my translation: 'The metaproject yes and no' throughout.

2   G. Mario Oliveri, *Prefabbricazione o metaprogetto edilizio* (Milano: Etas Kompass, 1968). See also Giuseppe Ciribini, *Industrializzazione dell'edilizia* (Bari: Dedalo, 1965).

3   Mendini, 'Metaprogetto sì e no', 4. This is in English in the original. It gives no reference for the text in quotation marks.

4   Manfredo Tafuri, 'Toward a Critique of Architectural Ideology', trans. by Stephen Sartarelli in *Architecture Theory since 1968*, ed. by K. Michael Hays (Cambridge, MA: MIT Press, 1998), p. 22.

5   Ibid., p. 22.

6   Alessandro Mendini, 'Possibilità per il metaprogetto edilizia', as an introduction to the essay 'Possibilità per la fabbricazione aperta', *Casabella*, 325 (June 1968), 38. (All translation by the author throughout.)

7   Ibid., 38.

8   Paolo Viola, 'Il metaprogetto edilizio come politica di progettazione', in Oliveri, *Prefabbricazione o metaprogetto edilizio*, p. 169.

9   Mendini, 'Metaprogetto sì e no', 8.

10   Ibid., 8.

11   Ibid., 8.

12   Viola, 'Il metaprogetto', p. 170.

13   Ibid., p. 170.

14   William Diebold Jr., *The Shuman Plan: A Study in Economic Cooperation 1950–1959* (New York: Frederick A. Praeger for the Council on Foreign Relations, 1959).

15   Competition brief pamphlet: *Per un Progetto di una unità d'abitazione fabbricata su scala industriale*, in *Gazzetta Ufficiale delle Comunità Europee*, no. 163, 4 October 1965, 1.

16   Enrico D. Bona, 'Possibilità per la fabbricazione aperta: Le indicazioni che si possono trarre dai risultati del concorso indetto dalla Ceca', *Casabella*, 325 (1968), 39.

17   Umberto Eco, *Opera aperta: forma e indeterminazione nelle poetiche contemporanee* (Milan: Bompiani, 1962).

18   Umberto Eco and Bruno Munari, *Arte programmata: arte cinetica: opere moltiplicate: opera aperta* (Milan: Officina d'arte grafica A. Lucini, 1962).

19   Lara Vinca Masini, 'Arte Programmata e prefabbricazione', *Domus*, 428 (July 1965), 13–15.

20   Alvin Toffler, *Future Shock* (New York: Random House, 1970). Italian translation *Lo choc del futuro* (Milan: Rizzoli, 1971).

21   Elémire Zolla, *Éclissi dell'intellettuale* (Milan: Valentino Bompiano, 1956).

22   On the other hand, seen as an obsession with technique.

23   Mendini, 'Dallo stile al metaprogetto', p. 175. Mendini refers to an earlier FAO report, *Inchiesta mondiale* (1957–1959), 1960. See Donella H. Meadows, *The Limits to Growth: 'A Report for The Club of Rome's Project on the Predicament of Mankind'* (New York: Universe Books, 1972).

24   Mendini, 'Metaprogetto: sì e no', 4.

25   Ibid., 13.

26   Ibid., 12.

27   Ibid., 8.

Part III
The construction site

Chapter 8

An introduction to Sérgio Ferro

Felipe Contier

Sérgio Ferro is a Brazilian painter, architect and professor, and one of the major intellectuals dedicated to questions of labour in art and architecture (Figure 8.1). Born in Curitiba in 1938, he studied and began his career in São Paulo. His interest in painting led him to the Faculty of Architecture and Urbanism (FAU) in 1957, which at the time was the only course in the creative arts available at the University of São Paulo (USP). At first, Ferro dedicated himself to the study of art history, completely oblivious to architecture. However, the effervescence of Brazilian architecture during the construction of Brasilia and the amazement caused by the architect and intellectual leader of FAU, João Vilanova Artigas, threw him and this younger generation of students and architects immediately into architectural practice.

While still a student, he formed a collective, along with his friends and main collaborators Rodrigo Lefèvre and Flávio Império. Together they would be known as the Arquitetura Nova group and they began an intense period of creative activity, encompassing painting, architecture, scenography, printmaking, theatre and

Figure 8.1
Sérgio Ferro at FAUUSP in 2012.
Photo: Ilka Apocalypse, 2012

theoretical studies. In 1959, Ferro and Lefèvre joined the Brazilian Communist Party, which at the time harboured much of the leftist intelligentsia and many prominent artists and architects, including Artigas and Oscar Niemeyer.

As Ferro was beginning his studies in Marxism, he also had the opportunity to design and build in Brasilia. It was then that he was exposed to the unspoken reality of the construction site, which seemed to him to be inconsistent with the humanist and emancipatory discourse of modernist masters. Ferro began to look for an answer in Marxist theory for the outdated and violent conditions of architecture's mode of production. At the same time, his interest in the history of art and architecture led him to investigate the formal and material techniques of modernism in a less passionate way, freeing him from the training he had received.

Being a brilliant student, Ferro became professor of art history at FAU in the year following his graduation, and that same year designed two experimental houses which, as one of Artigas's main disciples, earned his work inclusion in a chapter in *Arquitetura Contemporânea no Brasil*, the most important compendium of Brazilian architecture history.[1] At the Boris Fausto House (Figures 8.2 and 8.3) he experimented with industrialised components, whereas at the Bernardo Isler House (Figures 8.4 and 8.5), he designed a masonry-brick vault that tested his hypothesis on the most adequate construction solution to Brazil's economic and technical conditions.

Ferro's dialogue with Artigas started to diverge in the mid-1960s. Artigas was always mindful of the political meanings of architecture in history and economics, but he never gave up the artist's prerogative and his alliance with the progressive sectors of the bourgeoisie who supported the development of productive forces in Brazil. Based on the politicisation proposed by Artigas, Ferro and his colleagues sought to reverse the order of the project: departing from desired transformations in the relations of production to arrive at design solutions. In Ferro's studio, even though his colleagues were all artists, the aesthetic argument was forbidden. Instead of idealising the urban and formal result, the clients and their ideal budget, the labourers and their ideal materials, they took advantage of what was at hand, however precarious: wooden slats, low quality hollow bricks, small pieces of glass and unskilled labourers. This was a search for simple architectural solutions that could be immediately incorporated by the population, who in the Brazilian context largely build their own houses without architects. However, the result of these investigations was a non-conventional modern architecture, filled with a deep aesthetic sense.

During this period the catenary vault emerged as a mark of many of the group's projects. Its *raison d'être* was as a structural form that worked well under compression and, consequently, suited the use of rudimentary materials. Tables and benches were made in concrete, domes were made out of plastic buckets and open systems were put together from bike gear. Some of their projects had exposed electrical and plumbing systems that were fixed directly onto the façade with nothing more than a handful of concrete mix (Figure 8.6). In 1965, the Arquitetura Nova group was recognised with an entire issue of the architecture journal *Acropolis*. In 1967, during the military dictatorship, Ferro left the Communist Party and joined armed resistance groups. At the same time, he devoted himself to deepening his Marxist studies with prominent

Figure 8.2
Boris Fausto House in
São Paulo, designed in
1961 by Sérgio Ferro.
Photo: Ana Paula Koury,
1998

Figure 8.3
Boris Fausto House:
Ground floor plan.
Drawing: produced by
Ana Paula Koury for her
book *Grupo Arquitetura
Nova: Flávio Império,
Rodrigo Lefèvre e Sérgio
Ferro* (São Paulo:
Romano Guerra/Edusp,
2003).

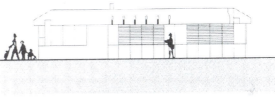

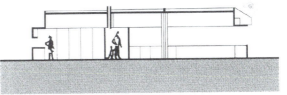

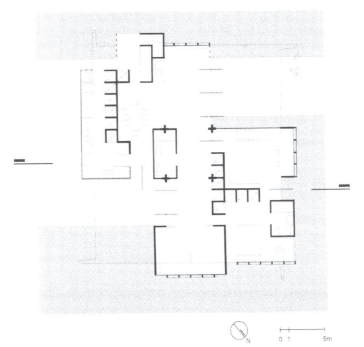

Figure 8.7
Cover of the first edition of *O canteiro e o desenho* by Sérgio Ferro (São Paulo: Projeto, 1979)

country's most impressive architectural texts, *O canteiro e o desenho*,[3] later translated into French as *Dessin/Chantier*,[4] or in English, 'Design/Construction Site' (Figure 8.7).[5] At Grenoble, he took over a leading role, introducing a multidisciplinary, horizontal methodology of teaching. He was also responsible for the first research initiatives at the School. Leading a group of young architects, he made a long and detailed study of the Monastery of La Tourette, exposing its site work and the consequences of the sculptural intentions of Le Corbusier for its construction.[6] Later, Ferro dedicated himself to study the Medici Chapel, interested in the meanings of labour in Michelangelo's sculpture and architecture.[7]

Ferro remains active – painting and writing – and a fierce critic of the separation between theory and practice. The modest amount of his published work is not proportional to its recognised value. Ferro's texts mix scholarship, originality and a disturbing relevance to the deepest – and at the same time most quotidian – issues of our profession.

Notes

1   Yves Bruand, *Arquitetura Contemporânea no Brasil* (São Paulo: Perspectiva, 1981).
2   Sérgio Ferro, *A casa popular/A arquitetura nova* (São Paulo: GFAU, 1972).
3   Sérgio Ferro, *O canteiro e o desenho* (São Paulo: Projeto Editores, 1979).
4   Sérgio Ferro, *Dessin/Chantier* (Paris: Éditions de la Villette, 2005).
5   In Latin languages, desenho/dessin has a double meaning: design and drawing. Ferro uses this word among other reasons because Artigas had a lecture called 'O Desenho', where he would explain the origin of the word as related to 'destiny', 'purpose', 'intention'. In Portuguese, the title is literally: 'The Construction Site and the Design'. In French, he chose the solidus (slash) intending it to be read as 'Design over Construction Site' or 'Construction Site under Design'.
6   Sérgio Ferro, Chérif Kebbal, Philippe Potié and Cyrille Simonnet, *Le Couvent de la Tourette* (Marseille: Parenthèses, 1987).
7   Sérgio Ferro, *Michel-Ange: architecte et sculpteur de la chapelle Medicis* (Lyon: Plan Fixe Édition, 1998).

have no intrinsic property other than that of establishing the necessary preconditions for the existence of the social system to which they belong; their presence – in itself devoid of significance – enables the social system to exist as a whole.[9]

The design of the finished product affects only – and only relatively – the circulation and consumption stages. Until the finishing of the product, design is a means (and not a neutral mediator, as we will see) to channel the fragmented work of the labourers into this stage at which it is ready to be marketed. At the level of the building site, the design is the mould into which 'idiotised' labour (in André Gorz's expression) is poured.[10] The shape and purpose of this crystallisation are irrelevant, for the time being; all that matters is the depositing of broken-down tasks in the one same object being formed. The product's design is mostly aimed at the heteronomous production – and this not so apparent function is the predominant one.

2c – In order to further elaborate on my last statement I will briefly return to production by manufacture. In manufacture (unlike the case of industry) operational know-how has not yet been transferred to machinery. Labourers are still the holders of this knowledge and responsible for the concrete progress of the operations. They sell their labour power to capital, but do so on the understanding that they will make their knowledge and know-how available to capital, without which manufacture cannot produce. Therefore the labourer's subordination to capital is merely formal. In terms of concrete work output, except for grave deformations due to the excessive fragmentation of the tasks, the workman would proceed (almost) in the same way in forms of production that are not subsumed to capital.

This feature of labour in manufacture has numerous important consequences. For capital, its merely formal subordination is a precarious form of subordination. The domination capital exerts, based on the appropriation of all the material means of production, has a flaw: it does not include the subjective means of production, knowledge and know-how. (We will see further on how the transfer from formal to real subordination, in the sphere of construction, is a simulacrum of transfer.) This flaw tends to weaken the domination, and the most extravagant devices are consequently employed to remedy such a flaw.

2d – According to Marx, 'since handicraft skill is the foundation of manufacture, and since the mechanism of manufacture as a whole possesses no framework, apart from the labourers themselves, capital is constantly compelled to wrestle with the insubordination of the workmen.'[11] If in formal subordination, the subjective means of production are still held by the labourer, incorporated in his knowledge, in his know-how and skills, they can be used as a weapon of resistance in his fight against capital. I repeat: without these means manufacture does not work, especially in the case of fundamental crafts up to the nineteenth century such as masonry and carpentry. Construction history is full of important strikes that paralysed construction activity for long periods and were organised by workmen from those crafts. (Friedrich Engels recounts in detail a long strike by carpenters of Manchester supported by the other building crafts, and insists on the employers' difficulties replacing strikers.)[12] David Harvey notes that these crafts can be monopolised and are as powerful as those tools of capital – but obviously in the opposite direction.[13] We will see further on how this flaw in subordination contributed to the emergence of modernism in architecture.

Since the beginning of the history of our post-medieval architecture, building sites have been favoured grounds for bouts of insubordination by workmen from these monopolisable crafts. Capital's devices against this insubordination – inseparable from formal subordination – are diverse, numerous and, as I said before, extravagant; unexplainable if we ignore the intricacies of manufacture, amongst which we must include design.

The implicit logic of the crafts, as created by the workmen's own tradition, has a certain range of forms compatible with this logic. Roughly, this range can be illustrated by Romanesque and Early Gothic architecture. Now, as Manfredo Tafuri noted, one of the concerns of the first architects was to ridicule and disqualify this range of forms and impose on buildings an *ersatz* classicism, masking the real construction that corresponds to such a range in a typical instance of symbolic violence.[14] Since then and to this day, even as manufacture is disfigured with side-products of real subordination, it is difficult to find works of a symbolic ambition in which design does not go against construction logic. I will return to this matter further on.

Another device, equally originated at that early stage, is art. Art (*ars*) used to be the name of all qualified crafts, without distinction. Since the early Renaissance, the drive of the fine arts to be admitted as liberal arts made the material labour of those artists a problematic one. It cannot be avoided, for without such a labour (at least until post-modernism) there is no work of art, and therefore there is no artist (also until post-modernism). But in order to become liberal artists, these artists should not work with their hands, which would be inadmissible in the field of liberal arts. Painting and sculpture struggled to find a way out of this impasse (a point that is dealt with in my recent book *Fine Arts and Free Labour*).[15] Architects, in turn, had less problems: they hadn't laid their hands on building since the high Gothic period . . . They drew and had models made for them – things that were not incompatible with their progress up the social ladder. Meanwhile, they obviously could not remain grounded in, and continue to reproduce, the same range of forms as manual labourers: they would risk glorifying precisely what manufacture sought to hide, its structural dependency on the labourers. Design therefore proceeds to seek in itself or in its history, forms that were external to the labourers' range of forms. But this range stems from the technique, the knowledge and the know-how that building manufacture employs to assure its own operation. An impasse still – which has not yet been solved by architecture as separated from the building site. To this day, design and (correct) construction are antagonists – contemporary architecture is testimony to this. The persistence of this contradiction should not come as a surprise to us: 'what has fallen out [in the sense of a quarrel] from a sole principle does not henceforth follow independent routes . . . instead the two never occur *separated* [Adorno uses the Ancient Greek word *choris* here].'[16] The split between design and building site, formerly integrated, leaves in each of these the void of its other. From then on 'the two

neve
attrib
expe
techi
is al
becc
ordir
disg
agai
tech
des
man
man
their
its f
and
anec
Tour
conc
writi
mon
of m

2e –
has
built
boar
pher
Ferd
at th
that
abov
that
build
post-
techr
mac
(Labo
build
trans
and
and
that l
and

tangible coincidence. Whoever commands a (*submitted*) *labour* focuses on contents determined by external elements, including Nature, which only imposes demands. Matter, then, is nothing but 'means of production' and the teleological action operated by the subject is not, according to Simondon, *essentially technical*. The operation gets lost amid external determinations of a *form* and a *content* that do not concern it.[19]

For Simondon, technical objects emerge in a world where our 'social structures and psychic contents' have been shaped and determined by the category *labour*.[20] But to which category of labour does Simondon refer – is it heteronomous labour or 'free labour'? Labour invariably emerges in his work in its heteronomous sense, as 'alienated labour'. In the present mode of production, we are used to the total subsumption of labour, and therefore it is essential to distinguish the category of labour from the idea of 'production'. Marx states that men 'indirectly produce their own material life' only when they produce 'their means of subsistence', but not when they 'labour'. Furthermore, Marx also indicates, as we have seen, how much technology can reveal about 'the mode of formation of his [man's] social relations, and of the mental conceptions that flow from them', precisely because it addresses the way in which man immediately relates to Nature when promoting the production of his life.

The *labour* to which Simondon refers in *Du mode d'existence des objets techniques* is not therefore the 'free labour' that Ferro describes when he reproduces, defends and repeats many times what William Morris claimed as the meaning of *art*, and that also allows me to advocate for a reconciliation between Simondonian thought and the Marxian text. It is precisely this notion of *free labour* – of a non-hylomorphic relationship with Nature – that encourages us towards a practical and didactic effort to overcome the gap between *technique* and *theory of architecture*. As Ferro insists, reiterating Morris:

> This is not a provocation: art, for us, is nothing but the expression of free labour. It is only natural therefore to study the free building site by drawing on the concepts of aesthetics.[21]

In the course of its *process of individuation*, a work of architecture leaves *traces* that allow us to substantially recompose the *modes of existence* implied in its fabrication. More than taking fabrication as the essence of architecture, redeeming these modes of existence (in the terms of the technical ensemble) means to take them again as the core of human becoming and, at the same time, to restore the social and political relevance of architecture.

Notes

1   Note that I refer here to the Brazilian context, to that multitude of architects who work in the building materials market, real estate companies, decoration shops, small contractors firms, etc., to whom the métier is only a 'plus' that helps them position themselves in the labour market.

2   Karl Marx, *Capital: A critique of Political Economy, Volume I, Book One: The process of production of Capital* (1867), www.marxists.org/archive/marx/works/1867-c1/index.htm (accessed 28 April 2015).

3   'Apparent because it would be impossible to dissociate the fabrication of architecture from the material facets that determine it.

4   Sérgio Ferro, *A história da arquitetura vista do canteiro: três aulas de Sérgio Ferro* (São Paulo: Grêmio da Faculdade de Arquitetura e Urbanismo da USP–GFAU, 2010), p. 13.

5   João Marcos Lopes and José Lira (eds), *Memória, trabalho e arquitetura* (São Paulo: Editora da Universidade de São Paulo, 2013).

6   Ferro, *A história da arquitetura vista do canteiro*, p. 115.

7   André Gorz, *Metamorfoses do trabalho: crítica da razão econômica* (São Paulo: Annablume, 2003).

8   Ferro, *A história da arquitetura vista do canteiro*.

9   Sérgio Ferro, *Arquitetura e trabalho livre* (São Paulo: Cosac Naify, 2006), p. 417.

10   Sérgio Ferro, Chérif Kebbal, Philippe Potié and Cyrille Simonnet, *Le Corbusier: Le Couvent de la Tourette*, Monographies d'Architecture (Marseille: Éditions Parenthèses, 1987).

11   Sérgio Ferro, *Michel-Ange: architecte et sculpteur de la chapelle Medicis* (Lyon: Plan Fixé Édition, 1998).

12   Gilbert Simondon, *Du mode d'existence des objets techniques* (Paris: Aubier, 1989).

13   According to Simondon, *transduction* is an operation where Being lags behind itself, causing tension, and where each element of the individuating structure informs, by analogy, the following elements, propagating the changes and mutations progressively. Gilbert Simondon, *L'individu et sa genèse physico-biologique* (Grenoble: Éditions Jérome Millon, 1995, p. 32).

14   Gilbert Simondon argues, in his *Du mode d'existence des objets techniques*, that a more careful investigation about technical objects and correlations less apparent between *schemes*, *elements* and *technical individuals* is necessary. He intends it to achieve – more than a technology, a *mechanology* – of these individuals, which would allow us to understand some aspects closer to the essentiality of a technical existence, beyond the pure objectivity of the functional aspects attached to them (Simondon, *Du mode*, 1989, pp. 47 and 48). Even if it comes to 'essentialities', Simondon's mechanology does not seem far from the 'critical history of technology' as meant by Marx – although understood as a 'reified ontology' of the technique:

> A critical history of technology would show how little any of the inventions of the eighteenth century are the work of a single individual. Hitherto there is no such book. Darwin has interested us in the history of Nature's Technology, i.e., in the formation of the organs of plants and animals, which organs serve as instruments of production for sustaining life. Does not the history of the productive organs of man, of organs that are the material basis of all social organisation, deserve equal attention? And would not such a history be easier to compile, since, as Vico says, human history differs from natural history in this, that we have made the former, but not the latter?
>
> (Karl Marx, *Capital: A critique of Political Economy, Volume I, Book One: The process of production of Capital* (1867), www.marxists.org/archive/marx/works/1867-c1/index.htm (accessed 28 April 2015))

15   'Technicity' is the character, the sign that is added to the composition of form and material in the process of individuation of a technical object. Technicity enables the communication between the technical object and the technical milieu in which it is inserted, informing the latter about the distinctive qualities of the former.

16   Gilles Deleuze, drawing attention to the work of Simondon, commented in an article published in 1966 in the *Revue Philosophique de la France et de l'étranger*: 'Et ce que Gilbert Simondon élabore, c'est toute une ontologie . . .' As cited in Gilbert Simondon, *L'invention dans les techniques – cours et conferénces* (Paris: Seuil, 2005), p. 348.

17   Simondon, *Du mode*, p. 241.

18   Karl Marx and Friedrich Engels, *A Critique of the German Ideology* (1845), www.marxists.org/archive/marx/works/1845/german-ideology/ch01d.htm (accessed 28 April 2015).

19   Simondon, *Du mode*, pp. 242–243.

20   Ibid., p. 249.

21   Ferro, *Arquitetura e trabalho livre*, p. 416.

Chapter 11

Factory processes and relations in Indian temple production

Megha Chand Inglis

Listen to this sound . . . tran tak . . . tran tak . . . tran tak. This is the sound of the hammer hitting the chisel. Carving factories big or small reverberate with this sound. For us 'tran tak' signifies Vishvakarma's presence for it is on his invitation that we dwell on the earth as craftsmen, having left Som [the moon], where we dwelt before.[1]

The intimate space of capital

When individuals from the Sompura community of hereditary temple builders of Gujarat, western India, speak of their present-day conceptions in relation to their long architectural lineage, narrations surrounding shifts in production processes inevitably come to the fore.[2] Notwithstanding historical transformations, notions of factory work and worship entangle in a way that invokes what thinkers of South Asian political modernity have termed 'heterotemporality' or 'coevalness' in conceptualising both the past and the present as simultaneously constituting the present, in a pre-analytical and un-objectifying sense.[3] As carriers of an embodied knowledge of crafting temples in stone for which no formal schools of architecture exist, the shifts are emblematic of certain negotiations this community has forged in exchange for its rise to global prominence. The assumed English title 'temple architect' instead of *sthapati* or *shilpi*, for instance, speaks of a struggle for global legibility as well as a particular way of worlding late capitalist contexts in an everyday tactical sense.[4] It is no coincidence that the emergence of this distinct title coincides with the emergence of the factory form in Indian temple production from about 1980.

This chapter is an attempt at capturing an idea of Indian political modernity out of a range of material and social practices from everyday life in the factories deployed for carving stone. It borrows frameworks posited by postcolonial historians of modern India, who invite us to think of 'relationships that do not lend themselves to the reproduction of the logic of capital'.[5] Dipesh Chakrabarty's readings of Marx's *Capital* in particular reveal elements of deep uncertainties built into the 'intimate spaces of capital'. These readings have been critical in my understanding of the relations of production in the carving factories of western India. Chakrabarty argues for a translational reading of history, in addition to charting historical transitions, which do not look for alternatives to the narratives of capital. Instead he argues that the globalisation of capital is not treated the same as capital's universalisation.[6]

All too often contemporary Sompuras are idealised through atavistic representations which insist on this very separation between craft and capitalist production, resonating with orientalist epistemic categories of colonial and nationalist imaginations from the late nineteenth and early twentieth centuries. In the case of heritage and conservation discourse in India they are viewed as bearers of unmediated 'traditional knowledge systems', obscuring the diversity of their practices.[7] In the case of ethnographic readings of their contemporaries – the *sthapatis* of South India – the primacy of the ritual mode of production over the capitalist mode is argued for.[8] In the case of their most visible transnational patrons, we are presented with a timeless dimension to the Indian craftsman's labour.[9]

Rather than obscuring the modernity, contradictions and heterogeneity inherent in the production of their temples, I treat the factory floor as a conceptual ground for claiming difference. Here the term factory – ubiquitous with modernity – is made its own through the affective and contingent relations of a range of constituencies on the ground. I borrow from Chakrabarty's frameworks in arguing that the embodied orientations and social trajectories therein can never be fully subsumed by the universal logic of capital, pointing to an 'excess' that capital needs but can never truly domesticate.[10]

This has involved me making relations with a network consisting of the current generation of Sompura temple architects, patrons, factory owners, technicians, contractors, supervisors and *karigars* in Gujarat and Rajasthan, and this chapter is based on informal interviews and site visits in and around a range of factories conducted during research field trips in 2012 and 2013. This last category of my informants – *karigar* – very roughly translates as 'craftsman' and consists of a critical workforce – certainly the largest – and the lowest paid in the entire temple production process, thereby suiting very well the needs of capital. Across the board in various scales of factories, I found that the idealised Sompura 'community' of temple makers was always already fragmented. The large workforce that it relied on comprised a new constituency, which did not come from long hereditary networks but consisted of men and women from the Bhil and Gharasiya tribes of western India. This workforce oscillated seasonally between field and factory and – much to the irritation of factory owners – between factory and factory to negotiate the best daily wage rates.

The tribal workforce had a double, ambivalent status. On the one hand they were referred to as *karigar*, which alludes to an acceptance of their relatively newly acquired skill, but at the same time this workforce was introduced to me through the terms 'labour', *nicch jati key log* (low caste), *adivasi* (tribal), *unpadh* (illiterate) *ganvaar* (uncouth), 'drunkards', and in one instance *jaanvar* (animal). The efficacy and influence of this doubly inscribed tribal workforce has been dramatic in the last thirty-five years, so much so that during my interactions with those above them, it was commonly acknowledged that '*adivasi karigar*' had become a category of its own, with its own generational identity around carving stone.

Formalising the factory form

Emerging in the Sirohi District of Southern Rajasthan in the opening years of the 1980s, the factory as a new formation in temple production formally reorganised work culture for Sompura temple architects. Its sub-district Pindwara in particular, today, is synonymous with factories that supply carved fragments for a global dispersal, to be assembled off site like three-dimensional jigsaw puzzles, an average temple requiring one hundred and fifty thousand individually carved pieces. An existing network of Sompura temple makers was already engaged in the area in small workshops. However the main sites of production were the temple construction sites themselves. Twentieth-century master builders like Narmada Shankar Muljibhai Sompura (1883–1956), Prabhashankar Oghadbhai Sompura (1896–1978), and Amritlal Mulshankar Trivedi (1910–1995) trained and organised entire teams of sculptors largely from the Sompura community on site, which is to say that the workforce was organised along caste, communitarian, kinship and skill networks.[11] The restoration of the medieval Dilwara temples, also in Sirohi District, from 1951 to 1963 is a case in point, where Amritlal Mulshankar Trivedi trained seventy-five Sompura sculptors in medieval stone carving. Expertise from these and other long-term projects percolated down to the initially unskilled tribal workforce that was brought into the fold of the Sirohi carving factories some twenty years later.

The emergence of the factories is intertwined with the transformation of Sirohi District's status from industry-less in 1983 to industrial-ised over the next two decades. The transformation was aided by the regeneration and development agency RIICO – the Rajasthan State Industrial Development and Investment Corporation Ltd (established 1969). This translated to significant tax breaks and heavily subsidised industrial plots, which were seized by the existing networks of temple makers and stone contractors. With the liberalisation of the Indian economy in 1991 and a surge in demand for temples from transnational diasporic communities located in the UK, USA and East Africa, the factory form offered the ideal offsite infrastructure for production. As a result, the Sompuras' expertise became focused in the conceptualising of temples, the production of drawings and the overseeing of management routines, while the expertise associated with carving stone came in the hands of the new constituency of *adivasi karigars*:

VT (a temple architect): Today there is no master builder available who has the ability to both draw and work directly on stone. Experts from my grandfather's generation could perform all roles. Today, I can draw, but I cannot carve. After a certain stage I get stuck.

Capital's abstractions

A key device through which factory processes are organised and time parameters ascertained is the 'layer drawing' system, which could be thought of as an 'invisible technical ensemble'.[12] The drawings are prepared by temple architects and CAD technicians from the Sompura community and form the basis of schedules of work and quantities. Labour is abstracted through homogeneous, repetitive work sequences: Stone arrival – Carving start – Carving OK – Polishing OK – Fitting OK (see Figure 11.2, right).

In the layer drawing system each piece of stone is drawn individually, numbered and given a unique name in the horizontal plane – the layer – and its relative position determined in relation to an overall plan (Figure 11.1). The layer drawing system serves different purposes. It is crucial for establishing complex management routines. It has a central place in preparing schedules of quantities and liaising contracts with clients and quarry owners (Figure 11.2, left). It helps divide work spatially, layers often being assigned to different factories so that works can take place concurrently.[13] Finally it is a critical piece of information for assembly in distant locations. Certain transnational patrons have devised software programmes that track the production of several temples simultaneously, by tracking the progress of each piece of stone on a daily basis.[14] In more modest outfits, the layer drawing system generates simpler paper-based management routines (Figure 11.2, right).

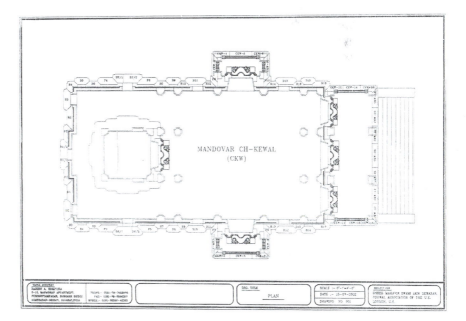

Figure 11.1
Layer drawing, plan. Oshwal Association of the UK

OSHWAL ASSOCIATION OF THE U.K.

LAYER:- MANDOVAR CH-KEWAL (CKW)

DATE:-26-12-2003

S.NO.	STONE NUMBER	STONE SIZE	PIECE	C.F.T
1	B1/1	2'-5 1/2" X 1'-8 1/4" X 1'-0"	1	4.14
2	B1/2	4'-4" X 1'-8 1/4" X 1'-0"	1	7.31
3	P1	4'-4 1/4" X 2'-0 1/4" X 1'-0"	1	8.79
4	P2	4'-4 1/4" X 2'-0 1/4" X 1'-0"	1	8.79
5	R1, R2	5'-8" X 1'-3 1/4" X 1'-0"	2	14.40
6	B2, B3	4'-9 1/2" X 1'-7 1/4" X 1'-0"	2	15.36
7	B10, B11, B12, B13	4'-9 1/2" X 1'-6 1/4" X 1'-0"	4	29.12
8	R3	2'-6 1/4" X 2'-5 1/4" X 1'-0"	1	6.14
9	R4	2'-6 1/4" X 2'-5 1/4" X 1'-0"	1	6.14
10	B4, B5, B9, B9, B14, B15	3'-5 1/2" X 1'-6 1/4" X 1'-0"	6	31.50
11	R5, R6, R7, R8	3'-4" X 1'-2 1/4" X 1'-0"	4	15.80
12	P3, P6	4'-7 1/4" X 1'-8 1/4" X 1'-0"	2	14.00
13	P4, P5	4'-7 1/4" X 1'-8 1/4" X 1'-0"	2	14.00
14	B6/1, B7/2	4'-4" X 1'-11 1/4" X 1'-0"	2	16.76
15	B6/2, B7/1	3'-5 1/2" X 1'-11 1/4" X 1'-0"	2	9.52
16	R9, R10, R15, R16	2'-6" X 1'-2 1/4" X 1'-0"	4	11.84
17	R11, R14	2'-11" X 1'-2 1/4" X 1'-0"	2	6.92
18	R12, R13	2'-11" X 1'-2 1/4" X 1'-0"	2	6.92
19	P7, P10	2'-3 1/4" X 1'-7 1/4" X 1'-0"	2	7.28
20	P8, P9	2'-3 1/4" X 1'-7 1/4" X 1'-0"	2	7.28
21	R17	4'-1 1/4" X 2'-1 3/4" X 1'-0"	1	8.80
22	R18	4'-1 1/4" X 2'-1 3/4" X 1'-0"	1	8.80
			46	259.63

TEMPLE ARCHITECT:- RAJESH A. SOMPURA

OSHWAL ASSOCIATION OF THE U.K.

LAYER:- MANDOVAR CH-KEWAL (CKW)

STONE NO.	B1/1	B1/2	P1	P2	R1	R2
ARRIVAL						
CARVING START						
CARVING OK						
POLISHING OK						
FITTING OK						

STONE NO.	B2	B3	B10	B11	B12	B13
ARRIVAL						
CARVING START						
CARVING OK						
POLISHING OK						
FITTING OK						

STONE NO.	R3	R4	B4	B5	B8	B9
ARRIVAL						
CARVING START						
CARVING OK						
POLISHING OK						
FITTING OK						

STONE NO.	B14	B15	R5	R6	R7	R8
ARRIVAL						
CARVING START						
CARVING OK						
POLISHING OK						
FITTING OK						

STONE NO.	P3	P4	P5	P6	B6/1	B7/2
ARRIVAL						
CARVING START						
CARVING OK						
POLISHING OK						
FITTING OK						

TEMPLE ARCHITECT:- RAJESH A. SOMPURA

Figure 11.2
Schedule of quantities (left). Schedule of work (right). Oshwal Association of the UK

During my fieldwork I was shown four of six factories in the industrial heartland of Pindwara run by a carving company established on the encouragement of RIICO's subsidies. The contractor owner of the factories was not from the Sompura community, but was well known within Sompura circuits for having the highest quality workforce. The factories were referred to as 'plots'. For ease of reference I will refer to them as Plots 1, 2, 3 and 4. The *adivasi karigar* workforce was engaged in different stages of production across the four plots for a multi-million-dollar temple project in the USA, with the last shipping container due out seven months later. Marble slabs had been shipped in from Italy, checked and cut to the right size in one half of Plot 4 using heavy-duty machinery. The cut stone pieces were then dispersed to Plots 1, 2 and 3 for carving. While Plots 1 and 2 had several hundred *karigars*, Plot 3 had only one technician, operating two recently purchased 'three axis' CNC machines imported from Italy. During my visit, torsos and heads of peacocks were being carved by the machines in rough outline, after which they were transported to Plot 1 for further refinements. The pressure of meeting shipping deadlines could be felt intensely in all four sites.

Capital's excess

In this conglomeration of factories, supervisors represented the disciplinary authority of capital over labour in nearly every sense. They stood aloof, patrolled the factory floor, not engaging in any unnecessary conversation (Figure 11.3). They maintained daily wage and attendance registers. Their main job was time keeping and ensuring that square blocks of stone were carved exactly to the details specified in full-size shop drawings. But in

Figure 11.3
**Factory supervisors,
Pindwara. Photograph:
Megha Chand Inglis**

everyday practice, the exercising of authority was not always a one-sided affair, tacitly understood by the supervisors, *karigars*, contractors *and* the temple architects with whose detailed drawing instructions the works were to comply. In other words power was rooted as much in the embodied and subjective practices of the *adivasi karigars* and their relations with the supervisors, as in the factory codes of surveillance.

The two supervisors – known as head *mistris* – who took me around Plots 1 and 2 were expert stone carvers themselves, describing their role as the *jod* (joint) between the temple architects and the *karigars*. Most Sompura temple architects I spoke to made weekly visits to factories to directly agree with *karigars* and supervisors the material nature of some of the qualities of carving they had in mind, while drawing in CAD, often working over pre-drawn motifs printed from their extensive CAD libraries. These qualities were *josh* (passion), *dum* (breath or life), *ubhar* (rising, swelling), *golai* (roundness), *gehrai* (depth) and *jhapat* (flight). As a matter of routine, factory owners instructed the best *karigars* to make plaster of Paris models that best translated these qualities, to agree the basic standard for others to follow on stone (Figure 11.4).

This interaction suggests that distance from the low caste *adivasi karigar* workforce was also accompanied by closeness and cross-communication, and that their low rank created no barriers when it came to their skill. Further, the supervisors' gaze had a built-in flexibility. In dealing with the most expert of *adivasi karigars*, the supervisors stood back deliberately, stating that the *karigars* knew best or that they didn't need instruction. There were fifteen such expert *karigars* in Plot 1, working with a workforce of two hundred, the former earning 500 rupees a day and the latter anything from 200 rupees upwards, depending on their skill.[15] For the majority of the workforce, both the contractor and the supervisors knew individuals by their names and were squatting and

Figure 11.4
Plaster of Paris model,
Kirti Maya temple,
Barsana, Uttar Pradesh.
Photograph: Megha
Chand Inglis

sitting beside them in dialogue, drawing and gesturing with a pencil or hammer and chisel. In gestures of reciprocity, the workforce referred to the contractor as *kaka*, a term of address usually reserved for senior male relatives. The supervisors were referred to by their first name followed by the suffix *bhai* (brother).

This collaboration in factory circumstances has resonances with pre-capitalist social relations involved in temple production. But following Chakrabarty's readings of Marx, the term pre-capitalist here is not used in a historicist sense, rather as a pre-analytical philosophical category, where the past, in practices of embodiment, comes into the modern. 'It does not come as a remnant of another time, but as constitutive of

Figure 11.5
Plinth of the Jasmalnath Mahadeva temple (twelfth century), Asoda, Gujarat (left). Plinth of the Kirti Maya temple (under construction), Barsana, Uttar Pradesh (right). Photograph: Megha Chand Inglis

a present.'[16] If we pay attention to the profusion of variation on the surfaces of medieval temples from North West India, a certain idea of labour is discernible (Figure 11.5, left). The trunk of one elephant sways this way, his neighbour that way, and so on. These variations suggest that the lowest in the hierarchy had a say in determining the detail and that this affect had agency. The collaborative roles that were being performed in Plots 1 and 2 were deeply resonant of those older embodied relations.

Seen from this perspective, the factory can be read as a negotiated space, as a crucible of encounters. Instead of rendering the *karigars* into mute witnesses to the discipline process, the factory relied on the subjective interpretations of the largest and lowest paid workforce as well as an exchange between the *karigars*, the supervisors, the contractors and the temple architects. This accessibility and exchange braided within surveillance codes was not bereft of its own contradictions:

> D R (a karigar): My name is D R. I am a Gharasiya. They call us *karigars*. I have been working here for twenty-five years. I do *gadhai* (carving). I learnt from other people who worked here. My father was a farmer. Our children will study. They will not do this. What they will do I do not know, but this much is clear to me, they will not do this.

Margins of contingency

The supervisors collaborated with two classes of *karigars* and as a matter of routine scrutinised and overwrote detailed shop drawings when it came to translating them into three-dimensional objects. Their combined subjectivity was instrumental in this reiteration. The two classes that the supervisors dealt with were *roop kaam karigars* and *nakshi kaam karigars*. The first class specialised in statuary, and were from Orissa, with their living arrangements consisting of rudimentary brick huts within the factory boundary walls. The second class were the local *adivasi karigars* that specialised in carving standardised repetitive patterns on the basis of full-size metal templates traced from CAD drawings. The two classes sat in different sections of the factory floor, for the *roop kaam karigars* exercised workmanship of greater risk and required quieter spaces to draw out the correct mood of the figures they carved.

OUP, 1991); M.A. Dhaky, *Encyclopaedia of Indian Temple Architecture*, vol. II, part 3, *North India: Beginnings of medieval idiom, c.AD 900–1000* (New Delhi: AIIS and IGNCA, 1998). See also Adam Hardy, 'Śekharī Temples', *Artibus Asiae*, 62, 1 (2002), 81–137.

3   Dipesh Chakrabarty, *Provincializing Europe: Postcolonial thought and historical difference*, 2nd edn (Princeton, NJ: Princeton University Press, 2008), pp. 47–72.

4   For a definition of tactics as opposed to strategy, I draw from Michel de Certeau, *The Practice of Everyday Life*, trans. by Steven Rendall (Berkeley: University of California Press, 1988), pp. 26–41.

5   Chakrabarty, *Provincializing Europe*, p. 64.

6   Ibid., p. 71.

7   See INTACH, *Charter for the Conservation of Unprotected Architectural Heritage and Sites in India*, www.intach.org (accessed 25 September 2014). For an argument on the colonial modern roots of such heritage-conscious postcolonial cultural formations, see Saloni Mathur, *India by Design: Colonial history and cultural display* (Berkeley and London: University of California Press, 2007), pp. 165–70.

8   Samuel K. Parker, 'Ritual as a Mode of Production: Ethnoarchaeology and creative practice in Hindu temple arts', *South Asian Studies*, 26, 1 (2010), 31–57.

9   See Kavita Singh, 'Temple of Eternal Return: The Swaminarayan Akshardham Complex in Delhi', *Artibus Asiae*, 70, 1 (2010), 47–76.

10   Chakrabarty, *Provincializing Europe*, p. 60.

11   Interview, B.K. Trivedi, Ahmedabad, April 2013. This view was held by all Sompuras interviewed.

12   I borrow this term from Adrian Mackenzie, *Transductions: Bodies and machines at speed* (London: Continuum, 2002), p. 11. Mackenzie's book elaborates on the writings of Gilbert Simondon who sought to redress the opposition between culture and technology. See Gilbert Simondon, *Du mode d'existence des objets techniques* (Paris: Éditions Aubier-Montaigne, 1989).

13   As an example, 1,526 *karigars* were employed in fourteen different sites across Gujarat and Rajasthan between 1993 and 1995, for the BAPS Swaminarayan temple, Neasden, London.

14   Interview, Sanjay Parikh, BAPS Swaminarayan Mandir, Ahmedabad, April 2013.

15   At the time of writing, 100 INR (Indian National Rupee) equalled 1 British Pound.

16   Chakrabarty, *Provincializing Europe*, p. 251.

17   This approach contrasts with those who argue that CAD-CAM processes give back to architects the status of the craftsman. See Jonathan Hill, 'Building the Drawing', *Architectural Design*, 75, 4 (2005), 13–21. See also Lars Spuybroek, *The Sympathy of Things: Ruskin and the ecology of design* (Rotterdam: V2 Publishing, 2011).

18   Sarat Maharaj, 'Perfidious Fidelity: The untranslatability of the Other', in *Modernity and Difference*, ed. by Stuart Hall and others (London: Institute of International Visual Arts, 2001), pp. 27–34.

19   I am grateful to Adam Hardy, Jaideep Chatterjee and Nick Beech for reading through drafts of this chapter and suggesting improvements. Thanks are due to Tania Sengupta and Katie Lloyd Thomas for their help during discussions. Conference attendance was supported by the Architecture Research Fund at the Bartlett School of Architecture, University College London.

Chapter 12

Construction sites of utopia

Silke Kapp

Utopias are pieces of literature that present new social totalities, with new political and economic institutions, new habits, new tastes, new labour conditions and – always – a new space. My question is, very simply: *How would these utopian spaces have been produced?*[1]

Most utopian writers do not explain this, concentrating on issues which they perceive in their own societies and from their own social position. As these authors are seldom building workers or familiar with construction sites, they do not worry much about them, or about the inner coherence between the production of utopian spaces and utopian labour arrangements. But we can derive the construction sites of a utopia from the few hints provided in the texts, the decisive general features (the built environment itself, the political structure, the division of labour, ownership and technology, for example), the context in which the utopia was written, and other references used by the author.

Why engage in such a tricky task? This idea first arose as a sort of marketing strategy for a critical theory of architecture, because architects (and students) enjoy discussing utopias, preferring to avoid discussion of building work and its social conflicts. Utopias are appealing to architects because, in one way or another, architects aim to create spaces in which life would be better than before (even if only a by a bit). In contrast, construction sites tend to appear in the architectural field only as a means to this noble end. Reflecting upon construction destroys architectural illusions, because it shows that even the best plan is a device for the conventional domination of labour, and that we, as designers, are responsible for this device. Most designs could never have been conceived, let alone carried out, under relations of production other than capitalism. Utopias magnify this crucial but largely obscured contradiction. Looking at their construction sites may get us used to envisioning not only how nice life could be once a building is ready, but also how life would be in the course of its material production.

The following presents this approach to utopias through commentary on just three of them: Thomas More's *Utopia,* written at the beginning of the modern era, and the utopias of Edward Bellamy and William Morris produced at the end of the (second) industrial revolution. I will briefly indicate some general aspects of these utopian societies, spaces, their solutions for labour, and their construction sites.

We may assume that these utopian construction sites are intended to perform somewhat lasting transformations on their material surroundings, thus requiring a considerable amount of work. In the real world this has almost always implied arduous physical labour, together with domination. Utopias can resort to a few basic schemes to solve this question (whether or not they address it directly). First, they can criticise *heavy* labour or the drudgery that causes bodily pain and social contempt. A simpler lifestyle, fair allocation of labour among all society members, shorter working hours, cooperation, or improved technologies are ways to *relieve* such a burden. A utopia can also concentrate on the critique of *alienated* labour, or the meaningless activity that disqualifies and isolates workers, labour that is done without any pleasure, only for the sake of an abstract exchange value. In this case, the answer is *emancipation* of labour (from capital, the state or any other oppressive relation), so that workers can themselves determine the means and ends of their working process. Still another possibility is to criticise *labour as such*, or the ideology of work as the only way to personal fulfilment and social recognition. The *abolition* of labour, due to improved machines, a benevolent nature or some other marvel would be the prospect in this case.

More's *Utopia*

A truly golden little book, no less beneficial than entertaining, of a republic's best state and of the new island Utopia was published by Thomas More in 1516,[2] in the context of an ascending merchant capitalism in Europe, enclosure of the commons in England, poverty, hunger, crises in crop production, unemployed soldiers (after the War of the Roses), humanist scholars, and the promise of the newly 'discovered' continent. More himself was in a delicate political position, as a Master of Requests and Privy Councillor.[3] We can never be sure which aspects of his text were intended as ideal images, criticism, satire or simply as jokes, beginning with the name *U-topia* (suggesting both 'no-place' and 'happy-place').

More's protagonist is a Portuguese travelling intellectual named Hythlodaeus (which means 'non-sense'). The Utopian society appears to Hythlodaeus as a happy Spartan monastery. There is no private ownership, no money, and no poverty. Reading and humanist studies are widespread. Everybody follows the same time schedule and uses the same outfit, and jewellery and other vanities are regarded as foolish. But the most important feature of this utopian society is the absence of any quantitative growth.

Population, economy, space, everything is stable and seems ready. There is almost no building activity besides preventive maintenance.

Utopia is a croissant-shaped island that equals Great Britain in size (Figure 12.1), and has a remarkable infrastructure of roads, bridges, fortifications, water supply, and fifty-four cities. They range from 70,000 to 140,000 inhabitants (equal to the population of London around 1500), and they all follow one and the same scheme, similar to a Roman colony, with four sectors, a regular grid, and a surrounding wall. But Utopia also has its own colonies on a nearby continent, which function as buffers against changes: when the population on the island increases, people move to the colonies; when it decreases, they return.

The burden of labour in Utopia is not too heavy because there are no idle classes or luxury goods and services. Agriculture is highly respected, and everyone works in it for at least two years, so that there is no social inequality between the city and the countryside. In addition, every Utopian applies him/herself to a specific craft. Six working hours a day is enough to produce plenty of everything needed for a simple life. Some unpleasant tasks are taken up as a sacrifice by a group of very religious people. The most degrading trade – butchery – is done by slaves (slavery substitutes for the death penalty, and is thus a 'humanising' measure). As for technological change, this is minor, based on common sense and careful resource management rather than on science.

But Utopia's historical records suggest that it was not always such a quiet place. The island was originally a peninsula. A king named Utopos conquered the indigenous population, and immediately ordered the cutting of the isthmus. He is said to have forced the natives and also his own soldiers to labour, so that the former might not think that he treated them like slaves. Then he defined the above-mentioned infrastructure, including the description of the urban configuration.

In antiquity 'cutting the isthmus' was a proverbial expression for aiming at impossibilities, because many powerful rulers tried to cut a channel through the Isthmus of Corinth, always failing due to natural or supernatural causes.[4] The episode shows how powerful Utopos must have been. But it also means that Utopia was founded as a kind of labour camp, the more so as its channel equals the English Channel in size, and its roads were probably built according to Roman tradition, which was still the best standard in More's time (Figure 12.2).[5] More tries to convince us that all this building was done without violence. But considering that in Ancient Rome road building was used as a punishment, why should these natives submit to such heavy and tedious labour if not by coercion?

Between Utopia's foundation as a labour camp and the republic's best state of absolute stability, there must have been still another phase of transition. We might suppose that this was when Utopians built all their public buildings – each city has two hundred meeting halls, thirteen churches, four hospitals and some other facilities – and replaced their first wattle and daub shacks for the two-storied stone houses with beautiful collective gardens that Hythlodaeus gets to know. It is likely that the crafts related to building flourished at that time, and that the whole society supported them, so that it would not take too long to get everything ready. It may have been the most interesting period for those Utopians who do not fancy the monastic life.

Figure 12.1
Great Britain and the
Island of Utopia,
following the shape
and size described by
Thomas More. Drawing:
courtesy Roberto
Eustaáquio dos Santos,
2015

Figure 12.2
Construction of Utopia's
infrastructure following
the Roman standard for
roads, bridges and cities.
Drawing: courtesy
Roberto Eustaáquio dos
Santos, 2015

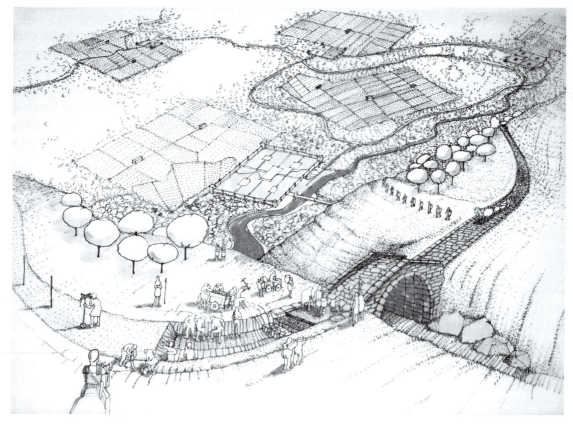

In summary, the material production of Utopia's space is inconsistent with Utopia's social order. Thomas More opposes heavy and despised labour, imagining a society in which labour would be relieved and well-respected, but he also imagines spaces that only hard dull work can provide – at least under the technological conditions he describes. Therefore construction must have taken place before the good life could begin, first in a long and brutal foundation period, followed by a better but still labour-intensive transition period. The Hippodamian plan of the cities illustrates this point: it symbolises equality and may indeed provide similar spatial conditions for all citizens after its completion, but the construction of a grid plan requires strict control, so that no differences are introduced spontaneously and no craftsperson is allowed to act at his or her own discretion.

Bellamy's *Looking Backward*

Almost four centuries later, in 1888, Edward Bellamy published *Looking Backward: 2000–1887*, which was to become a bestseller in the United States and abroad.[6] Bellamy's context is the city of Boston in a world of already 'globalised' industrial capitalism, urban expansion, financial crises, international labour movements, and violent repressions. Many people saw revolution as imminent, so that all sorts of competing proposals for a new social order were in debate: communism, socialism, anarchism, liberalism and conservatism, in every imaginable version.[7]

The protagonist of *Looking Backward* is the rich and well-educated idler Julian West, who travels to the year 2000 by way of a hypnotic sleep of more than a century (a fire destroys his house but spares the secret cellar where he is sleeping). West finds a society that appears to be a hybrid of the military and Disneyland. Eventually he learns that, after a short and peaceful revolution at the end of the nineteenth century, 'the Nation' had become the sole owner of any former private property. As a central planning and management unit, the Nation guarantees total economic equality by means of a grant that every citizen receives on a kind of 'credit card' (which operates more like a debit card).[8] Consumption is less conspicuous than it once was, but it still represents the better part of life, in contrast to production. In fact everybody seems to behave, think and feel like the middle class to which Bellamy himself belonged. For instance, everyone appreciates and supports music, literature and the fine arts, but as a consumer, whereas artistic production is reserved for professionals.

The utopian city of Boston has changed so much that Julian West hardly recognises it. Instead of pollution, slums, ugly buildings and ugly people, there are trees, parks and huge public buildings all over the place. According to Bellamy, these buildings are of a 'magnificent architecture', but his descriptions suggest that no new style has developed. Indeed they look just like the bourgeois parts of American and European cities in 1887 – symmetrical façades, axial entrances, monumental stairs, outer and inner surfaces solemnly decorated with sculptures, carvings, mosaics and murals. And Boston's family homes are mostly conventional and unspectacular houses or flats, which the citizens rent from the Nation for an amount defined by size and location. As for the modern factories and technical devices – such as automatic canopies to cover pavements when it rains or pneumatic tubes to deliver messages and wares almost instantly – these are rather concealed.

The labour question is solved in Bellamy's utopia by an 'industrial army', which follows a military code of honour and obedience. Every citizen has to enlist at the age of twenty-one, when he or she finishes school. In the first three years of working life, young Bostonians must take the harder jobs. Later, they may choose. Thanks to a complex central system, subjective vocations match objective needs, and the sacrifices related to different occupations are equalised by shorter or longer working hours. Productivity increases constantly by means of new technology and overall rationalisation, which ranges from the labour process itself to efficient distribution and waste prevention. Even so, people do not really like their work; they do it because it is their duty as citizens, and because they know that at the age of forty-five they can retire and have fun for the rest of their lives. Only artists, physicians, priests, journalists and professors (but not architects) work individually or in autonomous guilds, and are not subject to the rules of the industrial army.

As for Boston's construction sites, Bellamy assumes that the Nation decided not to put the new order in risk by building big projects immediately after the revolution.[9] Instead, they began with housing reform, reallocating families to create equal dwelling conditions. The construction of infrastructure and the magnificent public buildings must have started later, when the new social order was already completely established. It is likely that new technical devices relieved many operations in the construction industry, and that labour processes were gradually re-engineered by scientific studies and management. After all, Bellamy was a contemporary of Fredrick Taylor and Frank Gilbreth. The latter's motion studies in bricklaying, for instance, must have been brought to perfection in the year 2000, so that the bricklayers of the industrial army would work with machine-like efficiency. The monotony and tediousness produced by these rationalised operations in Boston remain hidden behind surface decoration, applied by professional artists.

The construction of Bellamy's utopian space is part of his ideal social order. In contrast to More's island, the renewal of the city of Boston is assumed to happen when the good life had already begun. The only problem is that, if art has anything to do with work and with freedom, there cannot be any art of building in this utopia. Architects are managers, and building workers are animated tools. The burden of labour is alleviated for the price of a deeper alienation. The abolition of labour could be achieved in this utopia if it were only a question of technological development. But it is not. Politically, freedom *from* labour is as unlikely as its emancipation, because there must always be real or invented necessities to keep people in check.

Morris's *News from Nowhere*

William Morris's *News from Nowhere or an Epoch of Rest* was published in 1890, two years after Bellamy's book, as a critical response to Bellamy's solutions to class struggle

Figure 12.3
Boston in 1872 (after the fire that destroyed the darker area); and, below, Boston in 2000, as suggested in *Looking Backward*, with neoclassical public buildings, orderly arranged parks, and free of slums, smoke and the wasteful means of production and distribution that characterises a free market economy. Drawings by Charles Richard Parsons, 1872, and courtesy Roberto Eustaáquio dos Santos, 2015.

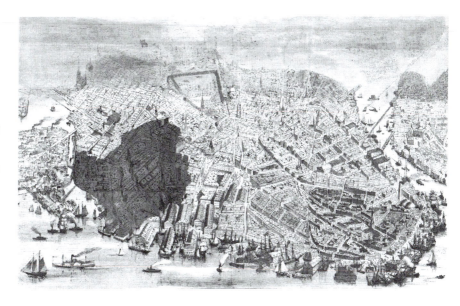

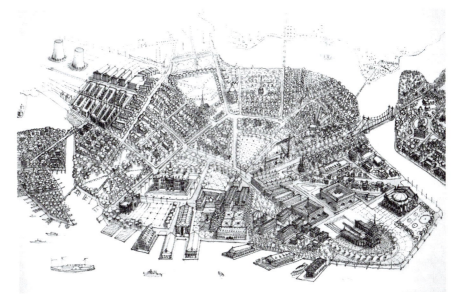

and his view of socialism.[10] *News from Nowhere* presents a unique utopia, because Morris, as an artist, craftsman, political activist, reader of Marx, and a theorist of art and labour, takes the material production of space as a key element for his utopian society, instead of just describing space as scenery.[11] Thus *News from Nowhere* pictures a much more radical transformation than Bellamy had in mind. *Nowhere*'s revolution took at least a century, and was anything but peaceful. In the process, people learned to feel, think and act differently. There are no nations, but self-organised communes (this is what communism means). Not only cash but also all accountancy in human interaction has been abolished. Individuals may live in traditional families or in whatever other form of cohabitation. Children are free; there is no educational system; anyone can learn at any age, and intellectual or scientific knowledge is just one among other kinds of knowledge. And people do not appreciate arts, as Bellamy's middle-class connoisseurs would, but instead produce it every day.

Morris's utopia takes place in London and on the Thames up to Kelmscott.[12] The landscape reveals reconciliation with nature: free-flowing clear waters – as the Counter's Creek 'rescued from its culvert'[13] – huge diversity of plants and animals, recovered woods, plenty of gardens and orchards, discreet infrastructure, and cities that merge smoothly with the surroundings. Every building is carefully placed and 'of a splendid and exuberant style of architecture' not copied from any other. If More's utopia is reminiscent of a monastery, and Bellamy's of Disneyland, *Nowhere* appears more like a summer holiday in the country before mass tourism.

Morris does not explain how labour is organised in this pure communism, because people associate freely, and define by themselves their ways of working together. Their individual and collective autonomy matured during the process of revolution. The former dominated classes first learned how to organise politically in networks, not depending on leadership. Later they also learned how to produce without bosses and centralised planning. And still much later, after a period of extreme utilitarianism, perfectly developed machinery, and almost no need for human labour, the most important change came about: having time and freedom of mind to look for new enjoyment, people realised that the material exchange with nature can be fun, and that making things with one's own hands and mind can be a great pleasure. In other words, they overcame the schism between production (as a sacrifice) and consumption (as a reward). They began to enjoy themselves in so-called 'easy hard work', which means 'work that tries the muscles and hardens them and sends you pleasantly weary to bed, but which isn't trying in other ways: doesn't harass you in short'.[14] And they rediscovered old handicrafts and invented new ones, leading to an artistic practice completely different from nineteenth-century institutions. *Nowhere's* skilfully wrought and expressive works are part of everyday life, not confined to an awesome sphere of fine arts, nor shielded against use and transformation. Ultimately, all this results in a different view towards technology: while people in *Nowhere* held on to machinery for 'all work which would be irksome to do by hand',[15] in many branches 'machine after machine was quietly dropped under the excuse that the machines could not produce works of art'.[16]

Building is one of the most appreciated activities in *Nowhere*. Some people – referred to as 'obstinate refusers' – even forgo the annual haymaking festivities, so as to continue with their building activities, and remain fearful of running out of opportunities for engaging in such artwork. It is usually done in smaller or larger groups, which organise autonomously, in accordance with the skills and experience of each craftsperson. The idea of a new building and its major lines are discussed in the commune, and then the group is free to decide what to do and how to do it.

William Guest, the protagonist of Morris's utopia, gets to know the construction sites of a road and of a house. In both, work goes on in a festive atmosphere, as if it were a play, supported by jokes, food, drink, and interestedly watching bystanders (no construction site is screened against public curiosity). The young men who make up the road-mending gang, looking rather like 'a boating party at Oxford',[17] take pleasure in the joint bodily effort or the kind of 'easy hard work' mentioned above. The house-building workers, besides enjoying the working process as such, also cooperate for another reason. Their aim is to redeem a beautiful landscape from the sins of the nineteenth century: 'the site has been so long encumbered with an unworthy [house], that we masons were determined to pay off fate and destiny for once, and build the prettiest house we could compass here'.[18]

The new house does not satisfy any immediate functional demand, nor does it supply a market or fulfil a public plan. It may later find more or less temporary users (in *Nowhere* people are not attached to one particular plot), but it is above all meant to improve the place where it stands. The group, composed mostly of middle-aged men and women, seems to function as an artists' collective. They share a rough idea of their common project, having decided, for instance, to make the house all of ashlar masonry and carvings, despite the difficult transport of the stones. However, there is no rationalisation, nor design, nor any other previous definition of details. Each individual can develop his or her imagination in the process. The division between design and execution, intellectual and material labour, creative geniuses and an uncreative mass does not exist. Even the word 'architecture' sounds strange to most people in *Nowhere*, while their slight hierarchy on the building sites is based on the recognition of craftsmanship, not on social domination.

A radically revolutionised understanding of nature, work and art underlies the production of space in *Nowhere*. Morris sees emancipated labour as a corollary of an emancipated society, and this kind of labour is what he calls *art*. At the same time, the emancipation thus envisioned is so radical that one may speak of an abolition of labour. Nothing that would usually be associated with labour (pain, boredom, compliance, domination) exists any longer. Work in *Nowhere* is done out of choice, not out of necessity. No one is compelled to do anything.

News from Nowhere has often been dismissed as idyllic, pastoral and nostalgic, in spite of the fact that it includes, not only machinery and electricity, but disagreement, grumblers, sadness and even murder, not to mention the history of fierce revolution. Maybe Morris's un-ironic representation of a joyful life causes embarrassment to us, because we tend to associate such images with margarine advertisements. But regarding the topic discussed here, I interpret *Nowhere* as a glimpse of what human space and its production can become if only freed from the commodity form. There would be no need to achieve final products, to satisfy standardised or exquisite wants, or to distinguish sharply between planning, production, distribution, and use. Instead, a continuous process of collective and inventive interaction with nature may take place.

Thomas More's utopia points to a pre-modern society with no growth and a space that is so immutable that there would seldom be any construction sites at all. Bellamy tries to set his utopia in the future, but in fact only amplifies the logic of his own present, regardless of historical agency. Human life and human spaces are as commodified as before, both in production and in use. Morris, in contrast to Bellamy, takes the risk of picturing a future after the future, i.e., an epoch which would no longer be deducible from his own present. Not only objective structures but also correlate subjective dispositions disappear. Morris knew Marx and Engels's critique of so-called 'utopian socialism'; already in 1884, Morris noted that the content of a better society can only be dealt with 'in negatives'. 'There are certain definite obstacles to the real progress of man; we can tell you what these are; take them away, and then you shall see.'[19] Even so, Morris makes the bold effort of trying to imagine what cannot be foreseen. Not for the sake of conducting people there, but to broaden their desire. In regard to architecture this means that instead of aiming at ideal products to stage an ideal society, we may envision a process of production of space which would itself be part of a free life.

Notes

1   The following is part of a larger project on the *Construction Sites of Utopia* currently in preparation. This project has been funded by CAPES, CNPq and FAPEMIG.
2   Thomas More, *Libellus vere aureus, nec minus salutaris quam festivus, de optimo rei publicae statu deque nova insula Utopia* (Leuven, 1516). I use the following editions: J.H. Lupton, *The Utopia of Sir Thomas More* (Oxford: Clarendon Press, 1895) and, Sir Thomas More, *Utopia or the Happy Republic: A philosophical romance*, in two books, trans. into English by Gilbert Burnet (Glasgow: Robert & Andrew Foulis, 1762).
3   J.H. Hexter, *More's Utopia: The biography of an idea* (Princeton, NJ: Princeton University Press, 1952).
4   Edward Dodwell, *A Classical Topographical Tour through Greece during the Years 1801, 1805 and 1806* (London: Rodwell & Martin, 1819), vol. 2, pp. 184–185.
5   Thomas Codrington, *Roman Roads in Britain* (London: Society for Promoting Christian Knowledge, 1919).
6   Edward Bellamy, *Looking Backward: 2000–1887* (Boston: Houghton Mifflin, 1888).
7   Jean Pfaelzer, *The Utopian Novel in America, 1886–1896: The politics of form* (Pittsburgh, PA: University of Pittsburgh Press, 1984).
8   Bellamy, *Looking Backward*, p. 87.
9   See Edward Bellamy, *Equality* (New York: D. Appleton & Co., 1897), a sequel written by Bellamy to clarify the ideas of the first book for both his followers and his critics.
10 *News from Nowhere* was first published as a weekly serial in *The Commonweal* (Journal of the Socialist League) between January and October 1890. An unauthorised book edition appeared in Boston in the same year. The first authorised book edition, for which Morris revised the text, was published in London by Reeves & Turner in 1891. I use here Morris's 1892 edition, including illustrations and marginalia, William Morris, *News from Nowhere or an Epoch of Rest: Being some chapters of an Utopian Romance* (Kelmscott: Kelmscott Press, 1892).
11 The literature on William Morris is immense and controversial. The most interesting interpretation of Morris's work and life remains E.P. Thompson, *William Morris: Romantic to revolutionary*, revised second edition (New York: Pantheon, 1976).
12 In 1871 Morris obtained tenancy of Kelmscott Manor, a building constructed around 1570 in the Cotswold village of Kelmscott, which he used as a country house until his death in 1896. He made the trip on the Thames from London to Kelmscott several times.
13 Morris, *News from Nowhere*, p. 31.
14 Ibid., p. 251.
15 Ibid., p. 139.
16 Ibid., p. 260.
17 Ibid., p. 66. Morris draws on Ruskin's enterprise in Hinksey, involving Oxford undergraduates in local road improvements, offering them the chance to experience non-intellectual work, at the same time benefiting local villagers. The road-mending episode is an addition made by Morris for the 1891 edition. See Alex Macdonald, 'The Revision of *News from Nowhere*', *Journal of the William Morris Society*, vol. 3, no. 2 (Summer 1976), 8–15.
18 Morris, *News from Nowhere*, p. 253.
19 William Morris, 'How we live and how we might live', *Commonweal* (1887), www.marxists.org/archive/morris/works/1884/hwl/hwl.htm (accessed 15 May 2015).

Part IV
The work of architects

Chapter 13

Architectural work

Immaterial labour

Peggy Deamer

Introduction

Architecture's eradication of a discourse of design labour's relationship to construction labour and with it any discourse of architecture as a type of labour itself is not accidental. It works in capitalism's interest that labour is erased from our consciousness: no more organised complaining about how profit is (not) distributed fairly amongst owners, managers, and actual producers! And it works that architects, as the originators of the bulk of the built environment and all the power that supposedly comes with it, have forgotten that they labour at all, convinced, as they are, that 'design' stands outside the dirty world of both labour and the political economy.

The loss of this awareness, this chapter argues, is not accidental but is the consequence of historical developments in capitalism itself, developments that can be described as moving from a concern for production to a concern for consumption and beyond. And clearly, leaving behind issues of production leaves behind that of labour as well.

To examine this problem of architecture's loss of labour discourse, this chapter is divided into two sections. The first is a historical overview of how capitalism left behind production as a concern and the effect this has on how architecture in different economic eras understood itself. Behind this romp through capitalist history is Ed Ford's observation in *The Details of Modern Architecture* regarding nineteenth-century versus twentieth-century workers:

> Insofar as 20th-century architects have concerned themselves with the social consequences of their work, they have focused on the way in which buildings affect the behaviour of their occupants. Insofar as 19th-century architects concerned themselves with the social consequence of their work, they

focused on the way in which buildings (and particularly their ornaments) affect those who build them. There is perhaps no greater difference between the architects of the 19th century and those of the 20th than that each group was so indifferent to the social concerns of the other.[1]

This is a profound observation, which can be linked to the idea, again, that this transformation of social interest in architecture only mirrors that of the economy in general, with the social concern for the builder/worker flourishing in a period where capitalism struggled with issues of production, management and labour; and the concern for the inhabitant/consumer linked to capitalism's preoccupation with consumption.

If this generally agreed-upon description of capitalism's evolving modus operandi is right, it is also problematic for the reason described above: leaving behind a concern for labour and its fundamental place in a humanist reading of political economy. The second section then explores where, today, architecture's understanding of itself can further expand in a way that takes advantage of capitalism's disguised return via the 'knowledge economy' (it is argued) to issues of production. This section will focus on how the introduction of new knowledge technologies allows architecture to reposition and empower itself.

Architectural work in history

The crisis in identity for the builders/makers in the nineteenth-century change from artisan to factory-based constructor is exemplified, as is well known, by John Ruskin – with his plea for the stonemasons' freedom to create and carve without machine-induced tropes of repetition and standardisation; by William Morris – with his *Morris, Marshall, Faulkner & Co.* workshop, employing artisans whose objects kept alive creativity while deploying mechanisation; and by Eugène Viollet-le-Duc – with his speculations about what artisans/builders of the past would do with the new materials brought on by industrialisation. Here, the concern for the production and the producers was paramount, as Ford makes clear, even as the significance of Henry Cole's Great Exhibition of 1851 housed in Paxton's Crystal Palace – which Ruskin condemned purely on the level of its mechanical production (it was building, not architecture) – signalled the role that consumption would play in shaping design's mission.

The fact that capitalism was handing the architecture industry a more complicated set of circumstances than these nineteenth-century theorists initially understood is demonstrated by the German *Werkbund's* 1907–1934 project, where design workers' satisfaction was increasingly aligned with – indeed, elided with – that of the consumer. Happy work was equated with quality work was equated with quality products was equated with a sophisticated consumer – which *was* the real subject being produced. On the one hand, this wasn't just capitalism in general; it was a specifically German response to nation building. Germany's rise to being the third most powerful economy led it to challenge England not just economically, but culturally. On the other hand, it was also capitalism's general realisation that production was connected to consumption and that the factory workers *were* the consumers who must have the purchasing power to buy the goods they produced. Supply needed to be balanced by demand.

Peter Behren's AEG factory, then, is less the icon of the *Werkbund* (although it does demonstrate new aesthetic concern for the place of work) than is his design work on AEG's logos and clocks. More iconic still are the display windows of the new department stores, windows that had intense cultural scrutiny and were the main subject of Germany's effort to create the sophisticated consumer. The marketing of the seller replaced the naming of the producer/labourer. Unlike the celebration of the industrial maker envisioned by Morris and marketed by his *Morris, Marshall, Faulkner & Co*, 'the actual manufacturer' in Germany, suggests Frederic J. Schwartz in his excellent analysis of the *Werkbund*, 'neither named nor recognisable by obvious visible characteristics of the object, disappeared from view in the market'.[2]

After the *Werkbund*, architectural concern for the maker, as Edward Ford has indicated, virtually disappears – with notable exceptions. However, the various ways in which industrialised construction was sublimated is its own lesson.

Between the First and Second World Wars, Taylorism and Fordism produced goods at an incredibly expanded scale, mobilising an ever larger and well-managed workforce. The love that architects showed for industrialisation at this time was enormous: Le Corbusier, Walter Gropius, Mies van der Rohe – the major figures of 1920s modernism, as we all know – saw their work as extensions of technology and industrialisation. But for the most part, this love rested on an object's ability to symbolise industrialisation, which in turn was of interest for signifying the new modern era. The interest, in other words, was not to adjust the design process according to factory-based labour techniques; rather, it was aestheticised to shape the new, modern citizen/inhabitant – clean, objective, and unsentimental.

Aesthetics, in other words, was the favoured technique of producing the subject of the new order. As a form of capitalist ideology, it supported consumption, and what was being sold to the new middle class was no longer shoes and clocks but architecture itself. Le Corbusier, with his *Neue Sachlicheit,* was ultimately interested in how the 'nakedness' of pure volumes embodied the 'naked facts' that the machine age had wrested from an over-determined and sentimental past. He wrote:

> Our eyes are made to see forms in light; light and shade reveal forms and the images of these are distinct and tangible within us without ambiguity. It is for this reason that they are beautiful forms, the most beautiful forms. Everyone is agreed to that, the child, the savage, and the metaphysician.[3]

Likewise, Mies's interest in industry collapses around the celebration of its new materials, not its trades or workers. He too is interested in the aesthetic effect on the new citizen. After much praise and focus on the significance of industrialisation for modern architecture and the new opportunities it offers, he writes: 'I discovered by working with actual glass models that the important thing is the play of reflections, and not the effect of light and shadow as in ordinary buildings.'[4] While this position on glass's role in the skyscraper has been linked to a 'critical' position on capitalist culture,[5] labour is nowhere to be seen.

The exception, of course, is Gropius. He alone linked architecture's goal to production and explored technology for its labour benefit. The uniqueness of this position in comparison to other modernists is actually startling, given their shared attraction to industrialisation. It is most clearly expressed in his poignant essay on the housing industry. According to Gropius,

> Modern technique might already be ripe for [prefabrication], but the building trade today is still using old methods of handcrafts in which the machine plays only a subordinate role. A radical re-formation of the entire building trade along industrial lines is therefore a must for a modern solution of this important problem. It must be simultaneously approached from the three angles of economy, technology and form; all three are interdependent . . . These are beyond the competence of the individual and can be solved only by a concerted effort in collaboration with numerous experts . . . The better we organise physical labour, the more the human spirit will be emancipated . . .[6]

After the Second World War, until the early 1970s, as Fordism morphed into corporatism and the nature of work went from dirty and unpleasant to clean, white and appealing – and as factory work itself was financially rewarded and union-supported, daily labour – as the definition of work – was replaced by 'careers' and the factory was replaced by the office. Architecture was assigned, again, with the task of producing this user/consumer – in this case no longer by essential epistemological object-forms, but by the construction of (corporate) American lifestyle.

Corporatism – an American phenomenon particular to its emergence as the dominant world power after the Second World War – took on the task of enacting America's cultural and not just military and economic hegemony. Defined in the shadow of the Soviet Union, whose socialism was intrinsically pro-worker, America's new work had to prove its equally humane, benefit-laden bona fides.[7] While this can be seen as sympathetic to the worker, invested as it is in a new form of managed production (especially with the Keynesian support of full employment), the American corporation's definition of social responsibility was *really* to guarantee that we all have access to consumer goods.

> Corporations have a responsibility, first of all, to make available to the public . . . quality goods and services at fair prices, thereby earning a profit that attracts investment to continue and enhance the enterprise, provide jobs, and build the economy.[8]

As Susan Buck-Morss has pointed out, similarities of consumer styles came to be viewed as synonymous with social equality; democracy was freedom of consumer choice – and to suggest otherwise was un-American.[9] Architecture in America was divided into the design of the corporate facilities that shaped workers' work and the design of the house that shaped their leisure time. Both showed the need for style and elegance, but it was the house that could do the real work of indoctrination. As John Entenza stated in the announcement of the Case Study House Program:

> We of course assume that the shape and form of post-war living is of primary importance to a great many Americans, and that . . . the house[s] . . . will be conceived within the spirit of our times . . .[10]

The returning soldiers, more than needing work, had to settle in, make house, and consume. And the Case Study Houses were architecture's *entrée* into that enterprise, bringing affordability, mass-produced materials, and the *cachet* of European-imported sophistication. These houses were ambitious about technology – the wartime industry had proved successful and now needed a new market – but they were intended to develop the new American buyer. The goal was surprisingly similar to that of the *Werkbund*: to shape the modern citizen in a transforming nation-state. America, like Germany in the early 1920s, must be modern. According to Entenza:

> Perhaps we will cling longest to the symbol of the 'house' as we have known it, or perhaps we will realise that in accommodating ourselves to a new world the most important step in avoiding retrogression into the old, is a willingness to understand and accept contemporary ideas in the creation of environment that is responsible for shaping the largest part of our . . . thinking.[11]

Things change radically with neoliberalism. The end of corporatism in the early 1970s and the emergence of neoliberalism marked the transformation in capitalism from a production/consumption model to a profit model, from productive capital to financial capital. The target is no longer a generalised, average citizen needing a modern outlook. It is consumption let loose from need, cultural or otherwise. Entertainment and novelty are the paradigm and the wealthy are its audience.

Nixon in 1971, delinking the dollar from gold, essentially ended the Bretton Woods accord that had been set up after the Second World War to stabilise world economies. In doing so, he set them free to float. As well as 'free trade', the deregulation of the Reagan and Thatcher era became a form of corporate protectionism, as regulations were seen as a 'burden' on large industries. Wealthy investors – financial capitalists – are allowed to be irresponsible and invent new forms of dominance. The '1%' ensure that wages are suppressed as they use capitalism to support their style of consumption, and the downward equalisation of wages and the rate of unemployment come to be accepted as 'natural'. The only threat is the emergence of new players in the world economy. The newly rich OPEC countries, after the 1973 oil embargo, control the commodity of choice. To regain dominance, the multinational corporations must provide innovation commodities and lead in the world of design, so that affluent consumers can distinguish themselves from their peers on the basis of purchasing consumer goods that are made only in small quantities and with high levels of 'design intensity'.

In architecture, formal novelty in the 1970s becomes an end in itself, set free from the need to address the user/viewer/consumer, let alone the producer. Novelty is demanded by the form itself; it is required by its own id. As Mark Wigley wrote in his contribution to the 'Deconstructivist Architecture' exhibition catalogue:

do. And there is alignment on who is a knowledge/immaterial worker: researchers, designers, advertisers, consultants, artists, media specialists, IT programmers, gamers, etc. And there is, to a large extent, agreement on what it implies for capitalism: that is, in the knowledge economy and the gift economy, the traditional link between goods and services breaks down and traditional economic theory becomes obsolete – since it is based on factors of production (land, labour, and capital) that are restraints rather than drivers – for both.

The distinction, then, to be drawn between knowledge work and immaterial labour is not between capitalism and socialism, but between that which capitalism chews on easily and that which it cannot easily digest. To guide contemporary work away from neoliberalism's grasp, subtle strategies need to be articulated.

This model of work is clearly appealing to architecture as it emerges from a profession based on Taylorist division-of-labour and corporatist hierarchies to one embracing open-source access, social media, rule breaking, and individual initiative. But to guide this work away from neoliberalism's grasp towards the original, more radical aims of immaterial labour requires extracting strategic distinctions.

One should foreground the 'radical autonomy' of the worker from the system in which they are placed. As *Autonomia* claimed, the worker exists as a person prior to their insertion into a labour context. The architectural worker should therefore play in the system, but use it to their own ends. As Maurizio Lazzarato, a principal theorist of immaterial labour, says:

> Industry does not form or create this new labour power, but simply takes it on board and adapts it. Industry's control over this new labour power presupposes the independent organisation and 'free entrepreneurial activity' of the labour power . . . Today, with the new data available, we find the microeconomy in revolt against the macroeconomy, and the classical model is corroded by a new and irreducible anthropological reality.[19]

One should focus on a technologically more transparent concept of labour. As the digital theorist Tiziana Terranova suggests, the digital commodities that come out of the immaterial labour, 'do not so much disappear as become more transparent, showing throughout their reliance on the labour that produces and sustains them'.[20]

One should see that this new work may not be paid, but has rewards in cultural cachet. It 'involves a series of activities that are not normally recognised as "work" . . . [those] involved in defining and fixing cultural and artistic standards, fashions, tastes, consumer norms, and more strategically, public opinion'.[21] This labour, after all, is not to be equated with employment and not all unpaid work is exploited. As Terranova also points out, the digital immaterial economy is an important area of experimentation with value and free cultural/affective labour not developed as an answer to capital needs but as a process of economic experimentation with caring and sharing as its own reward.

One should recognise labour *as* labour, one that binds worker to worker, whether blue or white collar. It rejects distinctions based on status or economic reward – which lingers in the knowledge worker (educated, Google-bound) – and enjoys labouring itself. If there is class identification here, it is one of worker solidarity.

One should celebrate 'collective intelligence' not as a means to an end but as an end in itself. The aim is the pleasure that the 'collective intelligence' offers the individual, not the organisation. As Pierre Levy, the cultural theorist and media scholar, writes:

> [Collective intelligence] is a form of universally distributed intelligence, constantly enhanced, coordinated in real time, and resulting in the effective mobilisation of skills . . . The basis and goal of collective intelligence is the mutual recognition and enrichment of individuals rather than the cult of fetishised or hypostatised communities.[22]

Hard to organise and impossible to monetise, the rhizomatic nature of collective intelligence thwarts capitalism's structural needs.

The relevance of the shared knowledge worker/immaterial labourer as a positive model for architecture should be clear. We have the possibility of emerging as workers who collaborate and share; who are autonomous, self-realising, and entrepreneurial; who form flexible partnerships, embrace change, and spurn excess making for the sake of just making; who understand that the traditional distinction between goods and services is obsolete. But to ensure that this entrepreneurial spirit and the leap into the 'gig' economy is not merely neoliberalism's opportunity to make precarity feel natural and virtuous, the architectural worker must side with the more radical elements of immaterial labour.

Enter knowledge parametricism, otherwise known as BIM, which foregrounds the information that lies behind design, accesses intelligence, not just form, and allows/demands collaboration. Within professional structures, it breaks down the distinctions and hierarchies that have haunted the profession, it broadens the meaning of design to include the process, and it makes us smart about issues that matter to the client (money and schedule). Across the professions, it highlights the equality between and co-dependence of the various AEC (Architecture, Engineering and Construction) disciplines, it links immaterial design thought to material production, and it empowers the constructors to recognise themselves as creators.

This is BIM's capability but it is not how it is currently deployed. Mostly associated with the efficiencies it offers in procurement and clash detection, it is dedicated to risk management. This use of BIM doesn't change the DNA of our current dysfunctional process, which not only keeps intact the division between designers and constructors but lends it an unproductive cultural overlay: the cool avant-garde of the formal parametricist vs. the geeky construction managers. Worse, it allows the economic advantages associated with these efficiencies to be accrued by the owner, not the architect. (Whether this is the fault of capitalist ideology or BIM's own mythology is an open question.)

Knowledge parametricism should instead instigate a reconceptualisation of architectural practice altogether, a recalibration along its immaterial labour potential. To overcome lingering class distinctions that accrue with a 'designer vs constructor' distinction, we can and need to consider the de-professionalisation of architecture: in sharing AEC knowledge, designers and constructors operate as a team, one that is disrupted only by the 'professional status' given to architects alone. In one fell swoop, we do away with all the hubris that supports our effeteness, and with that, our irrelevance.

We can and need to reconsider how and what we produce. Object making has to disappear as the goal of architectural labour. Rather, our labour produces knowledge – social, ecological, urbanistic, visual, performative, cultural, formal, and historical – that ensures the ongoing viability of the built environment. If we saw the delivery of knowledge (as opposed to the delivery of an object) as our area of expertise, certain consequences would follow: we would no longer be doing piecework; we would think about employees differently, no longer staffing for a particular (object-defined) job, but pursuing and nurturing the best and the brightest; and we might lose the (white male) star architect so associated with avant-garde object making.

We must have total transparency regarding not just our resources and data, but salaries and fees. Lawyers agree on what they pay associates, so can we. Realtors agree on what they charge, so can we. Let the client come to us not because we compete on fees and salaries (and thereby undermine the profession as a whole), but because they understand the difference in interests, background, quality, and aesthetics we offer. Let's raise our value by not competing with each other but with an economy that has figured out how to have us cheat ourselves.[23]

We can and need to embrace risk, not deflect it – risk that is of the unknown paths to power and redefined authorship; the risk of having our own money and prestige at stake in a project. Eventually, it means embracing the risk that comes with access to power and the siren song of money.

We must not race for more work for the sake of having more work. We need to evaluate whether what we are asked to do and where we put our time makes the world a better place.

Conclusion

It needs to be repeated: the immaterial labour/material labour distinction isn't merely a relabelling of the existing one between designer and constructor; rather, it clearly identifies the fact that there is immaterial labour (knowledge work) in all forms of production once we leave behind the manufacturing model of work. The contractors and fabricators, engineers and landscapers – they all think and they all design, just as architects do physical work to support their mental explorations. The validity of immaterial labour is less its contrast to material labour than it is the labelling of design as a type of work, indeed one that is linked to affective labour and care work. As this chapter has insisted, the dichotomy of designer versus worker, which immaterial labour is meant to overcome, is not only destructive, but also works in capitalism's favour. If we cannot identify as workers, we fail to politically position ourselves to combat capitalism's neoliberal turn.

Responding to the call of immaterial labour will not bring on the revolution, but it will direct capitalism into more responsible enterprises, build a 'commons', and stifle the divisions, rivalries, and competitions central to neoliberalism. Disrupting the mechanisms of capitalism is necessary even if each small victory eventually yields to co-option. We are in a position to not beat capitalism, but to keep it guessing, and to make it uncomfortable. We architectural workers only need to keep throwing up alternative forms of economic and social performance.

Notes

1　Edward R. Ford, *The Details of Modern Architecture* (Volume 1) (Cambridge, MA: MIT Press, 1990), p. 9.
2　Frederic J. Schwartz, *The Werkbund: Design Theory and Mass Culture before the First World War* (New Haven, CT: Yale University Press, 1996), p. 128.
3　Le Corbusier, *Toward an Architecture* (Los Angeles: Getty Research Institute, 2007), p. 29.
4　As quoted in Reyner Banham, *Theory and Design in the First Machine Age* (New York: Praeger, 1960), p. 268.
5　See K. Michael Hays, *Modernism and the Posthumanist Subject* (Cambridge, MA: MIT Press, 1992).
6　See 'Walter Gropius' "Housing Industry" (1924)', https://modernistarchitecture.wordpress.com/2010/10/28/walter-gropius%E2%80%99-%E2%80%9Chousing-industry%E2%80%9D-1924/ (accessed 4 September 2014).
7　On the USA and Russia, each having the 'other' by which to define each other, see Jodi Dean, *The Communist Horizon* (London: Verso, 2012).
8　*The Business Roundtable*, 'Statement on Corporate Responsibility' (October 1981), p. 12, as quoted in Ralph Gomory and Richard Sylla, 'The American Corporation', *Daedalus*, 2 (Spring 2013), www.amacad.org/publications/daedalus/spring2013/13_spring_daedalus_GomorySylla.pdf (accessed 10 September 2014).
9　Susan Buck-Morss, *Dreamworld and Catastrophe: The Passing of Mass Utopia in East and West* (Cambridge, MA: MIT Press, 2000).
10　John Entenza, 'Case Studies House Announcement, January 1945', www.artsandarchitecturecollection.com/architecture/case.study.houses/text.html (accessed 1 October 2014).
11　Ibid.
12　Mark Wigley, 'Deconstructivist Architecture', in *Deconstructivist Architecture*, ed. by Philip Johnson and Mark Wigley (New York: Museum of Modern Art/Boston: Little, Brown, 1988), p. 11.
13　See Jaime Stapleton, 'The Knowledge Economy and Globalisation: Internationalising Intellectual Property and the Fate of Critical Art Practice', www.jaimestapleton.net/aipkefive.pdf (accessed 21 September 2014). In addition, I have been aided in this discussion of neoliberalism and knowledge work by David Hesmondhalgh's 'Neoliberalism, Imperialism, and the Media', www.academia.edu/1534973/Neoliberalism_Imperialism_and_the_Media (accessed 2 August 2014).
14　Mark Getty, 'Blood and Oil', *The Economist*, 68, 4 March 2000, p. 68, www.economist.com/node/288515 (accessed 4 September 2014).
15　Patrik Schumacher, 'Free Market Urbanism: Urbanism beyond Planning', in *Masterplanning the Adaptive City: Computational Urbanism in the Twenty-First Century*, ed. by Tom Verebes (London: Routledge, 2013), www.patrikschumacher.com/Texts/Free%20Market%20Urbanism%20-%20Urbanism%20beyond%20Planning.html (accessed 30 November 2013).
16　Aleksandr Bogdanov, 'Puti proletarskogo tvorchestva (Paths of proletarian creative work)', *Proletarskaya kultura* (Proletarian Culture), no. 15/16 (1920), 50–52, trans. in *Russian Art of the Avant-Garde: Theory and Criticism 1902–1934*, ed. by John E. Bowlt (London: Thames & Hudson, 1976), pp. 178–182, as quoted in Catherine Cooke, *Russian Avant-Garde* (London: Academy Editions, 1995), p. 100.
17　I am indebted to Tiziana Terranova and her article, 'Free Labour: Producing Culture for the Digital Economy', *Social Text*, no. 2, 18 (Summer 2000), 33–58, http://web.mit.edu/schock/www/docs/18.2terranova.pdf (accessed 10 September 2014).
18　Peter Drucker, *Post-Capitalist Society* (London: Routledge, 1993).
19　Maurizio Lazzarato, 'Immaterial Labour', www.generation-online.org/c/fcimmateriallabour3.htm (accessed 3 August 2013).
20　Terranova, p. 48.
21　Ibid., p. 41.
22　Pierre Levy, *Collective Intelligence: Mankind's Emerging World in Cyberspace* (New York: Plenum, 1995), p. 13, as quoted in Terranova, p. 43.
23　I have spent the last four months studying antitrust laws and this claim would surely send me to jail if it were spoken at an AIA or RIBA convention. The secret is to have a third-party journal or academic institution do a survey publishing fees and salaries, identifying averages to which we architects just happen to subscribe. As long as there is no 'agreement', as long as it is 'tacit collusion' and not actual collusion, it is legal. Transparency is close to collusion, but it is not the same.

from medieval methods of construction: 'in that moment, the transition to a new technique of construction, a new organisation of society, and to new forms of expression in architecture takes place as a whole'.[20] Thus, Schmidt's understanding of typification went far beyond that of economists and state planners.[21] According to him, technical and economic demands could not be ends in themselves. Rather, they needed to be addressed alongside aesthetic and social questions, which should be given equal importance (Figure 14.2). Typification meant giving meaningful expression to a social process of production. In this process, architects would have to give up their autonomous and privileged position 'outside' construction so as to be reintegrated through collective forms of labour. At the same time, Schmidt remained deeply suspicious of the restructuring of the professional field under socialism, where socialisation and specialisation were driven chiefly by the demands of an elite of state planners and technical engineers.[22] He not only accepted but also embraced the architect's elevated position that originated in the Renaissance – after all, the architect ought to *intellectually* (and thus artistically) master industrialised construction. The experience in the Soviet Union and in the GDR, where the architectural profession was integrated with production (e.g. concrete panel factories) as part of the implementation of the so-called New Economic System in 1963,[23] had made him aware of risks such as lack of flexibility, complacency and loss of accountability. This may explain the above-mentioned cautionary note that architects, in contrast to his hypotheses from the 1930s, would not merge/dissolve in the 'house factory', even if the character of their work had already been drastically transformed.[24]

Collaboration: complex environmental design and the production of mass housing

By the late-1960s, more than a decade after Schmidt's arrival, architecture in East Germany had changed dramatically. Distinctly socialist architectural forms derived from

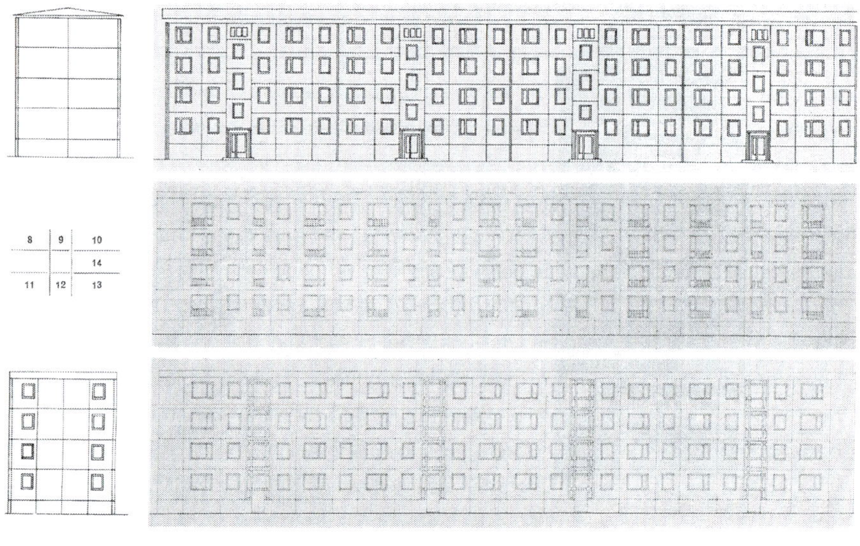

Figure 14.2
Alternative façade elevation proposals for housing type P1 by Hans Schmidt, 1963. *Deutsche Architektur*, 4 (1963), 205

Figure 14.3
Spread from the journal
Deutsche Architektur
discussing art in the
industrial prefabrication
of concrete panels, 1972.
***Deutsche Architektur*, 1**
(1972), 38–39

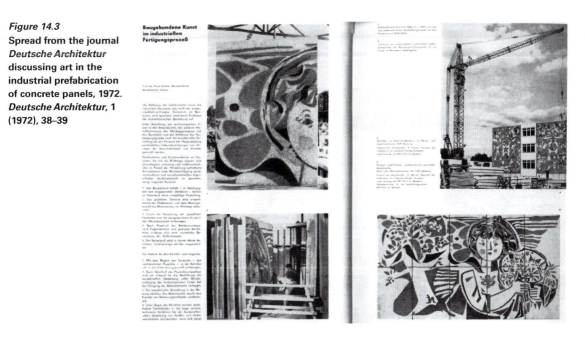

new industrial construction technologies had not developed. Instead, the rapid expansion of those technologies had created its own material reality. Nowhere else did this become more visible than in new towns such as Hoyerswerda, Schwedt or Halle-Neustadt, and in new housing districts in cities throughout East Germany. Their monotony and lack of identity was regularly and publicly denounced. In this situation, art became utilised under the official paradigm of 'synthesis of architecture and art' – in the way Schmidt deplored – as a tonic strategically applied to vast empty spaces and unresolved façades, in order to relieve their dull uniformity, and to add socialist content to an environment otherwise made up of bleak, technically determined objects (Figure 14.3).[25]

This approach was criticised by Flierl in numerous public talks, articles and other publications between 1967 and 1983, in which he developed his concept of complex environmental design as an alternative to the idea of synthesis.[26] He was familiar with the theoretical discourse as well as practice of architecture-related art through his membership in the Central Work Group Architecture and Art (ZAG), which existed from 1968 as a joint forum of the Association of Architects (BdA/DDR) and the Association of Artists (VBK-DDR). Between 1975 and 1983, he became the group's director. Flierl began to rethink the relationship between architecture and art in the context of industrialised construction in an article published in the journal *Bildende Kunst* in April 1968.[27] He argued that the concept of synthesis in its traditional form of creating a totality from two (sometimes more) objects, a building and an artwork, was no longer tenable. This was due to the transformation of construction methods within architecture, which led to a vast increase in the scale of architectural production from individual houses to ever larger realms of the built spatial environment.[28] As architectural labour became subject to qualitative changes – following the outlines earlier described by Schmidt – the relationship between architecture and art, too, had to be reconsidered, shifting the focus from the physical connection between building and artwork to

Figure 14.5
Model for design of seating landscapes using modular concrete floor slabs designed by Jürgen and Ursula Thierfelder, 1980. *Form + Zweck*, 4 (1980), 7

architecture-related art was founded in Berlin, whose goal was to facilitate contracts with individual artists and designers, and which provided them with atelier and workshop spaces to support the production process. Despite several efforts to draw up new contractual regulations in order to establish desired complex relationships between different environmental designers, such contracts were never engaged.[45] Worse still, conflicting interests and spheres of influence often led to tensions between architects and artists. While the latter were seen as unfit for interdisciplinary work, the former

Figure 14.6
Sun sail by Christian Tietze, 1980. *Form + Zweck*, 4 (1980), 8

showed little interest in artists' interventions in the design and configuration of buildings and complexes, and resisted collaboration whenever possible, arguing that project changes would be forbidden and threatening to systematically delay contracts for the realisation of artworks regardless of official regulations.[46] Finally, the participation of users often remained limited to finishing delayed landscaping works, or to building missing playgrounds and public areas.[47]

Few realised examples thus appear to hold up to the ideals of Schmidt and Flierl's writing. Despite participating in various competitions – the most prominent being the design of East Berlin's city centre in 1958–59, when Schmidt and Flierl directed a team of architects from the Institute for History and Theory of Architecture – Schmidt did not manage to realise any projects during his fourteen-year stay in the GDR.[48] He attempted to participate in design work several times and sketched out numerous alternative proposals to colleagues' projects – to analyse and improve their designs, and to stimulate public debate.[49] Similarly, Flierl's influence on architectural design remained limited and rather indirect. His interferences with the design and construction process of Berlin-Marzahn had little echo. Nevertheless, both Schmidt and Flierl sought to develop their theories in close proximity to and on the basis of critical analyses of architectural practice in light of its altered conditions of production.

Schmidt's notion of typification and Flierl's concept of complex environmental design both challenged existing social relations of production and uncovered the internal contradictions that characterised the production of the built environment in East Germany. At the same time, they claimed alternatives to the realities and limitations of building production under state-socialism by imagining different kinds of social relations. Yet, as the forms of collective labour they envisaged remained distant utopias, the corresponding architectural forms also never fully materialised. It often remains overlooked that the (re-)integration of architects into the social production process of industrialised architecture under socialism as envisaged by Schmidt and Flierl was only partly realised – their integration into a centrally administered top-down construction economy occurred, but with very little, if indeed any, political power and diminishing influence on public discourse. Once the collapse of socialism made visible its architectural failures, Western critics were quick to launch scathing attacks on East German building production as 'architecture without architects'.[50] In a somewhat paradoxical reflex, historical scholarship has attempted to restore the authority and subjectivity of architects in the face of their apparent disappearance in the industrialisation of construction by focusing on strong figures and signature architects such as Hermann Henselmann, by seeking to identify marks of individual authorship in standardised buildings and large-scale projects, or by invoking the figure of the dissident architect.[51] While much speaks in favour of such approaches, do they not also betray the collective character of architectural work in socialism? Whether and how the models developed by Schmidt and Flierl might speak to the complex assemblages that define contemporary architectural practice can only be part of a social debate. 'The question remains open',[52] Schmidt noted at a seminar in Venice in the summer of 1970, whether form might indeed still be imaginable as a social matter.

For Petrović, however, flexibility is imagined more than fulfilled because users don't profit from the possibility of having a choice:

> There are various solutions of 'flexible' secondary elements of the system, which enable the changes and 'flowing' of the spaces. Experiences however, show that the users rarely exert these possibilities for which they paid so highly (because such a flexibility also has its additional price!), and investors, as a rule, are much more likely to be interested in the starting price of the object, than in its later expenses of maintenance and reaching the flexibility.[23]

IMS is ultimately a system not a tool, for it opens a limited number of options for the secondary construction elements to be added to it towards completing a building. Users' freedom of choice here cannot result in their personal invention of components, but simply in a choice from the selection on offer by the specialised market.

Although in practice real alterations enabled by the IMS system were rare in socially owned flats in New Belgrade, the system's practical promise of adaptability strongly influenced New Belgrade architects in competition entries and design decisions. The expanded cost of social responsibility led the Marušićs to abandon their position as lead designers on the project, when the contractors suddenly decided to drop the IMS system in favour of a panelling system imported from France but 'by then already regarded as outdated'.[24] They believed the change compromised the flats, with smaller windows, and less flexible space dictated by the rationalisation of panel types and their dimensions, and inflexibly prescribed by the procurement process. The flexibility of the IMS system had been constructed upon the belief in the future self-managed alterations of the flats, that didn't actually take place in New Belgrade. The faith in this idea was in fact a speculative flexibility.

Formalising the flexible

Directed towards more adaptable solutions, Belgrade School tried to synthesise the ideas of flexible, convivial and individual space. We cannot say that the Belgrade Flat in any way increased the consciousness of the user towards the self-management ideals. The belief in flexibility as an indisputable positive value tended to abstract the IMS prefabrication system as the pure hardware that is so customisable. My interlocutors suggested that it allowed what they called 'crossword' or 'lego-like'[25] playful organisation of the bases. However, for IMS to transcend the flexibility of a hardware, and enable users' alterations, too, systemic change would have had to happen. New Belgrade architects' specialised tasks already contained means of architectural communication, which by their historical sedimentation within the discipline limit the possibilities of flexible and convivial tools for the non-professionals.

It was the specific combination in New Belgrade of self-management, the market stronghold for the IMS system and the principle of expanded communication that allowed the symbolism of the freedom to choose one's own self-determination to penetrate architectural production. The Marušićs were right that, in the project for

New Belgrade residential blocks 61–64, the principle of workers' self-governing could not directly influence their design. Baylon's examples of flat designs with expanded communication reflect more an absolute advantage of the private sphere over any further architectural intervention in organisation. Although self-management principles in fact support the belief in individuals' right to choice, expanded communication could not provide citizens with tools for conviviality, as it was not introduced in a social vacuum. Expanded communication was rather a bolt to fix what Evans described as the sociogenesis of the architectural design principle. Without questioning the bigger part of the design process which normalises the private sphere, while at the same time opening the other, limited one for future negotiation, the Belgrade Flat could offer only a minuscule version of how designers imagined future flexibility of organisation.

The 1:1 scale model of flat to be built in the new residential blocks 61–64 was exhibited at the Belgrade Building Centre. But according to the Marušićs the construction of apartment blocks was already advancing in New Belgrade and the exhibit of the prototype came too late for citizens to be involved in the decision-making process and make their voice count in the final design. So the Marušićs may well be right to deny the existence of self-management at the level of citizenship. However, the social responsibility of such projects was considered high, because of the many public competitions for housing under the social-ownership scheme, and architects and citizens were both aware of the social responsibility that such a project would convey.

Architects resorted to formal means, partly because they felt accountable for the social tasks they were institutionally not equipped to fulfil. This preoccupation resulted also from a normalised architectural education still prevalent today. It encourages a system of beliefs which give formal solutions political valency, inasmuch as it could be proved rational by culturally-specific standards: from lowering the costs of the building by cheaper construction to speeding the construction process. 'People need new tools to work with rather than tools that "work" for them', Illich avowed.[26] The only tools New Belgrade architects could reach for were the formal characteristics of pure dispositions of the zones of the flat. Even if wishing to espouse the Yugoslav self-managed individual, Belgrade 'architect-workers' disentangled themselves from the working class as a whole, at the same time creating the flexibility of performance as the norm. What was mediated was a specific cultural split: intellectuals drive the working class, yet separate from it by their own intellectual and aesthetic procedures, which necessarily introduces hierarchies of social relations through taste; these are closer to 'design for' the imagined flexibly-managed-self rather than 'design with' the self-management, as embraced by Illich and Gorz. The work they performed communicating the universal models *to* the citizens (rather than *with* them), detaches design faculties from the citizen, rather than creating that new self – the collectively-abstracted idea of socialist self-management.

Notes

1   Milenija Marušić and Darko Marušić, interview (Belgrade, 2013). Author's translation to English.
2   For example, architects Aleksandar Stjepanović and Mihailo Čanak, whom I interviewed in 2013, were involved in similar projects in New Belgrade in the 1960s and 1970s.

bias in history writing. If topics like parliamentary politics were preferred, women's overwhelmingly informal political participation could be overlooked.[2] 'Making women evident' was a political project.[3] Feminist historians developed invisibility as an analytic category to analyse the criteria driving historical inquiry and interrogate the sources routinely used as evidence.

Liberal feminist studies of women's participation in architecture rely heavily on quantitative evidence derived from official institutional demographics compiled from education institutions, professional associations and registration/licensing bodies.[4] Prevalent measures of women's participation in architecture relate to formal stages in a conventional professional career. These gated stages are variously understood as 'barriers that legitimise participation and occupational closure', as mechanisms of consumer protection, and as milestones of professional achievement and attainment.[5] Sourcing other kinds of evidence beyond these formal measures unearths a much larger female demographic and provides a different insight into women's participation. It also changes the criteria driving both historical inquiry and contemporary frameworks if we look beyond the legally mandated title of architect to see the women who work in architecture.

This chapter uses recent studies of the Australian architectural community to provide evidence to support the claim of women's large informal presence in architecture. Four different kinds of measurement will be examined: two traditional means of counting women in architecture after graduation – membership of the Australian Institute of Architects, and registration figures; and two non-traditional means – a large online survey, and the Australian census figures. Examining these four measures reveals gaps in all. Particularly striking is the absence of women in the formal means for counting architects. In Australia, women students successfully participate in education and have comprised approximately 40% of architectural graduates for at least three decades.[6] However, following graduation, women start disappearing from formal professional demographics: lagging in registration statistics and in the Institute membership categories available to registered architects. The tendency of women to 'disappear' as they proceed through the profession has been known for some time.[7]

'Disappearance' as the analytic frame for inquiries into women in architecture will be challenged in this chapter. The familiar question, 'Why do women leave architecture?' has driven important studies of women's attrition after graduation, but these inquiries are, naturally enough, concerned to understand how women are excluded from architectural institutions and how key professional gateways seem to be blocked. Looking afresh at traditional data sources, we can see that even these allude to an invisible pool of women in architecture – shadowy figures not present in formal measures.

Examining the recent membership records of the Australian Institute of Architects, Gill Matthewson found intriguing clues that suggested the presence of a large informal workforce. In 2013, women comprised 28% of overall membership but, as Matthewson observed, 'a minimum 65% of the women members are in membership categories that indicate they are not registered architects'.[8] This compares to 33% of male Institute members in these categories. Registration – the Australian equivalent of licensing – is another standard demographic used to monitor women's inclusion in the profession after graduation. In 2012, 21% of registered Australian architects were women. Women have comprised 40% of architecture student cohorts over the last twenty years, and a 21% registration rate *appears* to represent a significant decline in participation.

However researchers can look beyond registration figures and Institute membership rolls to find other statistical data on women professionals. The Australian state undertakes a nationwide census of its citizens every five years. The survey is our primary source for discovering women in architecture who do not register within the formal measures kept by architecture's institutions. The census collects data on all those who self-nominate as 'architects', and not simply on those who are registered as architects. The 2011 Australian census includes 4,138 women who identify as architects, yet there are only 2,079 registered women architects in the professional roles. In contrast, 10,836 men in architecture are identified through the census and there are 7,877 registered male architects. That is, half the women working in Australian architecture participate in the profession 'informally' (as do 27% of men).

In 2012 a qualitative study led and conducted by Justine Clark at Australian website Parlour, gathered 1,200 online survey responses of women in architecture and almost 900 male respondents. This aimed to reach a wide range of potential informants, including those not normally found via registration records or membership of the Australian Institute of Architects and those who had moved sideways into allied fields or had 'left' architecture. The women's survey confirmed the presence of large numbers of 'invisible' women. The survey data recorded that comparable to the 2011 census, only half the women respondents were registered architects, although 70% of the men surveyed were registered. Only half of the women respondents described their current primary employment as being in private practice, as compared to 78% of men. The survey reported that 706 women respondents described themselves as primarily working in architecture, while 635 worked in related fields.[9] The census and Parlour statistics cannot be neatly correlated, nevertheless, they indicate that both registered and non-registered women are working in a range of capacities and contexts. As much as a third of the Australian architectural workforce falls outside formal measurement. This pattern is intensified and magnified for women architectural workers, half of whom appear to be operating outside the legally mandated title 'architect'.

Large numbers of invisible women architects have been observed in an earlier study. In *Designing Women* (2000), Annemarie Adams and Peta Tancred drew on Canadian census data to observe that almost two-thirds of Canadian women in architecture were not registered.[10] Accounting for the experiences of these women and men requires a shift in focus, away from a rigidly bounded, legal identity category defining the 'architect'. In the next section we focus on ways in which researchers might construct a different picture of women's lives in architecture.

Career journeys

Women's working lives can be understood through the prism of the 'career journey', a model that shifts our focus from examining the static snapshot of women's participation.[11]

Constructing accounts of women's careers over time, allows researchers and participants to map changes and shifts as a woman's path intersects with key career milestones and life events. The career journey rather than the snapshot allows us to account for variations in experience of architecture, work, and sometimes gender disadvantage. It is also a useful model for capturing the patterns of women's formal and informal participation in architecture.

Variation in women's working lives is under-theorised in architecture, where the data is invariably organised around the category of 'women' as a starting point. Tensions exist between the homogeneous category 'women' and the specificity of singular experiences and the differences amongst women.[12] These differences are challenging for political attempts to speak on behalf of, and for, all women. Approaching women's lives in architecture through the model of the career journey helps provide a structure for capturing diversity and drawing out larger patterns.

Online surveys provide a new means to investigate the diversity of individual career paths after graduation. These surveys can access large numbers of participants and reach recipients outside official institutional networks. However, survey questions need to be designed to calibrate multiple ways of working. Parlour knew anecdotally about the rise of the 'portfolio' architectural career – where architects work across roles, as consultants, educators and in building design. Parlour also knew that working lives change over time; many people are involved in more than one field, or hold more than one position at any given moment. In response, the survey sought to discover women's multiple ways of working by asking about principal, secondary and previous fields of engagement, and employment contexts. The results unearthed a kaleidoscopic range of activities and fluid career paths.

Both the census and Parlour surveys confirmed that women are more likely to be salaried architects and are much more likely to be employees than employers. The complexity of women's lower rates of participation in the registration process and Institute membership is beyond the scope of this chapter, but women's over-representation in the employee category is linked to women's lower participation in architecture's formal structures. The 2011 Australian census recorded that 76% of women architects described themselves as employees, compared to 56% of men in architecture. Only 8% of Parlour's female survey respondents were employers, with the remainder being self-employed (14.6%), contractors (3.1%) or employees (56.6%). In contrast, 25.8% of Parlour's male respondents were employers, 21.6% were self-employed, 1.5% contractors and 45.9% employees. Many women are positioned differently in terms of workplace and professional agency. Capturing the detail of their everyday working lives challenges architectural historians and theorists to construct new accounts of architectural production *written from below*, rather than from above.[13]

The problem of making architectural women visible is further compounded by the ways some women shift in and out of visibility within the profession. Women are more likely to have atypical or flexible career paths, with multiple breaks, different levels of intensity and changing roles over the course of a career. Many also find it hard to re-enter the profession after a career break, or to maintain professional visibility after returning from a period away from formal work. This is particularly an issue for women who work in architecture whilst caring for children. Women architects are also more likely to move in and out of private practice and to work in related areas. The detail provided in the quantitative and qualitative survey responses reveals that these 'invisible' women have many different modes of engagement: a substantial number are working to all intents and purposes as architects within conventional practice, but without being registered, others with architectural backgrounds are working in non-traditional ways within architecture, and still more are working in a wide range of allied industries and related fields. Others have left the field altogether, or never managed to get a foothold after graduation. The Parlour survey of men revealed that some men are also working in these non-traditional ways. However, women form a much larger 'invisible' cohort.

Many women's working lives follow the pattern identified by the term 'non-standard' career paths.[14] By contrast, men as a group are more likely to follow a 'traditional' career path. The structures of the profession are still geared towards linear, rising career trajectories, to the detriment of many women (and some men), regardless of their talent, commitment, expertise and experience. It also means that women are less likely to be in a position to change these structures.

If many women (and some men) are working within architecture in 'un-sanctioned' ways, the boundaries that surround the profession are much less stable and more permeable than institutional structures would suggest. For some this informal participation is a means of professional opportunity and expanded impact and engagement, but for others it is the outcome of career disadvantage, disappointment and compromised professional identity. The presence of a large number of 'invisible' participants in the profession, and the diverse ways in which they participate, points to a significant mismatch between the profession's formal image of itself, the actuality of contemporary practice, and the mechanisms through which the profession's image is maintained and boundaries enforced. This mismatch has significant implications as the profession tries to adapt to a rapidly changing environment, in which all professions are under pressure. The decline of the regulatory state, the internationalisation of markets and the loosening of monopolies over knowledge are some of the historical factors remaking traditional professions in the twilight of the long twentieth century.[15]

Dana Cuff has argued recently that the role of the architect and the 'figure of the firm' is mutating as the profession undergoes major economic restructuring. She points particularly to the rise of large multinational architectural companies, rather than locally based partnerships, and their expansion into urban and infrastructure work undertaken by teams of multidisciplinary professionals.[16] These changes present further challenges to the structures that traditionally define professions as national boundaries blur.

In Australia, registration provisions also change across different state borders. The differences between individual Australian states are only one of the current difficulties facing the contemporary registration process. An architect's participation in the labour market no longer strictly conforms to jurisdictional models of registration, as contemporary architects increasingly work across nations or across international borders. Now architects are much more mobile in their search for labour markets. Workers in Australia are increasingly incorporated into Asian and South-East Asian Australian architectural offices. These are digitally linked but geographically distributed offices operating within the same firm. Young architects may follow sources of architectural work and temporarily or permanently move overseas. Australian architectural practices also employ architects who were not originally trained or registered in Australia. Contemporary architects have a geographical mobility that crosses the fixed boundaries of the registration domain.

Registration is the key boundary that reinforces and limits architecture as a profession in Australia. It is quite possible to work in architecture without being registered – the 'protections' offered mostly relate to the use of the name 'architect' – nonetheless, registration is still the dominant means of defining the profession. The Parlour research, and a separate concurrent Australian research project by Dr Susan Shannon, point to numerous issues in both the process of registration for architects in Australia and the perception of this process.[17]

The role of registration in a changing architectural landscape is a growing focus of research. Significant recent changes in the North American professional architectural landscape were identified by Cuff, including the growth of the super-sized firm, and a radical contraction in the number of small practices and the size of each practice's workforce. In Australia, under the recession practices have also shrunk and transformed.[18] Australian practitioners recently surveyed reported that employment with large firms and the specialisation of roles organised by large firms did not give apprentice architects access to the range of onsite supervision skills and other skills demanded for the registration log. The criteria for registration may need to change.

Many women – perhaps half of all women architecture professionals – and increasing numbers of men are able to work in architecture without being registered. Using American Institute of Architects data, Cuff observed that in 1997 in North America, of the 26% of two–four-person firms, half of them had only one licensed director.[19] Although the requirements vary from state to state in Australia, at least one director of an 'architectural' firm must be a registered architect. However there are career penalties accompanying a failure to register. Registration is the principal means of attaining professional visibility. Being registered gives formal recognition to years of hard work and study, it reinforces professional identity and it gives greater access to the traditional power structures through which reputations are made and influence obtained. While the legal structure of registration is only one form of recognition, other institutional systems of recognition and reward are dependent on the legal structure of registration. For example in Australia, registration sanctions entry of architectural work into the institutional award systems and regulates participation in the award juries.

Other models for formally legitimating professional architects exist and can be investigated as a way forward. Australian architect Jane Cameron suggests there are lessons to learn from the Institute of Chartered Surveyors, which offers registration under different areas of expertise.[20] In the Swedish system the major gateway into the architectural profession is via accredited tertiary education. The Swedish profession is overseen by a professional membership organisation which most students join in their first year.[21] The association offers levels of membership based on the degree of experience. Globally, architects who graduate and train in one geographical location and then practise across international borders also need to have their prior experience recognised. If registration is to continue as a meaningful part of the profession, the system will need to address both perception and process issues.

Even if registration practices change in the near future and formal measures for counting women change accordingly, we will also need to find the means to provide stories of women's working lives. Writing in 2000, Cuff forecast that, 'Professional unity will be further challenged by the increasing diversity among practitioners who call themselves architects.'[22] Contemporary architectural media and our modes of architectural history are dominated by top-down stories. We have few accounts of the lives of salaried architects or less visible practitioners or of firms that fall outside the media recognition system. In this last section of the chapter we turn to another means for counting women in, by locating oral history, past and present, as a key contribution to shading-in women's presence in architecture.

Presenting diverse stories of lives in architecture

This chapter's analysis of women's work in architecture has drawn on women's qualitative survey responses as well as quantitative data. Life stories have long been important quarries for feminism because of feminism's emphasis on experience as the place of gender formation. But the life story occupies a peculiar place in the discipline's models for theory and history production.

In an influential 1991 essay, Dell Upton called for an end to architectural biography as the explanatory history of architectural production and meaning.[23] He argued that this dominant form of architectural history as biography was bound to the emergence of the modern profession and served a legitimating function by sanctioning the monopoly of architects in the building market. If the driving method was biography, the storytelling mode was that of the great man and his works. Upton was objecting to a simplistic use of agency to explain the production and cultural meaning of environments. His critique was one of a number of revisionist approaches to architectural history writing in the 1980s and 1990s. Some historians sought to write histories of architecture from the bottom up by focusing histories on marginalised actors: communities, minorities, builders, patrons, clients, or occupant-focused histories. Feminist history was active in this sphere.[24]

The place of biography in architecture is currently undergoing a reassessment as oral history methods gain hold.[25] As we seek to expand the archive of voices in architecture we will need to revisit the debates about biography and architectural history. Documenting a range of lives in architecture expands accounts of architectural production and reveals the contribution of marginalised actors – women, Aboriginal, African-American, architects, salaried architects – to the making of architecturally sanctioned production. Biography or life-story texts are essential sources for sociological histories of the profession. Ensuring a range of voices is recorded in oral history projects is a new frontier for feminist activism. The splendid Art Institute of Chicago oral history archive holds interviews from a small, but very interesting number of women architects, and includes some history of their careers as salaried architects, but the collection has a strong focus on (male) practice directors and well-known firms.[26]

Early feminist histories of the 1970s consciously recovered 'heroines', a project that might seem like a female replication of the 'great heroes and their works' approach. Recovery projects also have another function for contemporary subjectivity. Feminist film theorists argued that identification with (fictional) characters was an important mode of twentieth-century subject formation. As teachers we experience delight from our women students when we schedule the writings of historically important women critics and women architects. Biographies provide models, ancestors, moments of recognition and mirrors.

Online written survey responses offer a glimpse of the varied lives of women in architecture and collect fragments of their voices. New conditions at this historical juncture, particularly digital media and social media, provide a means for diversifying the voices of architecture and presenting varied stories about a life in architecture.

The recent Australian discovery of larger numbers of women graduates in architecture than conventionally measured, echoes an earlier Canadian investigation. While both studies are very welcome their findings do not curtail architecture's feminist project. The profession still faces severe equity issues. As Lauren Berlant has observed, in most liberal democracies inequality is no longer formal (enshrined in law or policy) but informal (in behaviour) and, 'partial, contradictory and contested'.[27] Numerous reports have vocalised these informal problem spots in architecture: a significant under-representation of women in leadership roles, under-representation of women solo director firms, sexual discrimination, particularly around issues of pregnancy and parenting, sexual harassment, difficulties returning to work after a break for childbirth/child rearing, a culture dominated by 'presentee-ism' and long hours, and a reluctance to provide part-time or flexible work to employees. We will need to continue to measure progress in all these areas. The project of counting women continues to be critical.

Notes

1. Information is drawn from the 'Equity and diversity in the Australian architecture profession: Women, work and leadership' project, funded by the Australian Research Council from 2011 to 2014, led by Dr Naomi Stead, University of Queensland, and its website Parlour, www.archiparlour.org.
2. Judith Allan, 'Evidence and silence: Feminism and the limits of history', in Carole Pateman and Elizabeth Gross, *Feminist Challenges: Social and Political Theory* (Sydney: Allen & Unwin, 1986), p. 174.
3. Joan Scott, 'Feminism's History', *Journal of Women's History*, vol. 16, no. 2 (2004), 10–29.
4. A different licensing system exists in Sweden.
5. Registration Boards see their role as consumer protection.
6. See Gill Matthewson, 'Updating the Numbers: At School', www.archiparlour.org (accessed 15 January 2015).
7. Gill Matthewson, 'Women's Involvement in the Australian Architecture Profession: Building a Clearer and More Inclusive Profession', www.archiparlour.org (accessed 16 January 2015).
8. Gill Matthewson, 'Updating the Numbers: Institute Membership', www.archiparlour.org (accessed 15 January 2015).
9. Justine Clark et al., 'Technical Report and Preliminary Statistics: Where Do All the Women Go?' (unpublished paper, 2012); Justine Clark et al., 'Technical Report and Preliminary Statistics: And What About the Men?' (unpublished paper, 2012).
10. Peta Tancred and Anne-Marie Adams, *Designing Women: Gender and the Architectural Profession* (Toronto: University of Toronto Press, 2000); Anne De Graft et al., 'Why Do Women Leave Architecture?'

(Bristol and London: University of the West of England and the Royal Institute of British Architects, 2003); 'Consultations and Roundtables on Women in Architecture in Canada' (Royal Architectural Institute of Canada, 2003).

11   See Shuling Lu and Martin Sexton, 'Career journeys and turning points of senior managers in small construction firms', *Construction Management and Economics*, vol. 28 (February 2010), 125–139.

12   Sneja Gunew, 'Feminist Knowledge: Critique and construct', in Sneja Gunew (ed.), *Feminist Knowledge: Critique and Construct* (London and New York: Routledge, 1990), pp. 30–31.

13   Katrina Navickas, 'What happened to class? New histories of labour and collective action in Britain', *Social History*, vol. 36, no. 2 (2011), 192–204.

14   Karen Burns, 'Women in Architecture', www.architectureau.com/articles/women-in-architecture/ (accessed 12 January 2015).

15   Dana Cuff, 'Architecture's Undisciplined Urban Desire', *Architectural Theory Review*, vol. 19, no. 1 (2014), 92–97.

16   Ibid., p. 92.

17   Amanda Roan et al., 'Issues of Registration: Report from the ARC funded research project Equity and Diversity in the Australian Architecture Profession: Women, work and leadership' (unpublished paper, 2013). Susan Shannon, Naomi Webb, Yishu Zeng and Jena Holder, 'Why Architecture Graduates Do Not Register as Architects: A Quantitative and Qualitative South Australian Study, 1999–2011', *Creative Education*, vol. 5, no. 6 (September 2014), 1540–1558.

18   Cuff, 'Architecture's Undisciplined Urban Desire', pp. 92–97.

19   Dana Cuff, 'Epilogue', in Spiro Kostof (ed.), *The Architect: Chapters in the History of the Profession* (Los Angeles: University of California Press, 1977, updated 2000), p. 353.

20   Jane Cameron, 'Wanted Business Savvy Archipreneurs', Association of Consulting Architects, http://aca.org.au/article/becoming-business-savvy-archipreneurs (accessed 4 January 2015).

21   Amanda Roan and Naomi Stead, 'A "New Institutional" Perspective on Women's Position in Architecture: Considering the cases of Australia and Sweden', *Architectural Theory Review*, vol. 17, no. 2/3 (2012), p. 387.

22   Cuff, 'Epilogue', p. 356.

23   Dell Upton, 'Architectural History or Landscape History?', *Journal of Architectural Education*, vol. 44, no. 4 (August 1991), 195–199.

24   Dolores Hayden, *The Power of Place* (Cambridge, MA: MIT Press, 1997); Daphne Spain, *How Women Saved the City* (Minneapolis: University of Minnesota Press, 2001); Alice T. Friedman, *Women and the Making of the Modern House* (New Haven, CT: Yale University Press, 2007); Gwendolyn Wright, *Moralism and the Modern Home* (Chicago: University of Chicago Press, 1980).

25   Linda Sandino, 'Introduction to Oral Histories and Design: Objects and Subjects', *Journal of Design History*, vol. 19, no. 4 (2006), 275–282.

26   Chicago Architects Oral History Project, The Art Institute of Chicago, http://digital-libraries.saic.edu/cdm/landingpage/collection/caohp.

27   Lauren Berlant, *The Culture of Complaint: The Unfinished Business of Sentimentality in American Culture* (Durham, NC: Duke University Press, 2008), p. xi.

Part V

Economy

Chapter 17

Building design

A component of the building labour process

Jörn Janssen

My first attempt – at the 1967 international congress on the Theory of Architecture in Berlin – to have the term 'architecture' thrown into the dustbin in favour of building design (*Bauplanung*) was not successful.[1] I shall try again here, differently. Whereas in those days in Berlin, during the students' movement, I presented my case polemically, I shall try to do this now academically.

This procedure obliges me to start by presenting my theoretical approach applied to the definition of building design. In the next step I will outline the historical framework within which the identity of the 'architect' has taken shape and on which it depends for its integrity. Subsequently I shall trace this identity in the process of its historical emergence in the century of the English Revolution. Inigo Jones, Francis Russell and Covent Garden will then be considered as epitomising the birth of building design and a typical object at this stage. My sixth section will just briefly outline the consolidation of the profession of the 'architect' and its split from that of the quantity surveyor and the structural engineer. I conclude with the most recent specialisation in building design in the service of finance capital. It is questionable indeed whether the 'architect' as a distinct occupation can survive the 'bubblification' of capital and property.

The creative power of labour

Social history is in the first place labour history. Labour is the driving force and creative power in production as the process of appropriating natural resources for human sustenance and development. The unfolding of productivity is based on increasingly complex social labour relations in a process of historical transformation. The complexity develops in all dimensions – physical, mental, geographical – creating new products, services and occupations. Here we are concerned with a segment of production that can be traced far back to the arrangement of living space in caves or using plants for shelter in small communities. We focus here on the stage when building in particular, alongside agricultural labour, was already regulated by statutory wages and landholding had become private property. Our point of entry is 1563, when the Statute of Artificers consolidated wage relations as the universal form of the social labour process and the privileges of chartered trades – guilds – were decisively invalidated in England.[2] A typical example of an attempt to maintain control over a new sector of production by a city corporation, the claim of the Chartered Company of Bricklayers to be in charge of supervising and reaping the benefits of brickmaking failed in the 1630s, and brickmakers made their careers by developing large industrial companies.[3] Equally, building labourers, mainly bricklayers, rose up to the ranks of landlords through house-building and property speculation.

'Free' wage labour relations, as opposed to 'the subordination of one individual to another' under feudalism,[4] unleashed a process of productive innovation. Its most obvious features were a deepening and widening in the division of labour, including between physical and mental occupations associated with developing new means of production, and the exploration of new natural resources. With statutory regulation of wage-labour relations, England became the global centre of this transformation.

The rise and fall of the building designer

Within the framework of the division of labour in building production, the special occupation of a building designer emerged in England at a well advanced stage of wage-labour relations. Typically, this design function was initially restricted to the building of great residences for the royalty and nobility and the application of ancient forms as a 'renaissance' of classical antiquity identified with the ornamentation of façades copying Greek temples. It took building design about two hundred years to develop into a mature profession and to become organised in Britain in 1836 in the 'Royal Institute of British Architects' (RIBA). As a discipline of higher education and a legal requirement for building permission, building design became regulated and standardised. At the same time, within a wide range of application, it became increasingly specialised between urban and detailed construction design, as well as in relation to different destinations of built products, such as housing, offices, churches, schools, traffic and transport facilities, and so on. In most recent developments, 'architecture' – in the common understanding of being an art concerned with the visual appearance of buildings – represents only a small, shrinking segment of environmental and construction design. It is disintegrating as a coherent qualification and becoming divided into a number of separate occupations. Equally, the internal hierarchy of design offices divides employers and employees as well as different grades of employees. The field of the profession is also divided between employment in different sectors: public service, construction industry, property development, teaching and research, and last but not least, architects' offices.

Thus, in a wider historical context of building production, the 'architect' will be remembered as a passing configuration, particularly commissioned to confer lasting aesthetical value to products of the capitalist building industry. Postmodernism was perhaps the last effort to rescue this mission at a stage when its artistic foundations were about to disintegrate.

Building design in seventeenth-century England

The geographical centre of building production in seventeenth-century England was London. Two major developments concerning the building industry are characteristic of this century: the number of inhabitants rose from 200,000 to 600,000 and timber was replaced by brick construction. This building production, mainly of private houses, was first regulated by a number of successive royal proclamations relating, for instance, to their exterior form, internal measures such as height of ceilings, materials – brick walls and wooden ceilings – and urban development severely restricted to building only on existing foundations. Thus, urban and building design in London was directly the business of the crown, possibly with the advice of the 'Surveyor of the King's Works' and under the control of the 'Aldermen and the Justices of the Peace'.[5] Further details of construction and design were implemented by the builder-investor and the master-craftsman employed to carry out the work.[6] For larger projects the builder might also employ a surveyor.

After the Great Fire of London in 1666, building design became governed by Act of Parliament through *An Act for rebuilding the Citty of London* of 1667:

> There shall be only four sorts of building: first and least sort fronting by-lanes, second sort fronting streets and lanes of note, the third sort fronting high and principal streets. The roofs of each shall be uniform. The fourth and largest sort of mansion houses for citizens or other persons of extraordinary quality not fronting the three former ways.[7]

Numbers and heights of floors, building material and dimensions of walls and wooden structures were prescribed in even more detail than in the former proclamations, at least for the first three types of houses.

This building regime had little need of a profession specialised in building design, as also reflected in the contemporary literature. A telling title heads a booklet by Thomas Wilford published in 1659 on how to construct a house with bricks, timber and tiles and to possibly decorate it with columns: *Architectonice: The Art of Building, or An Introduction to all young Surveyors in common Structures.*[8] Another manual by Balthazar Gerbier of 1663 is more precise on the hierarchy of labour employed by the building investor: *Counsel and Advise to all Builders; For the Choice of their Surveyours, Clarks of their Works, Bricklayers, Masons, Carpenters, and other Work-men therein concerned.*[9] In this hierarchy of four levels – surveyors, clerks of works, master workmen, and journeymen and labourers – the architect's 'Art of Drawing and Perspective' was incorporated in the surveyor.[10] In an earlier *Brief Discourse Concerning the Three chief Principles of Magnificent Building, viz Solidity, Conveniency, and Ornament,* Gerbier explicitly ascribed 'the powers of the great Architect' to the surveyor.[11]

From a distance of three and a half centuries we can identify design as a component of the building labour process, first of all as part of social regulations in the transition from feudalism to capitalism. Standard houses were to be built according to rules developing at all levels in the complexity of the labour process and underpinned by royal proclamation. To the extent that a capitalist class took shape, its residential aspirations had to be respected above general standards as in the fourth type of 'mansions' according to the *Act for rebuilding the Citty of London.* This category consequently needed individual treatment by design professionals. This was how, according to Richard Neve in 1703, building design became 'Architecture: A Mathematical Science, which teacheth the Art of Building, being a Skill obtained by the Precepts of Geometry'.[12] However the roles were still in flux when the eighteenth century began, as apparent in the description of the

> Architect. A Master-workman in a Building, 'tis also sometimes taken for the Surveyor of a Building, viz. He that designs the Model, or draws the Plot, or Draught of the whole Fabrick; whose business it is to consider the whole Manner, and Method of the building, and also the Charge, and Expence.[13]

The case of Inigo Jones and Francis Russell at Covent Garden

Inigo Jones is generally known as the pioneer of architecture in England, working for the pioneer of urban development outside the City of London, Francis Russell, Fourth Earl of Bedford. A special Royal licence of £2000 allowed them to build the Covent Garden Square between 1631 and 1639,[14] according to the *Proclamation concerning New Buildings* of 16 July 1630.[15] Nikolaus Pevsner, a respected scholar in the discipline of building history, wrote in his volume on *The Cities of London and Westminster* about Covent Garden Square: 'Inigo Jones was its architect all round.'[16]

If we try to establish who was the designer of the square, we have the choice between three names: Charles I, Francis Russell and Inigo Jones, or to regard them as a team. Tracing the design of the individual houses would require recognition of the roles of all the leaseholders and master-craftsmen of the plots. To date, no particular payment to Inigo Jones for building design services or any designs for the square have been found.[17] The only outstanding piece of architecture in the centre of the west side of this ensemble is the church of St Paul's, commissioned and paid for by Francis Russell. Though no drawings of this church have ever been found, Inigo Jones is usually presented as its designer.[18] In fact the portico so closely resembles Vitruvius's description of the Tuscan Order that this may well have served as a model.[19] In his book on Inigo Jones,

John Summerson accurately described this design relationship: 'Palladio's and Barbaro's Vitruvian version of the Tuscan . . . appealed to Jones . . . at Covent Garden he constructed a full-scale realisation . . .'[20]

Inigo Jones, who lived from 1573 to 1652, had in fact a great impact on building design in England. He visited Italy repeatedly and studied Andrea Palladio's *Quattro libri dell'architettura* of 1570 thoroughly.[21] He adopted the 'renaissance' of the classical orders and imported them to his native country. His expertise in Italian architecture was the background to his appointment as 'Surveyor of the King's Works' in 1615, an office which he held up to 1643. It was also part of his office to oversee the building of Covent Garden. However, a special discipline or profession of building design as described by Richard Neve was not yet known in England during the lifetime of Inigo Jones. According to Thomas Wilford, ornaments to be applied by surveyors were typically 'Bay-windows, Belconies, Pirgilleines [pergolas] and sundry other things in Architecture'.[22] But this did not imply that they had to draw them. There existed standards and models – applied and perhaps improved, adjusted and varied by master-workmen.

On the larger scale, urban development around the City of London was under the command of King Charles I (1625 to 1649) and Francis Russell. Whilst Charles I was primarily concerned with the dignity of London as the residence of royal government and its improvement through bricks and stone instead of timber, Francis Russell was driven by the search for profits, through investment in real urban as well as rural estate. Building the Covent Garden Square was a project that suited the interests of both, the King as well as the Earl. But, whereas private investment survived the Civil War, royal authority was to be handed over to parliament, as in the *Act for rebuilding the Citty of London* after the Great Fire of 1666.[23]

The emancipation of the 'architect' in charge of building design

The example of Covent Garden demonstrates a regime that was to become dominant up to today – building as capital investment. It is this regime that gave birth to building design as a distinct profession. The 'architect' became the prime consultant of an investor. The architect was to provide drawings of future investment, which allowed building contractors to estimate costs and to carry out work according to the intentions of the developer. In turn, the architect commissioned engineers to calculate the stability of construction, and quantity surveyors to prepare the tender documents and check accounts. Nevertheless civil engineers received their Royal Charter (the Institution of Civil Engineers – ICE) in 1828, nine years before the central role of the 'architect' was eventually confirmed through Royal Charter (the RIBA) in 1837. Quantity surveyors did not receive a Royal Charter (the Royal Institute of Chartered Surveyors – RICS) until 1881, and structural engineers (the Institute of Structural Engineers – ISE) not until 1934.

It is interesting to note that 'architecture' assumed the identity of an applied art rather than a sector of engineering, though this varies between different countries and traditions.[24] At any rate, it is unquestionable that, worldwide, the 'architect' became the closest consultant to the building investors, whether private, public, or religious. In this function he or she represents the link between investment and production as well as the respective opposite forms of appropriation through ownership and labour. In the comprehensive building labour process – spanning commercial occupations related to investment at the top, and manual occupations related to production at the bottom – the architect provides academic skills supposed to generate or implement innovation and aesthetic appearance.

The 'architect' under finance capital

During the late twentieth century, building production reached a level of complexity which made it increasingly dysfunctional to carry out construction design as part of the business of the designer attached to the investor. As a result, larger projects came to be carried out under design and build contracts, by which the main contractor was commissioned to carry out the technical design including structural engineering. This is a simplified picture of often much more diversified contract relations between specialist services. Generally speaking, building design is in a process of disintegration, which does not spare the figure of the 'architect'. The most prominent people are usually those employed on the largest projects of investment. These are the buildings most visible to everybody in the townscape and, therefore, shown in the magazines of architecture and the general press with the names of the respective 'architects'. In the age of finance capital, these projects are typically skyscrapers for offices, banking and associated financial services. Thus, a segment of building design, dissociated from the production process and its structural complexities, has become 'autonomous', an expression coined by Aldo Rossi for the application of form without regard to gravity, the practicalities of production, or functional requirements.[25] This specialisation of building design on its 'hard core' of pure geometrical form in generating icons has most recently been termed 'hardcorism'.[26] Typical examples can be admired for instance in London (the 'Gherkin', the 'Cheesegrater' and the 'Walkie-Talkie') or in Beijing (the 'Loop'), designed by celebrities of the established avant-garde, Norman Foster, Richard Rogers, Rafael Viñola, and Rem Koolhaas. We find the same formal excesses dominating the buildings of World Fairs and Olympic Games. This architecture shares with finance capital that it is removed from its real conditions. Garcia Cruz and Nathalie Frankowski have summed up this movement: 'It [hardcorism] is an architecture after the disappearance of the architect.'[27]

Conversely, by far the major part of building design and its great variety of occupations is anonymous. It is divided and dispersed through competitive relations between client and contractor, public and private sector, modes of production technology, functional specificities of the built environment, and so on. But these occupations outside the limelight of fashions are indispensable for real life and lasting innovation in building production. They are an integral part of the building labour process.

Notes

1   Jörn Janssen, 'Verhältnisse zwischen Theorie und Praxis in der Bauplanung', in *Architekturtheorie: Internationaler Kongress in der Technischen Universität Berlin, 11–15 Dezember 1967*, ed. by Jörg Pampe (Berlin: Technische Universität Berlin, 1968).

2   'An Acte towching dyvers Orders for Artificers Laborers Servantes of Husbandrye and Apprentises' (1563) 5 Eliz. c.4, *The Statutes of the Realm*, IV, ed. by A. Luders and others (London, 1819), pp. 414–422.

3   See Jörn Janssen, 'The Transformation of Brickmaking in Seventeenth-Century London', *Construction History Newsletter*, 71 (2005), 1–9.

4   Marc Bloch, *Feudal Society*, trans. by L.A. Manyon (London: Routledge, 1962).

5   See the 'Proclamation of James I in 1603', in C.C. Knowles and P.H. Pitt, *The History of Building Regulation in London 1189–1972* (London: Architectural Press, 1972), p. 18.

6   Andrew Saint, 'Architect and Engineer: A Study in Construction History', *Construction History*, 21 (2005/6), 21–30 (at p. 23).

7   'Charles II, 1666: An Act for erecting a Judicature for Determination of Differences touching Houses burned or demolished by reason of the late Fire which happened in London', in *Statutes of the Realm*, V: 1628–1680, ed. John Raithby (s. l, 1819), pp. 601–603, www.british-history.ac.uk/statutes-realm/vol5/pp601-603 (accessed 22 May 2015).

8   Thomas Wilford, *Architectonice. The Art of Building, or An Introduction to all young Surveyors in common Structures* (London: Brook, 1659).

9   Balthazar Gerbier, *Counsel and Advise to all Builders; For the Choice of their Surveyours, Clarks of their Works, Bricklayers, Masons, Carpenters, and other Workmen therein concerned* (London: Thomas Mabb, 1663).

10   Ibid., p. 5.

11   Balthazar Gerbier, *A Brief Discourse concerning the three chief Principles of Magnificent Building. Viz. Solidity, Conveniency, and Ornament* (London, 1662), p. 23.

12   Richard Neve, *The City and Countrey Purchaser and Builder's Dictionary, or, The Compleat Builder's Guide* (London: Browne, 1703), p. 3.

13   Ibid., fol. 11.

14   'King to Attorney General Heath: "to prepare a licence to Francis Earl of Bedford, to build upon the premises called Covent Garden and Long Acre, with a pardon to the Earl, and such persons as he shall name, for offences committed against the proclamation for restraint of building upon new foundations."' Charles I, Vol. 182: January 1–20, 1631, in *Calendar of State Papers Domestic: Charles I, 1629–1631*, ed. John Bruce (London: HMSO, 1860), pp. 473–487, www.british-history.ac.uk/cal-state-papers/domestic/chas1/1629-31/pp473-487 (accessed 28 May 2015).

15   Knowles and Pitt, *The History of Building Regulation in London*, p. 22.

16   Nikolaus Pevsner, 'London I, The Cities of London and Westminster', revised edition, in *The Buildings of England* (London: Penguin, 1973), p. 351.

17   *Survey of London*, XXXVI: Covent Garden, General Editor: F.H.W. Sheppard (London: Athlone Press, 1970), p. 2.

18   See for example John Summerson, *Inigo Jones* (London: Penguin, 1966); and Vaughan Hart, *Inigo Jones: The architect of kings* (New Haven, CT and London: Yale University Press, 2000).

19   Vitruvius, *De architectura*, ed. by Daniele Barbaro (Venice, 1556), p. CXXVIII.

20   Summerson, *Inigo Jones*, p. 89, referring to *De architectura*, ed. by Daniele Barbaro, ch. 7, 'Della Ragion Toscane', pp. 121–126.

21   Bruce Allsopp (ed.) *Inigo Jones on Palladio, being the notes by Inigo Jones in the copy of I Quattro Libri Dell Architettura di Andrea Palladio 1601 in the Library of Worcester College*, 2 vols (Oxford: Oriel Press, 1970).

22   Wilford, *Architectonice*, p. 30.

23   Knowles and Pitt, *The History of Building Regulation in London*, pp. 30–33.

24   On the ambiguities of art and engineering in common understanding, see Saint, 'Architect and Engineer'.

25   Angelika Schnell, 'Von Jörn Janssen zu Aldo Rossi. Eine hochschulpolitische Affäre an der ETH Zürich', *ARCH+*, 215 (2014), 16–23.

26   Garcia Cruz and Nathalie Frankowski, 'Purer Hardcorismus. Wie wär's mit einem Manifest der perfekten Formen', *ARCH+*, 215 (2014), 26–33.

27   'Es ist eine Architektur nach dem Verschwinden des Architekten', Cruz and Frankowski, 'Purer Hardcorismus', p. 28.

from the demand side, from architects and engineers, towards a supply side dominated by capital-intensive materials and product manufacturers. Cement and gypsum producers, glassmakers, cladding systems makers, timber converters and roofing technologists are the knowledge leaders in their fields, as are water, electrical and mechanical system engineering firms in theirs. Production lies increasingly within oligopolies of well-capitalised global firms that manage their relations with the design professions, with the academies, with contractors and with regulators to their advantage. The intellectual property of modern construction resides to an increasing extent squarely on the supply side, mediated by selective access through information systems, technical education, legal protocols, and tools, such as CAD, CAM, BIM, and so on. Building designers and contractors, who trade in know-how and who use little capital, increasingly become mere contingent players within the new political economy.[6] This does not mean that design is unimportant – it remains a distinguishing cultural trait of construction – but its role is increasingly contingent on the realities of the new political economy. Architects and consulting engineers remain commercially valuable to developers and public clients mostly because of their social prominence. Well-educated, socially active and politically influential through their cultural activities, they are needed to impress and reassure decision-makers, even as their technical contribution to construction becomes ever more marginal. The future position of the design professions in construction will be quite unlike the paradigm of architectural practice still fondly promoted in the design academies.

The shift of knowledge to the supply side has taken roughly a century. It started around 1900 with the rise of new scientific materials, particularly steel and concrete. The high risks associated with their use had to be assumed by the entrepreneurs who promoted them. The professions were not automatically welcoming of new materials.[7] A tipping point in the ownership of intellectual property came with the advent of patent concrete building systems from 1890, a quite sudden phenomenon, widespread in both Europe and America. Patent holders did the research, developed the processes and gained commercial advantage through their mastery of technique. Although much of what they built – factories, infrastructure and agricultural buildings – was culturally invisible at the time, the pattern they established of industrial control over scientific knowledge and processes grew steadily among material and product manufacturing companies. Some modern materials, such as Eternit asbestos-cement, became vertically integrated producer monopolies.

While this shift to industry progressed, the design professions remained powerful for two reasons: because of the cultural/social position of their practitioners, and because of the trust placed in them by a great and demanding patron, the state. In the case of Britain, for example, before 1914 the general building industry had shown little interest in any scientific understanding of the performance, compatibility and durability of materials. As late as 1920 there were no specifications for building materials, apart from Portland cement and steel.[8] But after 1918 government began for the first time to take a serious interest in construction, in its potential to support post-war reconstruction, and in its promise as a productive industrial force.[9] Innovative construction methods and building research started to be sponsored by governments, and by the mid-1930s construction eventually began to be taught in universities.[10] Professionals were particularly prominent in these government initiatives after the Second World War, with the emergence of the welfare state, when a golden era dawned for architects and engineers.

During the 1950s the state's need to rebuild and to respond to a rapidly rising population elevated constructional professionals to a plateau of power and influence that they enjoyed for thirty years. Urgent need for construction of all types, but above all housing, propelled architects and engineers into positions of power as public servants, until by the early 1970s more than 50 per cent of the British architectural profession were directly employed by central and local government. The security afforded by their position, and the beliefs of modernists about the social power of architecture affected the professional outlook – what architects were slowly losing in terms of technical mastery of construction due to industrialisation they were making up for through their professed social concern for the end users of schools, hospitals, universities and housing.[11] They began to reconceptualise the designer, not as a master-builder but as a type of social engineer with the power and the responsibility to improve people's lives and thereby build a better world. The focus on this view of the task, the social and political potency it gave to architects, was mirrored by a relative neglect of traditional professional competences dealing with the more practical sides of construction.

The prediction and control of construction cost, and management of the construction process were early victims of this neglect, responsibilities that were enthusiastically picked up by quantity surveyors, emergent 'project managers' and contractors through design-build arrangements that challenged traditional professional roles in the name of cost certainty and technical know-how. The growing availability of proprietary building systems and materials, actively marketed, particularly to public-sector clients, further eroded the professional authority of architects.[12] Meanwhile in the academy, architectural teaching, a sort of parallel world of fashion and aestheticism, grew increasingly remote from practice and beyond the control of the professional institutions that pretended to regulate it. Practical subjects were dropped or subverted into pretexts for design; the burden of practical education for practice was shifted almost entirely onto the offices where graduates went for early experience.

The construction professions in the early 1970s generally failed to anticipate the inevitable backlash against their power and influence, a backlash born of the disruption of global markets following oil price increases, with dramatic inflation and uncertainty about resources that fuelled a revival of free-market economic ideology and that reflected deep hostility to professional monopolies. All professions, even the hallowed 'scientific community', came to be seen as creators of problems and generators of negative consequences. The very concept of professionalism was put under threat.[13] A decline in public trust and its replacement by an overriding notion of accountability led to a quite sudden hollowing out of the welfare state, as key elements of it continued to increase in relative cost – notably public housing, now being seen as unaffordable.[14]

The rolling back of the state that gathered pace during the late 1970s and early 1980s included divestment of a huge body of publicly owned and delivered intellectual and professional capital related to design, construction and management of buildings. Responsibilities were transferred, diluted or lost as quickly as physical properties were sold to the private sector. The procurement skills of clients were dismantled as previously responsible government departments enthusiastically deskilled themselves. Private design and consultancy practices were invited to compete for public work on the basis of price rather than experience or qualifications. Such 'rationalisation' of procurement processes became politically popular in the freewheeling and relatively prosperous 1980s and 1990s. The promise was that free market procurement processes would be tested against robust, empirically based criteria. Unfortunately, the criteria actually deployed in this process became increasingly biased towards supply-side considerations, e.g. easy delivery at low cost, unaccompanied by any attempt to measure the longer-term value to taxpayers, clients and end users.[15]

As the sharp outlines of the new economy came into focus from the early 1980s onwards, the design professions, particularly architects, found themselves poorly prepared in several respects. With regard to the practical world of construction, growing loss of control over cost, time and technique has left architects with seemingly little to offer their clients. These 'clients' are now often design-build contractors wedded to the accountability criterion, to whom designers are 'novated' through complex procurement structures. They are less and less likely to be representatives of building users or actual property owners.

The role of architects in social discourse has become increasingly the fulfilling of social expectations – a sort of role-play – the reassurance of decision makers (sometimes simply showing off to a bemused public). In terms of professional self-image things are even worse; the concerned social engineers with the people's best interest at heart have not actually increased their social and economic capital since the Second World War. They have missed opportunities, and their standing has declined relative to other professions. They have not embraced building science, failing to develop a body of shared knowledge about building use despite improved ways of doing so; they have kept the building industry at arm's length; they have not developed professional knowledge about the clients or the users of buildings; they remain indifferent to the systematic measurement of the performance of buildings over time;[16] and they are even feeble at representing the interests of clients and users of buildings, preferring to remain inside the 'ghetto' of architecture schools, design stars, self-regarding journalism and opaque theorising about design.[17] In short, architects have emphasised what seems to set them apart from the world of building rather than engage with construction, with activities that could give them a strong role in what Paolo Tombesi hopes could be a new construction paradigm of *flexible specialisation*, in which it is the design of a highly fragmented and variable process rather than an end product that is important.[18] Tombesi calls for all of building to become a branch of architecture rather than 'keeping architecture a privileged but inward-looking subset of building'.[19]

For young professionals now embarking on a career, there are formidable obstacles to increasing the value to society of their gifts and their intellectual capital.[20]

Traditional professionalism, the main way of institutionalising expertise in industrial societies, is under threat from several directions: technically through the commodification of design work by computers; and organisationally through the replacement of professional judgement by the elaborate bureaucracies of both client bodies and the multi-professional firms that serve them, where professional knowledge is encoded in the structures of the organisations themselves.

How then should young design professionals position themselves with respect to the realities of the new economy in order to maximise their social rewards? Is it too late to become a master builder or a valued social engineer? Has too much cultural capital been irretrievably lost by dropping or shunning practical skills? To revive Sir John Soane's ideal of the professional – as an ethical honest broker between supply and demand – would require strong public trust in the role to be effective and, as I have already noted, in the new economy, professional judgement is generally no longer trusted. Risk-averse employers now require legal or at least organisational excuses for all contractual decisions (vastly inflating transaction costs, by the way).

Approaches to the redefinition of professionalism must abandon notions of 'returning' to any former successful state for the simple reason that the new economy has already completely transformed the context within which such roles would be exercised. I think that a starting point for developing a new paradigm of architectural professionalism could be to abandon the conceptual obstacle of the designer as mediator between demand and supply. After all, that idea is inconsistent with other important alignments to be found within the structures of the new economy, where technical knowledge and intellectual property are widely distributed in often novel patterns. Ethical behaviour is possible on either side of any transaction.

Jeremy Till's engaging polemic, *Architecture Depends*, points out at length the extent to which architecture is now dependent on the new economy. In future, he proposes 'a move from the idea of the architect as expert problem-solver to that of architect as citizen sense-maker; a move from a reliance on the impulsive imagination of the lone genius to that of the collaborative ethical imagination'.[21]

Imagination is the key ingredient, of course, but it can and should be put in the service of supply just as much as of demand. The challenge for built environment education is to mark out both possible futures for its graduates, something it can only do after it cleans the stables of the present academy. In terms of future syllabus, there clearly needs to be a common core for both those who plan to work on the supply side and on the demand side, but then each needs to develop specialist abilities that reflect modern realities, from the assessment of needs, through the decision to build, to the construction and the long-term maintenance of buildings. There is a huge amount of work necessary to shift the cultural paradigm, and we had better get on with it; neoliberal economics is here for the foreseeable future.

What chances are there for radical change in the education of construction professionals? Unfortunately they are slim for several reasons, despite frequent and often ambitious attempts to reform professional education.[22] The main reason is the decline in political influence and authority of the professional institutes that to some extent control the schools through the formal validation of their courses. Although I have discussed mainly architecture, this observation applies also to the engineering disciplines. The accelerating shift of intellectual capital towards the supply side of construction is the principal cause, undermining the technical authority that underpins the professional institutes, and their position in society. They can speak, but they may not be heard.

Another, and in my view equally important, reason not to expect radical change in professional education is that it is a system that suits those involved with it very well. A strong cadre of teachers of design has grown up in schools of architecture, not so much practitioners lending their skills and experience to studio work, complementing the teachers of technical subjects, but rather specialists leading design studios whose reputations derive exclusively from their activities within the schools and who thus have a huge stake in its perpetuation. The design world created by successful teachers of design units is highly attractive to potential students who flock to their courses from around the world, drawn in by lavish publication of the work of the schools, by extravagant exhibitions of work at year end, and by rich esoteric architectural publishing. Fees are steep and thus the arrangement admirably suits the institutions that host the schools of architecture. The increasingly productivist ethos of tertiary education effectively licenses the institutions to ignore the academically doubtful content of the design courses.[23] The income stream is just too attractive. This is a hermetic and successful system that will not be displaced any time soon.

My characterisation of the educational milieu is perhaps caricatured, yet it clearly resonates with many practitioners who have to educate its often barely formed graduates and with the students themselves who lament their low pay and frustrating lack of usefulness to society. The problem arises because there is no coherent didactic structure to the teaching of architecture that is shared by all schools, let alone by the validating authorities.[24] Each school, whether or not embedded in a university, makes up its own manifesto. Battles continue to be fought over whether or not design is teachable. What to teach, how to teach it and even where to teach it, remain open questions. Meanwhile schools have increasingly lost the capacity to teach facts or knowledge while the construction industry is generally ignored or shunned. The teaching of design in units run by charismatic teachers discourages dialectic within schools, while at the same time encouraging unhealthy hero-worship. And the system of the educational milieu flourishes globally despite it being frequently challenged; in Britain RIBA-sponsored research recently showed more than 80 per cent of employers agreeing that schools put theoretical knowledge above practical ability and that students lack the knowledge to build what they design.[25] But the milieu is also defended by eloquent spokespersons for the mysteries of design teaching.[26] The struggle is far from over. At the first ever open meeting of the RIBA Council attended by students, academics and practitioners, it was agreed to scrap the professional practice module – Part 3 – of the approved curriculum in favour of more early years emphasis on legal and management aspects of architectural practice. This may be seen as a rearguard reaction from the world of practice and its regulation, responding to the mood expressed in the survey cited above.[27] But it is unlikely to shake the educational milieu nor to slow the more general marginalisation of the design professions.

Notes

1   See Mark Linder, *Projecting Capitalism: A history of the internationalization of the construction industry* (Westport, CT and London: Greenwood Press, 1994).

2   The processes of diffusion and institutionalisation are addressed in James C. Scott, *Seeing Like a State* (New Haven, CT: Yale, 1998); and Keller Easterling, *Extrastatecraft: The power of infrastructure space* (London: Verso, 2014).

3   'Global Construction and Engineering December 2013', Marketline Inc., http://store.marketline.com/Product/global_construction_engineering?productid=MLIP1059-0012 (accessed 12 May 2015).

4   Andrew Rabeneck, 'The Transformation of Construction by Concrete', in *Nuts and Bolts of Construction History: Culture, technology and society*, 3 vols, ed. by Robert Carvais et al. (Paris: Picard, 2012), pp. 627–635.

5   See Amy Slaton, *Reinforced Concrete and the Modernisation of American Building, 1900–1930* (Baltimore, MD: Johns Hopkins University Press, 2001).

6   Barrington Kaye already spoke of the 'bogey of dispensability' in Barrington Kaye, *The Development of the Architectural Profession in Britain* (London: George Allen & Unwin, 1963). Manfredo Tafuri picked up the theme of the architect caught within the structures of capitalism in the last chapter of his *Architecture and Utopia: Design and capitalist development*, trans. by Barbara Luigia La Penta (Cambridge, MA: MIT Press, 1976). The contingent position of the design professions is a major theme of Jeremy Till's polemic, *Architecture Depends* (Cambridge, MA: MIT Press, 2009).

7   Marian Bowley recounts the institutional arguments that resulted in Britain being about twenty years behind the continent in starting serious use of concrete. Marian Bowley, *The British Building Industry: Four studies in response and resistance to change* (Cambridge: Cambridge University Press, 1966), pp. 15–27.

8   F.M. Lea, *Science and Building: A history of the building research station* (London: HMSO, 1971), p. 3.

9   Andrew Rabeneck, 'The Invention of the Building Industry in Britain', *ArtefaCToS*, 4, 1 (2011), 93–121.

10 Imperial College ran a one-year postgraduate course for selected teachers of building in 1933–1934 (most of the lectures given by BRS staff), but only the Universities of Manchester and Wales (Cardiff) accepted building subjects as part of a degree course in the 1930s.

11 Andrew Saint, *Towards a Social Architecture: The role of school building in post-war England* (London: Yale University Press, 1987).

12 Stefan Muthesius and Miles Glendenning, *Tower Block: Modern public housing in England, Scotland, Wales and Northern Ireland* (New Haven, CT and London: Yale University Press and Paul Mellon Centre for Studies, 1994).

13 Attacks on professions and professionals were led by iconoclasts such as Rachel Carson, Jane Jacobs and, later, by Ivan Illich and E.F. Schumacher, who initially inspired politicians to legislate against professional privilege. Later waves attacked government welfare and spending in general, leading to the 'rolling back of the state'. See Harold Perkin, *The Rise of Professional Society: England since 1880* (London: Routledge, 1989), pp. 472–519.

14 Onora O'Neill, *A Question of Trust*, BBC 2002 Reith Lectures, Lecture 3 'Called to Account', www.bbc.co.uk/programmes/p00ghvd8 (accessed 20 May 2015).

15 Francis Duffy and Andrew Rabeneck, 'Professionalism and Architects in the Twenty-First Century', *Building Research and Information*, 41, 1 (2013), 115–122.

16 Bill Bordass and Adrian Leaman, 'Building Performance Evaluation in the UK: So many false dawns', in Wolfgang F.E. Preiser et al. (eds) *Architecture Beyond Criticism: Expert judgment and performance evaluation* (Abingdon: Routledge, 2015), pp. 160–170.

17 See Malcolm Millais, *Exploding the Myths of Modern Architecture* (London: Frances Lincoln, 1998); and Gary Stevens, *The Favored Circle: The social foundations of architectural distinction* (Cambridge, MA: MIT Press, 1998).

18 Paolo Tombesi, 'The Carriage in the Needle: Building design and flexible specialization systems', *Journal of Architectural Education*, 52, 3 (1999), 134–142.

19 Paolo Tombesi, 'On the Cultural Separation of Design Labor', in Peggy Deamer and Phillip G. Bernstein (eds) *Building (in) the Future: Recasting labor in architecture* (New Haven, CT and New York: Yale University Press/Princeton Architectural Press, 2010), pp. 117–136.

20 The challenges for professionals are well articulated in the important book, Dominique Foray, *The Economics of Knowledge* (Cambridge, MA: MIT Press, 2006).

21 Till, *Architecture Depends*, p. 131.

22 Educational proposals for architecture mostly start from critique of existing schools and practices. They come from the professional press and from within the institutions responsible for validating the offerings of the schools; the RIBA organised education conferences in 1924, 1943, 1958 and 2008, and it has an ongoing 'Educational Review' panel. The *Architectural Review* frequently contributes to the debate, notably with Peter Buchanan's 'What's Wrong with Architectural Education? Almost Everything', *Architectural Review*, 185 (July 1989), and his more recent twelve-essay series 'The Big

Rethink', launched in *Architectural Review,* September 2012, by editor Catherine Slessor. It is notable that none of these initiatives involves contributions from the wider construction world.

23   See Stefan Collini, 'From Robbins to McKinsey', *London Review of Books,* 33, 16 (2011), 9–14.

24   David Dunster, speaking at *Architectural Education: Global difference,* RIBA Conference, London, 16 September 2011.

25   RIBA, *Appointments Skills Survey Report 2014* (February 2015).

26   Neil Spiller and Nick Clear (eds) *Educating Architects: How tomorrow's practitioners will learn today* (London: Thames & Hudson, 2014).

27   Laura Mark, 'RIBA Moves to Scrap Part 3', *Architects' Journal* (25 March 2015), www.architectsjournal. co.uk/news/riba-moves-to-scrap-part-3/8680459.article (accessed 20 May 2015).

Chapter 19

Financial formations

Matthew Soules

Perhaps the single most important socio-economic transformation of the last three decades is the hegemonic rise of finance capitalism. While buildings and their subdivided increments have long functioned, at least in part, as assets to invest in, finance capitalism tends to amplify this function and, in the process, impacts the physical form and organisation of architectural space. The financialisation of architecture is now so widespread and normalised that it remains largely, and somewhat paradoxically, beyond scrutiny. It is possible to trace finance capitalism's effect on the built environment through many building types, but housing, as the real estate market's most prevalent investment vehicle, presents the phenomenon in sharpest relief. This chapter focuses on North American condominium towers, and those in Manhattan and downtown Vancouver specifically, as exemplars of unique spatio-financial formations designed to maximise the investment asset function to the point of displacing architecture's many other possible roles.

The rise of finance capitalism

Finance capitalism prefaces the pursuit of profit from transactions of, and investment in, financial instruments such as currency, bonds and stocks, as well as commodities such as gold and oil. It subordinates processes of production as a means to generate profit by replacing them with processes of investment. By definition, it is contrasted with industrial capitalism in which profits are pursued through the production of goods to be sold at

By removing key operation and maintenance responsibilities from individual owners, ownership becomes easier, and by extension, so does buying and selling, thereby increasing liquidity. This has a simple but profound implication – it enables ownership without occupation or even contact with a unit, propelling housing closer to intangible asset classes like stocks and bonds. As Harris states, a condo was 'self-contained and simple, could be owned from a distance, occupied or left vacant, and transferred in a market of highly fungible commodities'.[18]

The genealogy of financial form

The physical form and organisation of condominium's most prevalent architectural type, the point tower, is a means to further enhance the investment function of housing. And more specifically, the slender version of the point tower perfects the asset function because it displaces housing from the more complicated aspects of its physical context and enervates lingering human proximities, thus simplifying, standardising, and abstracting it as an investment product. In this simplified form, condominium units are more easily traded and their liquidity further increased. The tower's most elemental operation removes the unit of housing from the ground where it is susceptible to the unpredictability of public space and the potential nuisances and dangers of noise, pollution, and strangers. And the slender tower seeks to minimise potential social complications within the building itself. To achieve experiential isolation, the simple reduction of the number of discrete units per floor reduces the multi-sensory evidence of neighbour proximity in the dimension where it has the most potential: horizontally.

It is more difficult to mitigate the transmission of sound and odour in the horizontal than vertical dimension in multi-unit housing, and minimisation of discrete units on a floor lowers this transmission's potential. Other than vertical circulation, the hallway is the primary space to encounter different occupants, and the minimisation of units per floor diminishes the likelihood of this encounter. The small floor plate, in combination with market-based standardisation of unit size, inherently achieves the reduction of discrete units per floor. It can be argued that the slender tower exchanges the potential of social interaction for the value attributed to the view – a more quantifiable and less risky quality. Not coincidentally, the very same form and organisation that enervates sociality also optimises view production. Desirable views are achieved via small floor plate towers because of what they enable internally and imply urbanistically. The corner condition inherently maximises view potential through its multi-directionality and a small floor plate uniquely offers a high corner to floor area ratio. Additionally, when combined with strategic spacing between towers at the urban scale, the repetition of small floor plate towers affords ample view lines between towers when compared to the repetition of other typologies such as slabs or mid-rise blocks. Height itself maximises the reproduction of these ostensibly desirable attributes. Taken collectively, these straightforward organisational and proportional tactics amount to an architectural form of dense isolation. The enervation of social 'contamination' effectively abstracts

Figure 19.3
The historical development of New York City condominium tower slenderness. Drawing: Matthew Soules and Cam Koroluk

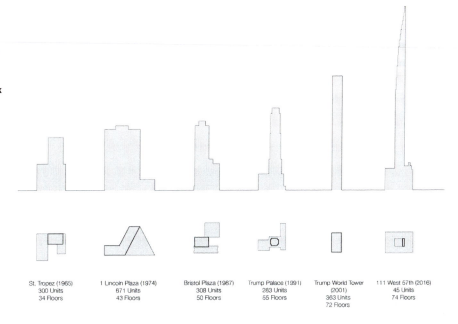

St. Tropez (1965)
300 Units
34 Floors

1 Lincoln Plaza (1974)
671 Units
43 Floors

Bristol Plaza (1987)
308 Units
50 Floors

Trump Palace (1991)
283 Units
55 Floors

Trump World Tower
(2001)
363 Units
72 Floors

111 West 57th (2016)
45 Units
74 Floors

domestic space and serves to remove it from collective entanglements and ultimately facilitates its post-social role – that of a tradable financial asset unto itself.

Avatars of financialisation: Vancouver and Manhattan

Vancouver is an exceptional case of financialised built form. 'The popularity of condominium defines Vancouver among Canadian and even North American cities', writes Harris.[19] The city's first condo was completed in 1970 but by 2010, 4,200 buildings comprised 98,000 condo units – a remarkable amount considering the city's approximately 600,000 residents.[20] Over the same period, property values have risen dramatically, to the point that the city's housing is now said to be amongst the world's least affordable – less affordable than New York and London.[21] This price escalation is commonly understood to be the result of speculative investment in a newly globalised market – 'nothing about [Vancouver's] economy explains why – in a city where the median income is only around seventy grand – single-family houses now sell for close to a million dollars apiece and ordinary condos go for five or six hundred thousand dollars', writes James Surowiecki in *The New Yorker*.[22] Of condos in the downtown core, approximately 55 per cent are not occupied by their owners, suggesting the 'strong role of real estate investors'.[23] While investor-owners typically rent their condos to tenants, there is an increasing phenomenon of those not bothering to do so, preferring to let the property sit empty to avoid the hassle and risk of renting. The result is that in downtown Vancouver's various new condominium districts approximately 15 per cent of units are owned but empty. In the Coal Harbour neighbourhood that number climbs to 23 per cent.[24] Not coincidentally, uniquely slender towers define these districts while zoning strictly regulates minimum spacing

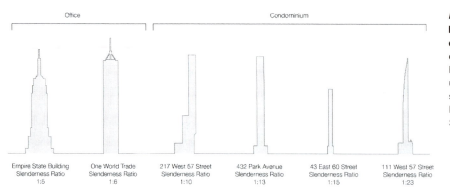

Figure 19.5
Numerous contemporary condominiums in New York City have unprecedented slenderness ratios. Drawing: Matthew Soules and Cam Koroluk

In revisiting Douglas Harris's key proposition that condominiums are by definition self-contained, simple, can be owned from a distance, can be left vacant, and are easily transferable, one can posit that condominiums themselves problematise the very possibility of an agonistic pluralism in spatial terms because they enervate the possibility of sensate contact between potential adversaries. After all, in the increasingly common manifestations of financialised architecture, in which significant numbers of condominium units sit empty as investments, actual human residents have left the premises, allowing capital itself to reside alone in a zenith of post-political architecture.

While finance capitalism pulls architectural space away from use value and toward an after-human condition of financial instrumentality it cannot make the transition from one to the other in entirety. The ostensible realism of real estate must remain for the logic of its financialisation to persist – and this reality is founded upon an ongoing material presence in the physical world. Architecture's post-political, financialised trajectory is therefore not a process of dematerialisation, but rather one of rematerialisation. As finance capitalism brings architectural matter into the orbit of heightened liquidity it reorganises its material qualities to make them perform more effectively in a financial ecology. In the 'false and fresh starts' of capitalism's ongoing development there will be any number of future rematerialisations that will bring to bear the simultaneous intimacy and estrangement that exists between capital and concrete.[36] In these subsequent conditions the physical reality of architecture will likely emerge into new formations that connect with capital in ways that further stretch the understanding of both.

Notes

1   Michael Hudson, 'The Transition from Industrial Capitalism to a Financialized Bubble Economy', *Levy Economics Institute Working Paper*, 627 (2010), www.levyinstitute.org/pubs/wp_627.pdf (accessed 28 April 2015).
2   Larry Neal, *The Rise of Financial Capitalism: International capital markets in the age of reason* (Cambridge: Cambridge University Press, 1990), p. 3.
3   Rudolph Hilferding, *Finance Capital: A study in the latest phase of capitalist development* (New York: Routledge, 2006), preface.
4   Fredric Jameson, 'Culture and Finance Capital', *Critical Inquiry*, 24, 1 (1997), 246–265 (at pp. 249–250).
5   Jameson, 'Culture and Finance Capital', p. 251.

6   Giovanni Arrighi, *The Long Twentieth Century: Money, power, and the origins of our times* (London: Verso, 1994), p. 1.
7   Jameson, 'Culture and Finance Capital', p. 246.
8   Ibid., p. 260.
9   Hudson, 'The Transition from Industrial Capitalism to a Financialized Bubble Economy', p. 4.
10   *World Development Report 2009: Reshaping economic geography* (Washington, DC: The World Bank, 2009), p. 206.
11   Hudson, 'The Transition from Industrial Capitalism to a Financialized Bubble Economy', p. 3.
12   *World Development Report 2009*, p. 206.
13   Saskia Sassen, 'When Local Housing Becomes an Electronic Instrument: The global circulation of mortgages – a research note', *International Journal of Urban and Regional Research*, 33, 2 (2009), 411–426.
14   Douglas C. Harris, 'Condominium and the City: The rise of property in Vancouver', *Law and Social Inquiry*, 36, 3 (2011), 694–726 (at p. 695).
15   Barbara Yaffe, 'Even Condos Becoming Out of Reach in Vancouver's Sky-High Housing Market', *Vancouver Sun*, 4 November 2014, www.vancouversun.com/business/Barbara+Yaffe+Even+condos+becoming+reach+Vancouver+high+housing+market/10154773/story.html (accessed 28 April 2015).
16   Brent Jang, 'Vancouver Real Estate Prices Break Records', *Globe and Mail*, 4 March 2014, www.theglobeandmail.com/report-on-business/economy/housing/vancouver-house-prices-hit-new-high/article17279408/ (accessed 17 February 2015).
17   Paul Goldberger, 'Too Rich, Too Thin, Too Tall?', *Vanity Fair*, May 2014, www.vanityfair.com/unchanged/2014/05/condo-towers-architecture-new-york-city (accessed 10 February 2015).
18   Harris, 'Condominium and the City', p. 714.
19   Ibid., p. 718.
20   Ibid., p. 719.
21   Demographia, *Eleventh Annual Demographia International Housing Affordability Survey: 2015*, www.demographia.com/dhi.pdf. (accessed 15 February 2015).
22   James Surowiecki, 'Real Estate Goes Global', *New Yorker*, 26 May 2014, www.newyorker.com/magazine/2014/05/26/real-estate-goes-global (accessed 1 February 2015).
23   Andy Yan, *Ownership, Occupancy, and Rentals: An indicative sample study of condominiums in Downtown Vancouver* (Vancouver: BTA Works, 2009), p. 7.
24   Andy Yan, *Foreign Investment in Vancouver's Real Estate Market* (Vancouver: BTA Works, 2013), www.slideshare.net/ayan_bta/btaworks-foreign-investment-in-vancouver-real-estate (accessed 15 February 2015).
25   For an extended discussion on Vancouver as model for contemporary urbanisation, see Matthew Soules, 'The "Liveable" Suburbanized City: Post-politics and a Vancouver near you', *Harvard Design Magazine*, 32 (2010), 141–148.
26   Goldberger, 'Too Rich, Too Thin, Too Tall?'
27   Skyscraper Museum, *SKY HIGH & The Logic of Luxury*, www.skyscraper.org/EXHIBITIONS/SKY_HIGH/sky_high.htm (accessed 15 June 2014).
28   Juliet Chung and Alyssa Abkowitz, 'Ackman Leads Group Paying $90 Million for Manhattan Penthouse', *Wall Street Journal*, 16 May 2013, http://blogs.wsj.com/moneybeat/2013/05/16/ackman-leads-group-paying-record-price-for-manhattan-penthouse/ (accessed 15 October 2014).
29   *The Chelsea* was designed and constructed as co-op housing, but shortly after its completion it was converted to a hotel.
30   Slavoj Žižek, *The Ticklish Subject: The absent centre of political ontology* (London: Verso, 1999), p. 199.
31   Chantal Mouffe, 'Which Public Sphere for a Democratic Society', *Theoria: A Journal of Social and Political Theory*, 99 (2002), 55–65 (at p. 55).
32   Ibid.
33   Ibid., p. 58.
34   Ibid.
35   Richard Sennett, 'Capitalism and the City', lecture at ZKM Center for Art and Media, Karlsruhe, Germany, 11 November 2000, http://on1.zkm.de/zkm/stories/storyReader#dl1513 (accessed 15 September 2012).
36   Jameson, 'Culture and Finance Capital', pp. 249–250.

Part VI
Law and regulation

Chapter 20

French architects' use of the law

Robert Carvais

Twenty years of researching French law have led me to try to figure out why most French architects hate the law. Why in particular do they resent its most significant embodiment, that is to say the overall set of rules comprising technical standards and legal rules, even though – according to the 1977 law – architects create 'for the common interest'? It might seem strange that, burdened by law with extreme responsibility, they are not satisfied or even interested in the prime authority which the state endows upon them. The curriculum of architecture schools barely includes any legal – or economic – knowledge. Law classes are mostly reduced to two months of intensive studying during the post-degree's 'sixth year', granting architects the accreditation to project management in their own name (*Habilitation à la Maîtrise d'œuvre en son nom propre* or HMONP). Architects are biased against the law as if it were the devil incarnate, despite knowing its crucial role in society (concerning contracts, liability, ownership, public order, etc.). But they persist in considering regulations as excessive and *a priori* constraints.

The aim of this contribution is to show how, through precise situations, recent and old, French builders (mason-contractors, and then architects) handle the legal constraints regulating their work. By legal constraints we are specifically referring to construction law (regulating public and private building) and urban planning law. Both these fields – at least in France – are always subordinate to the fundamental principles that govern public and private law alike; principles that are mostly written (and at times not) and found in constitutional, administrative, civil law, etc. Moreover, French law belongs to the family of Civil Law and differs from Common Law mainly in the lesser – but not entirely negligible – role of case law as a source of law. The law before 1804 (which we call Ancient Law) was organised entirely differently from the Civil Code (modern French law enacted after the Revolution), and was of an entirely different nature. But in both ancient and modern cases, fundamental principles, laws, by-laws, jurisprudence, contracts and customs have always added up to what we generically refer to as the 'law'. Hence, when we use the term we are referring to law in general, except when we explicitly mention one in particular.

In spite of the belief increasingly held by architects that the law bridles their creativity, it is worth noting and stressing the fact that architects have always known how to deal with current laws and to work unrestrained. Contrary to what they often think, law is not, and never has been, a personal constraint but a framework meant to protect public interest and always prepared to negotiate with the intents of individual projects, provided that the largest number of citizens are respected.

Through the historical situations uncovered by our work, as well as in contemporary examples, which are not directly linked to these historical examples, but approaching law in a similar way, we identified two methods used by builders to feel free as creators in spite of constraining rules. The first method was born from the activities of project managers, either mason-contractors or architects (or both). The second method originated from the world of lawyers, who granted citizens – architects in particular – some leeway regarding the legal concepts of the rules. In the first place, we will discuss the two means by which architects manipulate the rules to their advantage. On the one hand, they can downright ignore them, even if they are ultimately placed under the condemnation of the law. Court records describe some such occurrences, but how many others remain undetected by the law? And on the other hand, some architects take advantage of the vagueness, or even silence, of the law to reach their goals. In this case they interpret the standards, as lawyers do by trade, using any and all the philological tools to have the rule comply with their creative ambition (analysing the text; discussing the spirit of the law, based on history, casuistry, or the rule's alleged purpose; relying on logical interpretations, using maxims or mechanisms of argumentation such as *a contrario, a fortiori, a pari*). Clearly, at this stage, knowledge of law is essential.[1]

Secondly, and assuming that the law is not meant to impede architects but rather to show them how to comply as best as they can with the social rules defined by their elected representatives, lawyers can provide architects with tools which facilitate their creative actions (or at least do not limit their scope). Two situations can occur. On the one hand, a judge can, for a specific case, interpret the rule in a loose way that is favourable to the architect's freedom. On the other hand, a lawyer in his role as legal creator can implement lax concepts when drawing up a law. This allows for a flexible application of the law and non-categorical attitudes, affording citizens more freedom of action. Architects – and in particular town planners – benefit more frequently from such writings of the rules.

We will discuss these four scenarios based on examples drawn from the seventeenth- and eighteenth-century legal archives of French institutions supervising the construction world, in particular *La Chambre des Bâtiments* (Chamber of the Building Trade). We will try to substantiate their persistence in time by expounding modern examples of these solutions.

The strategies of architects

Civil societies, in this early twenty-first century and on a global scale, are prone to show their discontent towards the democratic order that their governments propose, or sometimes even impose. Whether they call themselves 'dissenters', 'indignés', 'rebels' or 'resistance fighters', their intent is to challenge social and/or legal rules. These protests can be carried out single-handedly or collectively, and in the latter case these expressions of discontent often occur as members of a trade organisation. Architects, who are surprisingly uninvolved in politics, seldom demonstrate in the streets. But they have an undeniable ability to disobey as creators, either by choosing to deliberately disregard constraining rules or standards, or by circumventing the law, allowing them – at the same time – to avoid the law and to show it all due respect.

Disregarding, distorting or breaking the rules

In Paris during the *Ancien Régime* there was a specific organisation in charge of judging, supervising and regulating construction activities. At the time, contractors – tradesmen, masons, and carpenters – and architects were equally entitled to project management. Since the Middle Ages the *Chambre des Bâtiments* (initially called *Juridiction de la maçonnerie*, the masons' court) was assigned with ruling on disputes, organising the supervision of works in the capital city – and even beyond – and regulating the technical standards of the art of building. We systematically read and analysed the *Chambre des Bâtiments* archives covering the period from 1670 to 1790, whether dealing with justice and police records, police reports or ensuing regulations.[2] Thus, we singled out recurrent defects and the building community's attempts to prevent them. We established three major types of weaknesses, relating to solidity, preventing fires, and hygiene. These were diversely located in buildings (foundations, walls, openings, posts/pillars, roofing, framework, chimneys, stairs, and cesspools) as a result of three very precise characteristics: poor building materials, poorly established connections, and malformations.

The year 1694 charts the contents of the official general rules of construction, the first 'reduction into art' of construction. Those were attributed to the future judge

Table 20.1
Evolution of types of defect found on Parisian building sites before and after the 1694 by-law

	1678		1694	1723		1753		1783	
Defects breaking the rules for:	n	%	**%**	n	%	n	%	n	%
Solidity	293	77	**66**	69	73	44	82	268	90
Preventing fires	79	21	**24**	26	27	10	18	31	10
Hygiene	6	2	**10**	0	0	0	0	0	0
Total	378			95		54		299	

Jean Beausire, mason and subsequently King's Architect, who transcribed the recurrent disorders in the form of proscriptions. During the eighteenth century the proscriptions relating to preventing fires decreased while those relating to the solidity of buildings constantly increased. This result shows the relative efficiency of rules and the fact that many project managers did indeed comply with fire rules but continued to build contrary to the laws of stability and safety. They avoided these constraints by openly breaking the rules. Some were never detected or sued.[3]

Nowadays too, architects sometimes defy all the legal constraints of construction. In that respect the example of building on Reunion Island is surprising, to say the least. The *Plan Local d'Urbanisme* (PLU, local town planning scheme) for the capital city, Saint-Denis, was drawn up by organisations knowledgeable and competent in terms of town planning and the protection of historical monuments. Having analysed the city's framework they considered that in addition to the historical monuments there were street blocks, houses and commercial buildings which held heritage or aesthetic value, and decided that they ought to be preserved for future generations. If unfortunately any of these came to be destroyed they were to be rebuilt identically. The basic premise was to preserve the historical heritage. The guiding principles reached by consensus were protected. Today, however, due to property, real estate and speculative pressure, all of this has been turned over. The very people in charge of applying it deprived the PLU of its substance, and new arrangements were made. Small ones first, until the day when a 'brilliant' mind invented the Neo-Creole style. The style, which has thrived for the past ten years, epitomises the art of cosmetics and sham. A place where a creole hut once stood is swept clean. Instead, a little concrete house is built and camouflaged with wooden planks. The new construction complies neither with setting, nor building methods or interior layout: from the heritage standpoint, aesthetics are disregarded and the PLU trampled, and the result is a complete perversion of Creole architecture.[4] Somewhat more subtly, architects can also sidestep the rules that restrict them.

Sidestepping the rules

Architects can choose from many possibilities to avoid the rules: they can use tricks to evade them by taking the opposite stance, or by using them in a different context – or they can interpret the rules by discovering something favourable where the law states nothing.

During the seventeenth and eighteenth centuries, master masons long sought for the ideal chimney.[5] In the beginning, the length of flues prescribed by the regulations was 'too strong', to the extent that the only solution chimney experts could suggest was to 'make wythes that would shorten it.' By the mid-eighteenth century, the masons' jurisdiction had taken the 'wiser' decision to differentiate, as in the 1771 rules, dimensional constraints of pipes according to the room's size – hence the chimney's – and according to the construction's age, so as to spare the owner compliance upgrades that would be too costly. But as the Crown Prosecutor aptly noted: 'Which law does greed not seek to elude?'[6] Contractors interpreted legal instructions in the least constraining way possible. Because they knew that in certain cases chimney pipes could be downsized to two feet, they downsized them all. Initially the measure was meant to allow for more flexibility towards the owners of older houses, to relieve them from the financial burden of rebuilding a floor. It turned out to be catastrophic for recent houses. Contractors were unusually keen on distorting that rule in new buildings, seeing that 'thanks to this short measure they carry [buildings] to a higher level in stories', thus raising the risk of fire due to nothing more than their pernicious desire to increase profits.[7] Architects managed to find and use a legal flaw to their advantage, despite the danger it represented.

Likewise, Patrick Bouchain analysed the articles of the French Civil Code chapter on the 'right of accession relative to movables' in order to discover ways for renters to appropriate their dwelling in a reversible and shared manner.[8] Couldn't this notion of 'accession' benefit the less privileged, allowing them to break free from the standards of social housing? According to Bouchain, 'property of use' would allow inhabiting a place to be considered a gratifying activity. Dwellings would gain 'added value' by virtue of being used by renters who would embellish or improve the dwellings. Nicolas Michelin's reasoning was similar when he invited lawyers to revisit the notion of common areas in co-ownership, through the right of enjoyment or conventional easements. These could give the general public access to places that are theoretically private and as a result would showcase architectural heritage. In the current context of immoderate residential conversions, using the right of enjoyment would allow architects to turn lifeless places into areas of social life.[9] Examples of the architects' propensity to disobey the law are not in short supply. But they are not alone. Lawyers have at their disposal a vast array of procedures inherent to the specific mechanisms of their field.

The tools of lawyers

During any legal argument and beyond the formal syllogism, which allows the rule of law to be applied to the facts of a situation in absolute terms, two intellectual operations are unavoidable: qualifying and interpreting. Thanks to the latter in particular, lawyers are afforded the means to modulate the harshness of the rule. And architects often stand to benefit from this. In practice, lawyers are always equipped with adequate techniques of interpreting the law, which provide architects with the means to endure rules and standards with more or less comfort. A judge will for instance be asked to pass judgment in court, and in light of the circumstances, can decide to mitigate the rigours of the law. The author of rules, a legislator or administrative authority, might deliberately let vague concepts be included, in order to obtain a less restrictive validation of the rule and more consensus from those involved.

The judge mitigates the rigours of the law

The customary laws of France under the *Ancien Régime* specified which persons were required to carry out the upkeep of a building according to their status as owner in relation to the other owners above or under them, as renter in relation to the owner, or as usufructuary in relation to the bare owner, as dowager or beneficiary. But when the question was to determine the portion of income and benefits which any religious person ought to devote to the repair and upkeep of churches or other buildings assigned to the sick, poor or pilgrims, the customs were divided: at times they spoke of a quarter, at others of a third; 'in order for the surveyors who are named to visit it to be able with more certainty to do their report, letting the Honorable judges give a ruling following their prudence'.[10]

Coming back to the present, the orders aiming to shorten construction times undeniably represent a step forward, but they have organised a complex system, sometimes ambiguous, committing a major part to the judge's interpretation.

The order of 3 October 2013,[11] relating to the development of housing construction, allows the public service issuing a building permit to depart from the local town planning scheme, in order to promote social diversity in areas where there is an imbalance between supply and demand. The rules that can be departed from are clear (size, density, parking), which is not the case for the conditions of the expected results. What is meant by 'building mainly destined to housing' or by 'harmonious integration to the urban environment' (article L. 123-5-1 1° of the French Code of Town Planning)? Only jurisprudence will make it possible to decide and it is hard to imagine the courts discussing these criteria!

Another order of 3 October 2013,[12] establishing an incorporated procedure for housing, known as PIL (*Procédure Intégrée pour le Logement*), also includes imprecision, affording judges a large margin of interpretation. The order is based on a work-in-progress concept of town planning. The idea is to adjust and to make compatible the entire town planning documents to carry out 'a development project or a construction, including mostly housing with a common good characteristic'. Here the scope for intervention is unclear.

By organising a double restriction (in time and space) to the interest in bringing proceedings, the order of 18 July 2013,[13] which aims to push back against abusive appeals, is tantamount to a multiplication of procedural obstacles for the petitioner. In reality the text, here again, gives the judge an enormous margin of interpretation at all stages of the proceedings. 'He [the judge] can pronounce a partial repeal of the attacked authorisation or postpone his judgment until the expiration of a term which he himself will have set to regularise the documents.' He can also order the author of the malicious recourse to pay damages to the permit's beneficiary if the latter has suffered from an 'excessive harm, exceeding [his] legitimate interest'. These notions, undefined, give a sense of the subjectivity that can benefit the architect.

The legislator introduces soft concepts

Always, or at least as early as the seventeenth and eighteenth centuries, the law, customs and regulations have included technical and legal terms requiring explanations. These soft, flexible concepts called for distinctions, which gave way to more or less constraining interpretations. For instance, customs differentiated the nature of the activities devoted to the upkeep of buildings. We noted five questions concerning this type of issue. First, what was the general framework to solicit a lawyer? Would he address the question of maintaining his own property or property belonging to someone else? Secondly, differences were made concerning the nature of the upkeep: the 'necessity' vs. 'usefulness' criterion was imperative. Thirdly – and this would seem normal – would upkeep include 'heavy repairs' opposed to 'light works'? What would this feature – apparently quantitative – really refer to? Fourthly, would the previous criteria of necessity require that the works be carried out very quickly? Finally, would the requirements of ordinary repairs be opposed to the degradations over time, or to those due to weather? In other words, how would 'dilapidation' by time and natural hazards impact the requirements of upkeep?[14]

Today, the law often seeks to let thrive the creative and innovative dimension of town planning projects. And this flexibility of application is obtained by using the fundamental concept of 'compatibility'. Town planning law is known for being at times rigid (compliance), and at others flexible (compatibility), but it is mostly intended to regulate projects (the concept is cited 223 times in the Code of Town Planning).

Like any legal system, standards are ordered according to the level of authority: at the top, the state rules (general concepts, national town planning regulations, exposure to noise scheme, coastline scheme, mountain zone scheme, territorial development directives), under these, the 'inter-communal' rules (pertaining to groups of municipalities), and under these, the municipal rules (in the local town planning schemes). This hierarchy of standards introduces the two crucial notions mentioned above – compliance and compatibility. When a document must comply with a superior standard, it must apply its provisions and respect them. The compatibility requirement is much less constraining. The inferior document cannot result in foiling the superior rule's application. There is more room for manoeuvre and flexibility in order to preserve the purpose of projects. According to the well-considered doctrine:

> compatibility is a flexible notion closely linked to specific considerations and sustained by the desire not to challenge the general notions of the project while also avoiding to freeze the details of its realisation. In this way, it is possible to digress from the project but absolutely not to impede it.[15]

The overarching project at the top of the scale cannot be jeopardised while the local individual project is not limited but guided by the compatibility concept.

For instance, being compatible with the town planning concepts set out in articles L. 110 and L. 121-1 of the Code of Town Planning is required of the authorities drawing up local town planning documents. The compatibility relation is less strong than that of compliance, but it does allow judges to cancel documents comprising provisions incompatible with these concepts. This contentious control is normal and not limited to manifest errors of assessment (as in the case *Conseil d'Etat*, 10 February 1997, *Assoc. défense des sites de Théoule*).[16] The provisions of article 121-1 do not apply to individual authorisations directly, but they are binding for any town planning document.

From a general and timeless standpoint – and beyond the interactions discussed a while ago or the metaphors uttered elsewhere – it seems to me that law and architecture should not be opposed but rather complement and understand one another. In November 2011, the Order of Architects in France (CNOA) launched a manifesto 'emphasising the right to architecture for all' (such was their slogan). It is always surprising to hear the highest professional institution in France state that: 'architecture is in danger . . . because regulations always override architecture'.[17] Building regulations only represent the technical standards of construction law. The very institution criticising them simultaneously forgets to remind the Ministry of Culture (supervising Architecture Schools) of coordinating law and economy in the architectural curriculum, relegating a compressed form of these topics to the final year of studies. This eminently political question would deserve more attention from the state, in order to foster the political empowerment of architects, and for them to become fully-fledged subjects of law.

Notes

1   Interpretation is one of law's fundamental mechanisms. On its role and methods, see all the general works introducing law. See Pascale Deumier, *Introduction générale au droit* (Paris: LGDJ/Lextenso editions, 2011), pp. 112–128. The more cases of astutely complying with rules an architect knows, the better he is equipped to find a technical solution respecting construction law. See Roberta Grignolo, *Diritto e salvaguardia dell'architettura del XX secolo: Law and the Conservation of 20th-Century Architecture* (Mendrisio: Mendrisio Academy Press/Silviana Editoriale, 2014).

2   Robert Carvais, 'La Chambre royale des Bâtiments: Juridiction professionnelle et droit de la construction à Paris sous l'Ancien Régime' (unpublished doctoral thesis, Université de Panthéon-Assas, 2001, to be published, Genève, Droz); Robert Carvais, 'La Chambre des Bâtiments: Juridiction de police', in *Les sciences camérales: Activités pratiques et histoire des dispositions publiques*, ed. by Pascale Laborier and others (Amiens: Université de Picardie Jules Verne, CURAPP/PUF, 2011), pp. 331–382.

3   Robert Carvais, 'Le règlement de Jean Beausire (1694): Droit et réduction en art de la maçonnerie', in *Réduire en art: La technologie de la Renaissance aux Lumières*, ed. by Hélène Vérin and Pascal Dubourg-Glatigny (Paris: Editions de la Maison des sciences de l'homme, 2008), pp. 336–362.

4   DPR 974's Blog, Défense du patrimoine architectural de la Réunion, Pour une architecture raisonnée et respectueuse: De l'art de contourner les règles, https://dpr974.wordpress.com/2010/09/08/de-l%E2%80%99art-de-contourner-les-regles-%E2%80%80%A6/ (accessed January 2015).

5   Although Paris never suffered anything like the great fire in London, regulations about chimneys were numerous and churned out at a steady rate.

6   National Archives (AN), Z1J 144, fol. 35, 1 March 1771.

7   Robert Carvais, 'La classification des actes du fonds judiciaire de la Chambre des Bâtiments: Une application à l'époque moderne de la hiérarchie post-révolutionnaire des pouvoirs', *Histoire et Archives*, no. 4 (1998), pp. 31–130 (at pp. 102–104).

8   Patrick Bouchain, 'Le domaine des possibles', *ArchiSTROM*, no. 3 (November 2011), no. 4 (January 2012), no. 5 (March 2013).

9   Michel Huet and Amélie Blandin, 'La notion de parties communes: le regard du juriste', in *Nouveaux Paris: La ville et ses possibles*, ed. by Nicolas Michelin (Paris: Picard, 2005), pp. 156–165.

10 Antoine Babuty Desgodets, *Extrait des Coutumes génralles et particulières de France, et des Gaules, en ce qui concerne les servitudes réelles, les édifices, et bâtimens: et le fait des raports des jurez, avec un Recueil d'arrests, concernant ces sortes de matières, tirez de plusieurs arrestistes, et de différens Parlemens*, Bibliothèque du Sénat, Ms 94, fol. 189 v°.

11 Order no. 2013-889 of 3 October 2013, relating to the development of housing construction, www.legifrance.gouv.fr/affichTexte.do?cidTexte=JORFTEXT000028025706&fastPos=2&fastReqId=453445414&categorieLien=id&oldAction=rechTexte (accessed January 2015).

12 Order no. 2013-888 of 3 October 2013 relating to the incorporated procedure for housing, www.legifrance.gouv.fr/affichTexte.do?cidTexte=JORFTEXT000028025629&fastPos=3&fastReqId=1639511296&categorieLien=id&oldAction=rechTexte (accessed January 2015).

13 Order no. 2013-638 of 18 July 2013 relating to contentious town planning matters, www.legifrance.gouv.fr/affichTexte.do?cidTexte=JORFTEXT000027727904&fastPos=1&fastReqId=703763510&categorieLien=id&oldAction=rechTexte (accessed January 2015).

14 Robert Carvais, 'Entretenir les bâtiments, une préoccupation juridique essentielle sous l'Ancien Régime', in *De l'entretien quotidien des édifices à la conservation du patrimoine bâti aux époques antique et médiévale*, ed. by Charles Davoine, Maxime L'Héritier, and Ambre Péron (Paris: Université Paris 8/ENS, Musée d'art et d'histoire de Saint-Denis, 2014).

15 Jean-Paul Gilli, Charles Hubert and Jacques de Lanversin (eds), *Les grands arrêts du droit de l'urbanisme* (Paris: Sirey, 1989), p. 146.

16 The provisions of article L. 121-10 of the Code of Town Planning require authors of local town planning schemes for towns that include noteworthy sites to make the building developments compatible with the preservation of those sites, www.legifrance.gouv.fr/affichJuriAdmin.do?oldAction=rechJuriAdmin&idTexte=CETATEXT000007927368&fastReqId=1102150765&fastPos=1 (accessed January 2015).

17 www.architectes.org/connaitre-l-ordre/actions-de-l-ordre/manifeste-pour-le-droit-a-l-architecture-octobre-2011 (accessed January 2015).

Chapter 21

The architectural discourse of building bureaucracy

Architects' project statements in Portugal in the 1950s

Ricardo Agarez

When asked to examine the fortunes of modern architecture in the last century, we tend to draw on two main sources: the visual records of the design and/or realisation of architectural works, and the published written discourse they generated. If given the opportunity, architects presented their work in architectural media, using their own words, and this, processed by critics, historians or journalists, often became an established account. Other kinds of material, such as private correspondence and oral testimony, may occasionally complement this account; but the position of a given object in architectural culture is still largely determined by its edited presentation. As a result, a divide frequently emerges between the actual conditions of architectural production and the critical discourse developed around (outside of) it.

If we stay close to the record of those conditions, however, we may find a different scenario. In quotidian procedures of architectural practice, in specific contexts, that separation collapsed, and a space for exchange was improvised within the boundaries of everyday building production, employing its internal mechanisms. As a case in point, this chapter investigates the traces of debates on modern architecture's principles left in the records of building bureaucracy in Portugal in the 1950s. There, planning and funding applications presented to state agencies and city councils included documents that not only portrayed the functional and technical aspects of the project – as they do in other countries – but also deployed aesthetical, ethical, philosophical and even political arguments in support of private and public building initiatives. These design *memoires* or project statements, called *memória descritiva* in Portuguese, were written by designers (architects and others) rather than by applicants (clients). They were meant not for publication or circulation of any kind but to be read only by a small circle of planners and officials in planning or funding assessments; extracts were occasionally used if such works were published. While some of these texts may bring to mind the genre of architectural competition entries, their audience was limited and removed from public scrutiny, confined to civil service offices – which in turn produced their own, statement-based replies and arguments, disputing or accepting proposals and initiating unedited exchanges on architecture's fundamentals. Unlike its mediatised counterparts, this debate develops very close to the industrial, pragmatic aspects of architectural practice.

In this chapter, I examine the role of these records in the analysis of architectural culture within the framework of bureaucracy. Can this unedited discourse-generating exchange be seen as an alternative arena for disciplinary debate, created by those who – like most of the designers and assessors involved – did not employ conventional forms of dissemination but still wished to convey their concerns and beliefs? Is this ultimately a space of proximity between the critical discourse developing in the discipline's 'higher spheres' and the real conditions of day-to-day production, codified and regulated, and so often belittled by those who practise and investigate architecture?

Words

> We envisaged a building . . . that would have been sensed before it had been seen because it is equal in spirit to other built masses that can be found, everywhere, in the Algarve, where Man has spontaneously created an architecture that is organic and alive, [whose particular] character [stems] from his logical use of materials and, most importantly, from his concept of dwelling, which he feels in his blood [and] leads him to calve flesh of his own flesh [just as] a female cannot but give birth to anything other than her own child . . . always bettered and more apt to live in her native environment.[1]

With these words, the architects Jorge Chaves (1920–1982) and Frederico Sant'Ana (1921–1961) described and submitted to the planning authorities their 1959 design for the Garbe, one of the first seaside hotels in the south of Portugal. In their *memória*, the architects seemed just as concerned with detailing the operation and construction principles of the hotel, as with exposing their views on how modern architecture should relate to, and employ the lessons of, vernacular building traditions. This had been a popular topic among Portuguese architects since the turn of the century and particularly in the 1950s, and a pertinent one in the context of the Algarve, where those traditions were well alive and a given for early tourism infrastructure.[2] Although the text was later quoted in a review of the building,[3] the architects themselves never published their thoughts on this or any other work, instead using the *memórias* as their only vehicle.[4]

While this almost too graphic description referred to a project of considerable impact and had multiple purposes,[5] the use of the statement to record architectural ideas was common across the full gamut of scales, types and ambitions of building. Describing a pair of twin houses in a side street of Faro, the Algarve's capital, architect Manuel Gomes da Costa (b. 1921) wrote in his 1952 planning application:

> A house that is the exact combination of useful spaces, usefully placed for the body and the spirit, will be 'biological reality'. [With the adequate] balance of dimensions, surfaces and volumes, harmony of materials and colours, it will be 'sensitive' and 'intellectual' reality.[6]

Costa might have tried to mark, with this well-learned Corbusian rationale, the contrast between his intellectual understanding of modern architecture and that of his engineer and house-builder competitors, in the limited context of 1950s Faro. His somewhat inflated explanation, to be read by those very few officials in charge of assessing the proposal, did not have to be so elaborate; but Costa, having designed over 400 buildings throughout the Algarve, never published a single word of his own.

The *memória descritiva* appears therefore as a consistent means of expression for architects, who used it to detail their 'architectural stance' (*partido*, as it was known in Portugal in the 1950s). This form of architectural writing is the only surviving record of the thinking behind the practice of the majority of Portuguese architects in the twentieth century.

Although I am tempted to include it in the description category that Adrian Forty called 'apologies and manifestos' – where designers or clients 'tell you why [the building] has to be like it is'[7] – I also note its absence from current investigations into the relationship between language and buildings. In this expanding field, the analysis of how words are used to describe and discuss architecture beyond matters of 'architectural language'[8] is being complemented with the study of alternative sites of written expression in characteristic texts – specifications, building legislation, design guides, office documents, competition and client briefs, manifestos, criticism and media – as *genres* with specific linguistic strategies.[9] Instances of the 'evaluative discourse' that 'makes aesthetic, functional and moral judgements on buildings' inside and outside of the profession are also under scrutiny.[10] Yet it remains difficult to find the architects' quotidian writings and attendant bureaucratic responses discussed in any detail, in either form or content: as products of architectural practice that are neither entirely private nor public – not strictly a record of design production or of its dissemination – they elude categorisation and conventional analysis of modes of discourse in architecture.

Control

What, in the Portuguese context, might have driven architects to elaborate on their formal-aesthetic 'stance' in such a narrow-scope medium? Private building initiative in Portugal had been subject to central government control since 1850.[11] Along with comfort, safety and salubriousness standards, the 'decorum' (propriety) of buildings framing public roads and streets had been a concern enshrined in national regulation since 1864, and ministries and municipalities were asked to maintain it by granting or withholding building permits.[12] The 'prospect' of a building was regulated through the permit mechanism, with local and central agencies sharing responsibilities in varying combinations over time,[13] and officials at all levels consistently entitled to assess the aesthetics of a design proposal. In Lisbon, this capacity was specified in the city's nineteenth-century by-laws[14] and reinforced in the new building code of 1930, which included a full chapter on the 'aesthetic conditions' required.[15] The national building code, focused at the start of the century on reining in real estate speculation and its nefarious effects on public health and salubriousness,[16] imposed new measures in its 1951 rewrite to ensure that 'minimum aesthetic requirements' were fulfilled.[17] Such was the belief in local and central authorities' ability to regulate the matter that when the building permit procedures were reformed and simplified in 1970 by national law, and the onus of verifying compliance with building codes was essentially transferred to designers, the single most important prerogative left to city officials was the appraisal of the 'external expression' of designs submitted.[18]

There was no mention of a specific 'project statement' being required in the nineteenth-century codes, and when it first appeared in national law, in 1909,[19] and in the Lisbon by-laws, in 1913,[20] the *memória descritiva* was defined as the element of the project submitted to building permission where materials, construction techniques and structural calculus were to be specified. To this date I have found no rule or by-law determining that design principles were to be justified in writing. However, since existing regulations placed such strong emphasis on the elevation and its role in valorising public space, it is not surprising that even the short application 'requests' used before 1909 often referred to composition issues – and that, at least from the 1920s on, the *memórias* presented to Lisbon municipality systematically included a paragraph on the 'architectural stance'.

In the face of regulations that clearly insisted on the aesthetic key, the need to argue for design choices was embedded in quotidian bureaucratic procedures and possibly seen as an *unstated requirement* by both applicants and officials. The widespread use of these documents and their specific regulatory framework points to one of their inherent purposes: to anticipate the need for justification in instances of aesthetic judgement, establishing an exchange of arguments on a subject that permeated all layers of public control.

Arguments

In the 1950s, these statements were written by architects, engineers and master-builders, in support of works that later entered the canon, of buildings whose history was never made, and of proposals that remained unbuilt; produced by the few architects who found ways to have their designs and rationales published in journals and monographs *as well as* by those who did not. The architect and urban planner Manuel Laginha (1919–1985) was in the latter group for most of his career,[21] and the example of his *memórias* and bureaucratic correspondence (Figure 21.1) suggests how such documents could be part of a discursive strategy that argued for change: originating not in the

CAMARA MUNICIPAL DE LOULÉ

APROVADO

sessão de___ de_____ de 19 _

MEMÓRIA DESCRITIVA

Consta o presente projecto duma Casa de
Habitação desenvolvida num só piso que fica elevado do
solo sêrca de um metro, e modesta, é certo, mas planea-
da sôb um conce·ito de lar pouco divulgado ainda entre
nós.

A quási novidade reside no predomínio ní-
tido dum compartimento a que os ingleses chamam" sala
de viver" e que nós poderemos chamar" sala de família"
A importância que lhe atribuimos provém da análise às
necessidades que tem tôda a casa de se apetrechar com
uma peça que sirva para a reunião da família e do reparo
nos inconvenientes que existem, na maior parte das vezes,
quando essa reunião se tem que fazer numa cozinha ou num
soturno quarto de costura. Esta grande peça que tem amplas
janelas na fachada principal que volta a sudoeste, funciona,
a um tempo, de sala de entrada pela singular disposição
dum móvel fixo, sôbre que corre uma espéssa cortina, de sala
de estar com fogão e·de pequeno escritório; e liga amplamen-
te para um recanto onde funciona a sala de jantar com liga-
ção para um terraço e para um corredor onde vai dar todo o
serviço de quartos e banho. Para êste terraço, voltado a
nonoeste abre, além daquele corredor, uma pequena cozinha

Figure 21.1
Arch. Manuel Laginha,
'Uma Casa de
Habitação. Memória
Descritiva'. Project
statement for the Aleixo
house, Rua Maria
Campina 145, Loulé,
dated 11 March 1946.
The first paragraph
reads: 'This project is for
a single-storey house . . .
certainly modest, but
designed following a
concept of home not
yet common among us.'
The architect then
proceeded to elaborate
on his innovation.
Instituto da Habitação e
da Reabilitação Urbana,
Lisbon

published public sphere but within the circles of bureaucracy, through both drawn and written arguments. This strategy may help to explain the passionate tone in many of these writings.

Having embarked on a civil service career himself, Laginha came to know official circles from within, and this may have prepared him (better than others) to argue his points as fiercely as he did. His 1952 design for a multi-family house in Estrela, Lisbon was complicated by the plot's awkward shape and inconvenient conditions dictated by adjacent constructions, which led to a *memória* largely devoted to justifying the points of non-compliance with building regulations. Words on the façade composition were fewer, but still enough to describe in detail how receding the entire elevation from the plot boundary created room for deeper balconies, shielded from the busy street by a checkerboard of concrete posts, metal mesh and greenery that went towards both the 'plastic enhancement' of the composition and the 'privacy' of residents (Figure 21.2). When city officials objected not only to deviations from plot use limits but also to the 'architectural stance taken, considering the local atmosphere' – referring to the contrast between his modernist proposal and the neighbouring late-baroque Estrela basilica – Laginha redrew the layouts but not the elevations, supporting his choice with a strongly worded *memória*. The façade, he wrote, can only be seen as part of a whole, the all-encompassing 'architectural synthesis', and to assess it in isolation is 'unfair and inconsequential'. Architecture must express the functional, economic, social and technical challenges of its day: this was so with the pyramids in Egypt, and the rational reconstruction of Lisbon after the 1755 earthquake – but not with 'sugary' replicas of past architectures. 'Conveying the local environment's message, unfettered', he wrote, 'is one of my missions as the project's author, so that I can then take all inherent responsibilities for my work'. Laginha saw nothing in his building's context that could influence the design positively, claiming ironically to have given the basilica his 'best consideration' by devising generous balconies from which the monument could be fully appreciated.[22] The project was subsequently approved and built.

Laginha's engaged tone was not due to this being a high-profile commission. It was a run-of-the-mill speculative development in 1950s Lisbon, and the form chosen for this correspondence was not uncommon, nor was its content. While he used the second version of his *memória* to defend his territory from perceived official interference – a common trope for post-war Portuguese architects – Laginha used the first version to anticipate criticism regarding his failure to comply with the then-recent 1951 building code, configuring another recurrent purpose for these documents: to dispute existing legislation.

Project statements are evidence of the parts that private initiative and architects played in internal debates, prompted within Lisbon's municipal bureaucracy by specific planning applications, that led to substantial adjustments to local policies in the 1950s.[23] Under the umbrella of the much-evoked argument favouring modern architecture as the true expression of its time,[24] designers often pushed a different agenda, serving their clients' interests: to take full advantage of the plot's revenue potential – for example, by reducing floor heights and adding floors to what more conservative munici-pal plans admitted. Architects Lima Franco (1904–1970) and Gonzalez Potier's (b. 1922)

Figure 21.2
Arch. Manuel Laginha, multi-family house in Rua Domingos Sequeira 11, Lisbon (1952–1954). View of the street elevation, with the Estrela basilica in the background. Instituto da Habitação e da Reabilitação Urbana, Lisbon

residential and commercial ensemble for a (very high-profile) block in central Lisbon (Figure 21.3) is one clear example of this process: their elaborate *memórias*, arguing for the obsolescence of pre-war, pompously neo-baroque municipal design directives, and for the need to update them along clearly contemporary lines (with 'an architecture of our time, sober and balanced'), in reality also pushed their dimensional and regulatory limits to extract economic advantages formerly impossible to obtain. Here as in other cases, the municipality agreed to renounce its own out-dated 'architectural stance' prescriptions much sooner than it accepted the excess in construction volume – proving that what was at stake was the real estate speculation encroachment on public interest,

Figure 21.3
Arch. José de Lima
Franco and Manolo
Gonzalez Potier,
residential and
commercial building
ensemble on the eastern
edge of Parque Eduardo
VII, Lisbon (1952–1956).
View of the elevations
on Avenida Fontes
Pereira de Melo. Ricardo
Agarez

not the choice of a conservative or modernist design. In fact, the general tenor of the officials' response, from the lowest-level planners to the mayor, was dismissive of all attempts to exceed those limits but in clear support of a modernist approach to complete the block: 'The [municipal] Architect's Office believe it is our duty to uphold that sound and long-lasting principle according to which Architecture, more than any other art, must express its own time.'[25]

The *memórias* were therefore important not only as vehicles for architects to express their design principles laterally to publication mechanisms but also, and importantly, as documents of the not-so-subtle process through which modern architecture's proclaimed ethical and aesthetical code of practice was put to the service of the development and construction industries.

Laginha was certainly a player in the 1950s speculative building game of chess, with its unwritten rules, arm-wrestling with officials and inherent pursuit of profit. Public commissions were rare and developers were much-needed clients who, moreover, were ready to embrace modernist designs along with their standardised, industrially produced materials and optimised construction techniques. Yet while economy was a factor, Laginha's *memórias* remained persistently focused on his strategy for change: namely, from what he saw as superficial pastiche to a more sophisticated understanding of building traditions in his native Algarve.

This argument was central in the social service and childcare centres of Olhão and Loulé (1951–1958), two of the foremost pieces of post-war architecture in the region. Laginha claimed to have derived his aesthetical stance for the less-known Loulé project 'naturally' from the region's economic and natural conditions, and to have applied the 'purest and most eloquent expression' of traditional materials and techniques, invoking vernacular forms not through 'petty fripperies' but abstractly, with large whitewashed surfaces and hollowed ceramic panels[26] (Figure 21.4).

Prompted by criticism from the Minister of Public Works (who expressed his 'absolute aversion to the type chosen – of exhibition pavilion – for the design'[27]), Laginha

Figure 21.4
Arch. Manuel Laginha and Rogério Buridant Martins, social service and childcare centre in Loulé (Faro, 1951–1958). View of the family assistance unit and gardens. Instituto da Habitação e da Reabilitação Urbana, Lisbon

added a statement in which he defended his 'lightweight' solution and interpreted any reticence as due to the 'emotional shock' caused in those who were more used to examples of 'the so-called Portuguese style', weighty and impenetrable to nature. 'In contrast to the rigid majesty of palace-like buildings, where gardens merely serve to fill residual spaces', he wrote, 'this building will embrace the playgrounds and gardens as integral to it [thus] clearly expressing its primary function – to house children'.[28]

Uninhibited by ministerial reluctance, Laginha's words suggest another possible dimension to the inflamed project statement: political resistance and/or resistance to political interference, performed within the sphere of a dictatorial government. Politically engaged (to the left), Laginha may have had this in mind in his reply to an outspokenly conservative minister.[29] But just how consequential was this form of (passive) resistance, played out as it was so close to the source of political decision, where arbitrary aesthetical judgement could take place, unimpeded? As it happens, the social centre in Loulé was built as planned, and paid for partly by the state, with the minister's assent. This might mean that Laginha's strategy was entirely successful, but it also signals how the conservative/modernist style debate in 1950s Portugal was less decisive than we are often led to believe today – with economy and pragmatism (again) playing a much more important role than issues of architectural stance.

This chapter is a first attempt to interpret a particular kind of writing by architects, to be found in building bureaucracy.[30] It aims to identify essential lines of form and meaning in documents that have previously escaped scholarly attention, focusing on how they testify to the encounter of the designer with his or her cultural, political and regulatory frameworks, and on how they constitute an important alternative source for insights into the architectural cultures behind less-known objects and practices. Although many routes for enquiry remain open, my investigation of the *memórias* supporting everyday architecture in Portugal in the 1950s allows for some preliminary observations to be drawn.

In most cases, the *memórias* were evidence of the designer's desire or need to convey his or her architectural thought in a private (unpublished) written discourse that complemented a drawn proposal: this was the case in Chaves and Sant'Ana's seaside hotel and in Laginha's Estrela building and Loulé social service centre. On a less apparent level, they were also evidence of a necessity – perceived by many designers – to address the regulatory scaffolding of design and building practices, trying to prevent reversals in the bureaucratic assessment of their proposals by anticipating the consequences of officials applying both stated and unstated rules; the investment in elaborate explanations regarding the aesthetical stance, and their frequently inflamed tone, can be seen in this light. Still less clearly presented, but equally important, was these writings' potential as instruments of political dispute, at a moment in time (the 1950s) when pre-war nationalist architecture, closely associated with the dictatorship, was denounced both in public and private spheres in Portugal. Lastly, the *memórias* testify to the involvement of modernist designers in the advancement of modern architecture's formal agenda in parallel with the economic development of the construction industry, illustrating how legal constraints devised to balance public and private interests were actively resisted by architects. The statements in support of the everyday multi-family residential projects in Lisbon, as well as of the seaside hotel in the Algarve, should be read bearing in mind the often undisclosed (and sometimes openly presented) intention of designers to push for economic benefits under the guise of aesthetic or stylistic arguments.

My discussion of the Portuguese *memórias* also raises peculiar ethical questions. These documents are neither strictly private nor public, often being written for a private purpose and audience but being presented to and deposited in a public institution. When treated as historical material and discussed publicly, what happens to their 'juridical' status? Furthermore, what might have been the 'real' intention of their authors in this regard? As pointed out in a recent (public) discussion about these texts, they evoke the image of the 'message in a bottle', something written with an undetermined, secondary intention: to be, or not, read again; to be, or not, found.[31] These architect-authors, not knowing if their words would ever be read beyond their original purpose, might nevertheless have expected that to happen, eventually: to many of them this was, after all, the only vehicle for a written architectural expression.

Notes

1   Jorge Chaves, Frederico Sant'Ana, preliminary design statement, 5 February 1960 (Lisbon, Jorge Chaves's Papers).
2   See Ricardo Agarez, 'Regional Identity for the Leisure of Travellers: Early Tourism Infrastructure in the Algarve (Portugal), 1940–1965', *The Journal of Architecture* 5, 18 (2013), 721–743.
3   Rui Mendes Paula, 'Hotel do Garbe', *Arquitectura*, 83 (1964), 100–110.
4   This use is clear in Chaves's work for an important Church charity in Lisbon; cf. Ricardo Agarez, 'De Regra, Renda e Desenho. Arquitectura para a Misericórdia de Lisboa *c.*1960', in *Património Arquitectónico* (Lisboa: SCML, 2010), 83–95.
5   To have the facility not only approved by central and municipal planners but also labelled as 'tourism utility' ('Utilidade Turística'), a status that entailed significant tax exemptions.
6   Manuel Gomes da Costa and Bento Viegas Louro, project statement, 24 April 1952 (Faro, CMF/ SAO-127/1952).
7   Adrian Forty, 'Architectural Description: Fact or Fiction?', in *When Architects and Designers Write/ Draw/Build/?*, ed. by Jørgen Dehs, Martin Esbensen and Claus Pedersen (Aarhus: Arkitektskolens Forlag, 2014), p. 201.
8   See Adrian Forty, *Words and Buildings* (New York: Thames & Hudson, 2000), and Anne Hultzsch, *Architecture, Travellers and Writers* (Oxford: Legenda, 2014).
9   See Dana Cuff, *Architecture: The Story of Practice* (Cambridge, MA: MIT Press, 1991); Rosario Caballero, *Re-Viewing Space: Figurative Language in Architect's Assessment of Built Space* (Berlin: Mouton de Gruyter, 2006); Robert Imrie and Emma Street, *Architectural Design and Regulation* (Chichester: Wiley-Blackwell, 2011); Tilo Amhoff, Nicholas Beech and Katie Lloyd Thomas, 'Further Reading Required', *Architectural Research Quarterly* 3, 16 (2012), 197–199; and Forty, 'Architectural Description'.
10 Thomas Markus and Deborah Cameron, *The Words Between the Spaces* (New York: Routledge, 2002), pp. 93–99.
11 Ministerial order, 21 August 1850 (MR).
12 Decree, 31 December 1864 (MOP).
13 Decree, 6 June 1895 (MOPCI); Decree, 20 October 1898 (DGCI/RI).
14 By-law code of 17 June 1869 (CML); By-law code of 30 December 1886 (CML).
15 By-law, 28 August 1930, in Notice of 6 December 1930, Chapter VI.
16 Decree, 14 February 1903 (MR, MOPCI).
17 Decree no. 38.382, 7 August 1951 (MOP), preamble and articles 121 and 127.
18 Decree no. 166/70, 15 April (MI, MOP).
19 Decree, 6 May 1909 (MOP), article 6.
20 By-law, 15 May 1913 (CML), article 3.
21 Some of his early works in the Algarve were published with his own, often unattributed descriptions: see, e.g., the magazine *Arquitectura* issues 26 (1948) and 35 (1950).
22 Manuel Laginha, additional project statement, May 1953 (Lisbon, CML/AI-36.084/52).
23 See Ricardo Agarez, *O Moderno Revisitado. Habitação Multifamiliar em Lisboa nos Anos de 1950* (Lisboa: CML, 2009).

24 See, e.g., Rebelo's 1950s pamphlets denouncing the fallacy of modern buildings disguised as historicist pastiches, in *João Correia Rebelo: Um Arquitecto Moderno nos Açores*, ed. by Ana Tostões and João Vieira Caldas (Angra do Heroísmo: IAC, 2002).

25 Cit. in Agarez (2009), pp. 110–111.

26 Cit. in Ricardo Agarez, 'O Centro de Assistência Social Polivalente de Loulé no Arquivo do Arquitecto Manuel Laginha', *Monumentos*, 23 (2005), 176.

27 Minister's assessment, 1953.07 (Lisbon, IHRU/DGEMN/DSARH/ED–3.17/18).

28 Manuel Laginha and Rogério Martins (1920–1997), second additional project statement, 1953.07 (Lisbon, IHRU/APML-NP871).

29 José Frederico Ulrich (1905–1982), minister between 1947 and 1954, is known for his conservatism, in contrast to his modernism-friendly successor, Eduardo Arantes e Oliveira (1907–1982).

30 My ongoing research project *Bureaucracy and Discourse in Everyday Architecture, 1930–1970* is a comparative study of the architectural culture in bureaucracy circles of Brussels, Lisbon, London, Paris and Rome.

31 A suggestion offered by the American artist Corin Hewitt at the British School at Rome's 'Celebration of Modern Studies' day (22 October 2014).

Chapter 22

Regulatory spaces, physical and metaphorical

On the legal and spatial occupation of fire-safety legislation

Liam Ross

Metaphorical spaces

In *Capitalism, Culture and Economic Regulation*, Leigh Hancher and Mick Moran developed the concept of 'regulatory space', an analytical construct that described a new approach to the study of regulation in liberal-democratic, capitalist political economies.[1] The need for such a concept was, according to the authors, that at the close of the twentieth century the discourse on regulatory governance was trapped within the problematics of 'regulatory capture', the concern that governmental initiatives authorised by public bodies tended to be enrolled, re-directed, and re-purposed to serve the interests of private companies. Hancher and Moran's argument was that the literatures on 'capture' limited the horizons of analysis and critique through two fundamental assumptions: that there *exists* a sovereign authority that reliably represents a definable public interest; and that regulation is its instrument to assert that interest *against* private gain. Hancher and Moran suggested that such assumptions are anachronistic and inadequate for the complexity of a neoliberal context in which, for example, the most commonly adopted vehicle for the advancement of private interest is the public company, and in which governmental roles traditionally associated with the state are intentionally deconstructed to create opportunities for entrepreneurial activity.

They drew on the metaphor of space to describe an alternative conception, because it allows regulation to be thought of as something that defines an *area*, as opposed to a line. While the term 'regulation' takes us back, etymologically, to the king, to the ruler, and to the drawing of lines,[2] Hancher and Moran wanted to describe the activity of regulation as something that was concerned with achieving agreement *between* multiple parties. Regulations, they told us, describe an 'issues arena' of common concerns whose limits are defined less by sovereign decision, more by the concord and discord between a wide range of actors. The spatial trope offered them a way to describe this arena that, like an architectural plan, constructs uneven allotments of space through partitions that enforce carefully designed forms of inclusion and exclusion. Further, they described regulatory regimes through characteristic spatialities. Emerging from different historical and geographical specificities, public/private divisions fall along different lines from place to place. But most importantly the trope allowed them to stress the notion that regulation is there to be *occupied*; its lines define legal opportunities whose effects are steered less by governmental intent, and more by the actors who take advantage of them. Their concept of regulatory space has created its own discursive opening, and since 1989 a rich literature has emerged, describing the process of regulation as a territorial struggle, which constantly redraws the frontiers, outposts, and mobile boundaries between that which we call public and private.[3]

While Hancher and Moran use the term 'space' in a strictly metaphorical sense here, the issues they describe nonetheless have a relationship to *physical* space; the discursive formation of our common issues arena has a degree of congruence with the material formation of what we call public space. Physical space is often both the *object* of our governmental problems, and the *means* of our governmental actions; it is one of the common things about which matters of concern emerge, a necessary vessel within which to meet and form agreement, but also the medium through which laws are applied in reality. That is, while 'space' might serve as a *metaphor* for law, law and space are already mutually inscribed: legislation must be written into space in order to take effect, and specificities of the physical are already inscribed into and presumed by our legal rationalities. This chapter engages with Hancher and Moran's term, then, in order to take their metaphor literally. It considers the complications created by exchanges between the physical and legal, so as to stress the agency of space, and of design, in the shaping of our governing-mentalities. It does this in two stages. The first part, 'Legal spaces/physical spaces', offers an illustrated history of the formation of the City of Edinburgh's built fabric and fire-safety legislature. Using the example provided by this city – home of many innovations in fire-prevention and rescue – it seeks to demonstrate the reflexive relationship between legal and spatial structures; one is not the cause of the other, but rather their development exhibits causal circularity. The second part, 'Occupying fire-safety legislation', uses this extended conception of regulatory space to make a detailed study of a specific regulatory ambition: the limitation of 'travel distance'. This example highlights fundamental theoretical and technical problems associated with the contemporary drive towards performance-based standardisation, and identifies their contradictory spatial consequences.

Legal spaces/physical spaces

Prior to the development of urban centres in Scotland, there was no specific legislature concerning fire-safety in the country. Fifteenth-century Scotland was a country of

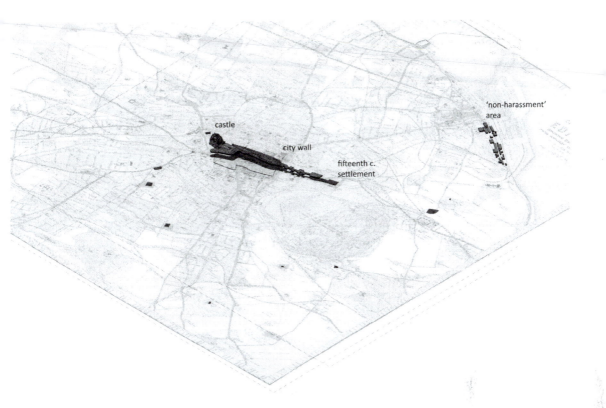

'non-harassment'
area

castle

city wall

fifteenth c.
settlement

Figure 22.1
Fifteenth-century
settlement of Edinburgh
and contemporary
'Non-Harassment'
Area (based on John G.
Bartholomew,
Chronological Map
of Edinburgh, **1919).**
Drawing: Liam Ross

isolated farmsteads, and fire was seen as a matter of personal responsibility, if not divine retribution. But the increased risk associated with densely settled communities gradually prompted recognition that communal assistance and precautions were required. The first of these was James I's Scottish Act of 1426, which prohibited the storage of flammable materials near or above fireplaces, imposed a curfew (*couvre-feu*) on the carrying of open flames from house to house, and banned 'common women' from living within the towns, or visiting men there (Figure 22.1). Open-flames, hay, and prostitutes were taken to be the sources of inflammation, and by banishing them to the outskirts of the town, the risk of ignition was reduced.[4]

It was not until two hundred years later, in 1621, that the Improvements Act also recognised the flammability of building materials, decreeing that, 'to prevent fire, the houses of Edinburgh shall be roofed with slate, lead, tile . . . instead of straw or boards'. The first physical and legislative infrastructure for fire-fighting were also established that year, when a further act made provision for 'the supplying of water to the city from a distance'. It took sixty years to build the damn at Comiston, the castle-hill reservoir, and the connecting mains, but by 1681 Edinburgh was one of the first cities to have 'fire-points' on pipes running to its ten public wells.[5] The continued expansion of the Burgh meant that seventeenth-century Edinburgh, still defined by its city walls, had reached such a height that egress, and vertical spread of flames, became significant risks. In 1674 the city empowered the Dean of Guilds Court to draw up Scotland's first set of building standards, which included a ruling that limited all buildings in the city to five storeys (Figure 22.2). It would take Geddes' late nineteenth-century conservative surgery to bring the Old Town (which reached fourteen storeys in height) into compliance with these standards, but they set the vertical limit for further extensions to the city.

In 1703 a devastating fire engulfed Parliament Close, the Royal Exchange, the Bank of Scotland and part of the Advocates Library, driving over two hundred families from their homes, and the city responded by forming a municipal 'Company for Quenching Fires'. The empowering act suggested, with great humility, that while 'God in his great mercy put a stop [to the recent fire], the council judges it their duty to lay down methods, and provide means, that through the blessing of God may prove effectual for preventing the like, or greater conflagrations'.[6] This municipal company consisted of part-time officers, provided only with crowbars, axes and buckets, but during the eighteenth century an increasing number of private enterprise brigades developed, set up by insurance companies as a means to spread the financial risk associated with fire. These companies – which formed the beginning of the city's insurance industry – commissioned an extensive and detailed mapping of the city, to allow fire-risk to be ascertained at a distance. Fire-insurance plans, similar to Goad's later city maps, were the most detailed surveys ever made of our urban centres, including information about the material composition of buildings, and – for the first time – stating occupant activity, providing a new kind of governmental visibility and knowledge base (Figure 22.3).

By the early nineteenth century this privatised system had come to be viewed as counterproductive; multiple companies often showed up to the same fire allowing uninsured buildings, or those insured by rivals, to burn. This led to the formation in 1824 of the Edinburgh Fire Engine Establishment, the UK's first full-time and professional municipal fire-fighting service, under the leadership of James Braidwood, designer of the first dedicated fire engine, and author of the first training manuals for firefighters. Braidwood shaped the service as we recognise it today, building dedicated stations for engines and live-in staff across the city. Becoming involved in building permissions, the fire services came to define the dimensional standards through which fire-risk could be understood, measured, and limited. Edinburgh's Central Fire Station (Figure 22.3), completed in 1900, provides something of an index of this new relationship between technologies of rescue and architectural design. Its five-storey tower, for instance, used for drying hoses, and testing 'horse-ladders', sets a visible limit to the surrounding buildings' eaves-height, both representing and ensuring their safety. Its courtyard pit indexes the maximum depth from which atmospheric pressure can be used to draw water, training staff to visually gauge which rivers and ponds were suitable. And the building was located – as Braidwood insisted all stations were – at the top of a hill, using its potential energy to reduce the response-time of the new hand- or horse-drawn 'squirts'.

It was not until the twentieth century that detailed regulations concerning the interior arrangement of buildings emerged, and these began in response to a well-publicised and documented fire at the Empire Palace Theatre, in 1911 (Figure 22.4). Although the entire cast was killed, three thousand spectators escaped unharmed. The event was taken to be a 'good' fire, and the building a model of design for fire escape. According to anecdotal reports, the spectators escaped within the duration of the National Anthem, played by a quick-witted conductor in order to maintain decorum.

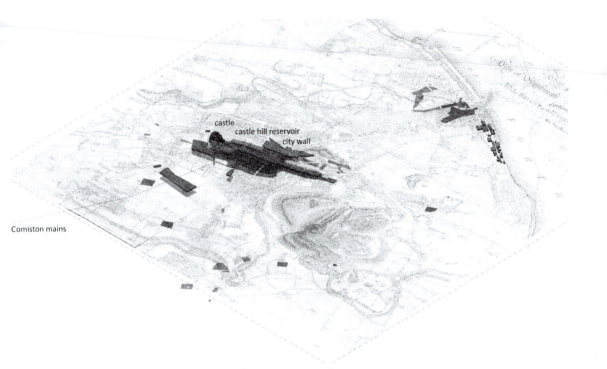

castle
castle hill reservoir
city wall

Comiston mains

Figure 22.2
Seventeenth-century settlement showing mains, reservoir, wells and eaves-height (based on Robert Kirkwood, *This Plan of the City of Edinburgh and its Environs,* **1817). Drawing: Liam Ross**

These anecdotal accounts continue to form the evidence base of a number of contemporary and international building standards. Since then, 2.5 minutes has been widely adopted as a standard for the safe egress time. Scotland's own standards for travel-distance are a derivation of this temporal standard, calculated on the basis of minimum permissible door-width, average national shoulder-width, and presumed walking speed; their purpose is to ensure that it is possible to calmly exit any building in Scotland within the duration of the National Anthem.[7] It would not be until the Second World War and post-war reconstruction that, conceived of as part of a broad programme of social insurance, both the fire services and fire-safety legislation would become fully nationalised. But by the early twentieth century Edinburgh's municipal standards had already established the fundamental principles of fire-safety legislation; structural fire-precautions, control over flammable building materials, and the facilitation of escape through limiting the depth of the plan.

Edinburgh's development demonstrates the historical and geographical specificity of its built fabric and legislative frameworks, as well as the mutually formative effects they have had on one another. Fire safety legislation was an important way in which the physical fabric of Edinburgh was shaped and re-shaped, contributing to its distinct spatial character. It enforced the notion of the city as having a clearly defined interior, from which peoples, activities and materials could be excluded to a spatially and legally looser periphery. It limited the upward expansion of the city and defined today's prevailing eaves-height. It changed relations of proximity and distance by irrigating the dense interior with materials brought from afar. It described the contours and materiality of the city as a topography of risk in a way that informed construction practices and patterns of urbanisation, as well as developing the increments – response time, fire-points, ladder-height and hose-length – through which fire-risk could be both understood and designed. But fire, in its interaction with the materiality of the city, was also the material cause behind a re-shaping of dominant governmentalities. In the period discussed, this reads as a trend toward an increasing collectivisation of risk; from the ethics of personal responsibility in fifteenth-century Scotland, to the formation of the Burgh or city as a responsibility-bearing agent, the formation of selective, profit-making prudential communities, to the universalisation of their role through local public bodies.

The history of fire safety in Edinburgh – at least up until the middle of the twentieth century – might be seen as a chapter within broader processes of governmen-talisation that operate through specific technologies of 'solidarity'.[8] That is, the physical space of the city is not a transparent delegate for governmental ambitions, any more than law is the simple writing of its emergent codes. The fabric of the city is an active participant in these processes of formation, and its physical and metaphorical spaces interact in ways that create reflexive-effects; moments of dramatisation, contradiction and unintended consequence. James I's blurring of material and erotic forms of ignition, for instance, demonstrates the capacity for apparently technical measures to accommodate ideological stowaways, ones which make an uncanny return in today's 'non-harassment' zones, which – as the city expands and gentrifies – continue to displace prostitutes into an unfortunate spatio-legal category alongside out-of-town storage facilities (Figure 22.1). While this act temporarily reinforced the physical and legislative boundaries of the city, these boundaries led to a vertical expansion that increased fire-risk, and so prompted the acts that would lead to horizontal sprawl (fire is both automobile and elevator in this 'race' for the city). Private-enterprise fire services were acknowledged as practically counterproductive, but they nonetheless created the legal space within which Edinburgh's insurance industry was established, as well as datasets that today continue to afford property-mapping services their knowledge base.[9] And just as the technologies of fire-rescue reframed the physical contours of the city in terms of a gradient of risk, they also found ways to enrol these gradients as an ally in fire-safety measures.

Occupying fire-safety legislation

Hancher and Moran's emphasis on *occupiability* provides a useful contact point within this literal-metaphorical slippage because it helps identity the particular actancy of space in the formation of this arena. The physical occupiability of space overlaps with, but is not identical to, the metaphorical occupiability of law. No set of building regulations can fully predict or prescribe the potential of the built, and any building holds possibilities that remain open to be appropriated. It is to this degree that we could understand the physical fabric of the city as a site of legal appropriation, invention, and accident, just as much as of inscription. Contemporary debates over the possibility of a performance-based form

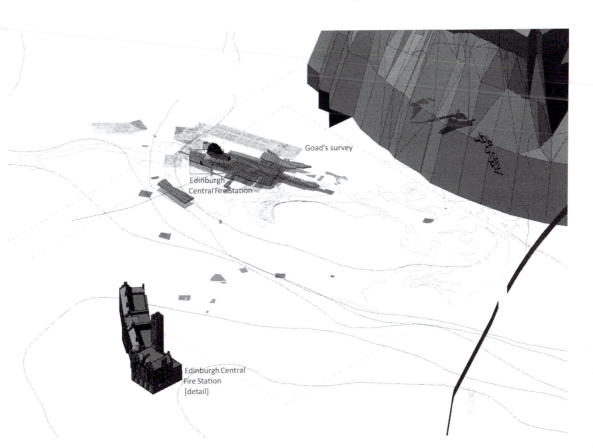

Goad's survey

Edinburgh
Central Fire Station

Edinburgh Central
Fire Station
[detail]

Figure 22.3
Insurance plans,
topography and inset of
Central Fire Station
(based on Charles Goad,
Insurance Plan of
Edinburgh, **1892).**
Drawing: Liam Ross

of fire-safety legislation offer examples of how physical and legal occupiablity diverge, and can come into conflict, in such processes of mutual formation.

The drive towards a performance-based mode of legislation began to develop alongside a critique of post-war planning and architecture. Universalising programmes of building standardisation, like the building practices and architectural styles they supported, came to be understood as autocratic and inflexible, lacking either an evidence base to support their assumptions, or the flexibility to address specific situations. This critique did not emerge, however, through a public concern for safety. As Vincent Brannigan narrates in his work on performance-based fire-safety codification, the critics of prescriptive standards were academics and professionals within the fire-safety community, people for whom it was of both scientific and commercial interest to develop more verifiable means of measuring and engineering for fire.[10] Emerging forms of fire-growth and egress simulation promised to provide the basis for modelling and designing to such parameters. Prescriptive codes had also lost favour within the architectural design community where, rather than offering a utopian potential, they came to be experienced as limits to the individual designer's creative freedom. Likewise, clients were often hostile to regulations, seeing them as a costly and unnecessary burden. More generally, though, we could situate this critique of prescriptive building standards in the context of the widespread problematisation of government occurring in Western Europe and the USA at that time. For the emerging neoliberal governmentality, prescriptive regulatory regimes were precisely the forms of clumsy government that undermined political economy, and should be transferred to the private sector. Emerging in this context were calls for a performance-based form of codification that was based upon scientific fact, created opportunities for design flexibility, and promised a reduction in the cost of building, and the cost of government. It was of interest to scientists, engineers, designers, clients and regulators alike. As Hancher and Moran suggest, the development of performance-based forms of codification cannot be understood as the result of a public voice making demands for the common good; indeed its claims do not pertain to safety at all. The regulatory space of contemporary fire-safety legislation was defined by a set of overlapping sectoral interests for the improvement of scientific and academic rigour, the expansion of professional competencies and markets, and for political reforms.

The common ground that unites this coalition of actors might be framed through their concern for 'economy'. Good government is here an economic government, one that governs as much as it needs to, and no more. Accurate engineering is likewise an economic engineering, one that specifies that which is necessary, and no more. The promise of performance-based regulation is that *less* regulation is good for political, scientific and financial goals, and that economy offers a common 'truth procedure'[11] for politicians and engineers, as well as clients. Architects and architecture played a not-insignificant intermediary role in the formation of this coalition. Building design is here the 'boundary object' through which these diverse concerns overlap; the common thing around which this coalition of actors gathers, and through which they form agreement.[12] Architects not only suggested they were capable of offering that resolution, but likewise claimed that less regulation would free them to do so more efficiently and effectively, conceiving design itself as a means to synthesise purely scientific and practically political concerns.

The problem with this promise, and with the ambition for a performance-based mode of fire-safety more generally, is that its social and technical aspects do not overlap seamlessly, because safety is a discursive entity, not something that submits itself to empirical definition. Socially acceptable levels of safety vary from time to time, and place to place, in response to particular focusing events. Any attempt to establish a scientific basis for their performance-specification therefore encounters a fundamental epistemological problem. As Brannigan shows in 'Fire Scenarios or Scenario Fires? Can fire safety science provide the critical inputs for performance-based fire safety analyses?' this problem surfaces in the technical challenges faced by performance-based codes.[13] Computational modelling for egress and fire-spread are themselves based upon assumptions, standards and codes, often the same codes upon which prescriptive standards are based.[14] Fire-safety science is yet to offer a more scientific basis upon which to define safety. As such, while performance-based codes have opened up new markets in design speculation and created opportunities to trade off margins of safety, they are limited to saying that, on the basis of an increased number of assumptions, a particular configuration is 'as safe' as a prescriptive solution.

However, despite depending upon existing standards, performance-based standards nonetheless create fundamental changes in how they *look* and operate. The

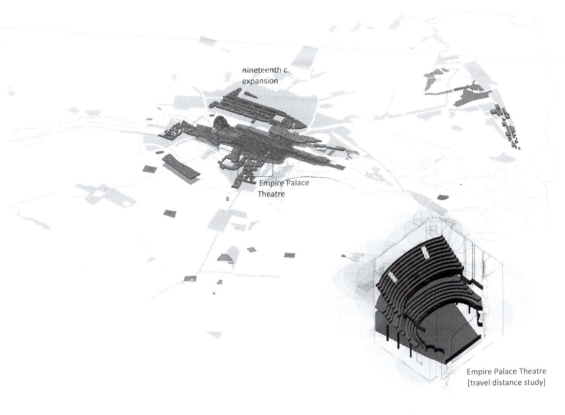

nineteenth c.
expansion

Empire Palace
Theatre

Empire Palace Theatre
[travel distance study]

Figure 22.4
**Nineteenth-century
expansion and inset of
Empire Palace Theatre
with travel distance
measurements.
Drawing: Liam Ross**

social decisions behind prescriptive standards are scientised within such codes, coming to look like technical facts, if not being buried completely within computational models. This change in appearance parallels and enforces a real shift in the locus of decision-making. Performance-based modes of standardisation transfer decision-making away from the nominally accountable arena of legislation, to the private context of design consultation. In practice these forms of statutory compliance are employed as a means of eliminating prescribed margins of safety through the creative deployment of approximations and assumptions. This practice may occasionally support the specification of design solutions that we would consider dangerous, but what it always achieves is a privatisation of social decision-making. That is, this change in the technology of government brings with it a change in rationale, and perhaps also what we could call a change in subjectivity. Regulation changes from an activity in which we recognise common threats, and develop universalised means to counter them, to one through which we make calculated decisions balancing individual opportunities for profit and loss. But of particular interest in this context, it also implies changes in the legal occupiability of physical space. Since reductions in margins of safety are gained by increasing the specificity of design-model assumptions, it is logical that as such processes of regulation are mainstreamed, new forms of regulation will be required to ensure that the built reality complies with these models in terms of use, furnishing and occupancy levels. Thus, in this case, the creative freedom of the designers is bought at a cost to the freedom of the occupant. The metaphorical loosening of our regulatory space implies a reflexive tightening of our physical spaces.

Notes

1   The term is defined in the editor's concluding chapter, 'Organising Regulatory Space'. Leigh Hancher and Michael Moran, *Capitalism, Culture, and Economic Regulation* (Oxford and New York: Oxford University Press, 1989).
2   The verb 'to regulate' comes into English language through the Middle French *regler* – to control, order, regulate, govern, to mark with lines drawn with a ruler – having a close relation to the contemporary *ruiller* – to preside over, decide, determine, decree, and to mark out, specifically in senses relating to building.
3   I am paraphrasing McDermont who extends the 'regulatory space' literature by bringing the concept into dialogue with thinkers such as Henri Lefevbre, Michel Foucault and Bruno Latour. See Morag McDermont, 'Territorializing Regulation: A Case Study of "Social Housing" in England', *Law & Social Inquiry*, 32 (2007), pp. 373–398.
4   '[N]o hemp, lint, stray hay, heather nor broom be put near the fire, nor above the flame in houses with fires . . . common women shall be put to the utmost ends of the town where there is least peril of fire . . . no fire be fetched from one house to another within the town except within a covered vessel or lantern.' 'Records of the Parliaments of Scotland', www.rps.ac.uk/static/bottom_frame.html (accessed 14 October 2014).
5   For a more detailed account, see Lothian & Borders Fire Rescue Services' own publication, Alexander Reid, *'Aye Ready!': History of the Edinburgh Fire Brigade, the Oldest Municipal Brigade in Britain* (Edinburgh: South-Eastern Fire Brigade, 1974).
6   Ibid., p. 7.
7   For a more detailed study of this event, and the resulting regulation, see the author's contribution to Els De Vos, Johan De Walsche and Marjan Michels, *Theory by Design: Architectural Research Made Explicit in the Design Studio* (Brussels: Academic & Scientific Publishers, 2013).
8   I use the term here with François Ewald in mind; through the emergence of our welfare states, post-war European governments increasingly took on both the role and the rationale of social insurer. Their principal discursive object, then, was no longer 'justice' so much as 'solidarity'. François Ewald, *L'Etat providence* (Paris: B. Grasset, 1986).
9   Goad's maps were recently acquired by Experian, see www.experian.co.uk/goad/goad-plans.html.
10 Vincent Brannigan, 'Fire Scenarios or Scenario Fires? Can fire safety science provide the critical inputs for performance based fire safety analyses?', *Fire Safety Science*, 6 (2000), 207–218.
11 I am drawing here on Foucault's genealogy of neoliberal government, a process he describes – in another spatio-legal exchange – as one in which the 'marketplace' becomes the site of verification for governmental policies. Michel Foucault, *The Birth of Biopolitics: Lectures at the Collège de France, 1978–1979*, trans. Graham Burchell (London: Palgrave Macmillan, 2010).
12 I adopt this concept from Actor Network Theory in order to describe building design as something which, by virtue of its relative immutability, allows the differing opinions of a range of stakeholders to come into relation. See S. Leigh Star, 'This Is Not a Boundary Object: Reflections on the origin of a concept', *Science, Technology & Human Values*, 35 (2010), 601–617. More broadly, in stressing the importance of the built environment in shaping our governmentalities, I am following ANT's prescription to foreground the actancy of the non-human.
13 Brannigan, 'Fire Scenarios or Scenario Fires?'
14 Speed of egress within computational modelling, for instance, must assume a speed of escape, and most frequently adopts the same stately standard defined by the 1911 fire. Needless to say, this standard represents more to do with the common currency of patriotism in Edwardian Britain than any material phenomena of fire, or egress.

Chapter 23

Common projects and privatised potential

Projection and representation in the Rotterdam Kunsthal

Stefan White

From properties to projects

'Intellectual property' in the UK and much of the world divides creative knowledge into three types; 'Distinctive identity' or design protection, 'Original expression' or copyright and 'Useful idea' or patent.[1] Traditionally, architectural knowledge has been protected using design protection and copyright, with patents the preserve of engineering and science. However, Rem Koolhaas and OMA have produced a number of faux patent applications. The one examined here is called 'Loop-Trick' and refers to the Rotterdam Kunsthal (1992) as its 'initial application'.[2] In *S, M, L, XL*[3] OMA describe how the Kunsthal design originated in a 'previous design for the same site'[4] taking the form of a challenge: 'How to imagine a spiral in four squares?'[5] The resolution of this question appears to be what the Loop-Trick patent attempts to protect as a 'Useful idea' as indicated in Figure 23.1 and in the overlay of the Kunsthal form on to the 'patent' drawing shown in Figure 23.2. However, when OMA's Rotterdam Kunsthal was completed in 1992, architect Gareth Pearce walked around the building and felt so strongly that his student project design for the Docklands Town Hall (DTH) had been used in the design of the Kunsthal that he subsequently brought a copyright infringement case against OMA.[6]

Making use of Gilles Deleuze's critique of representational thinking and Robin Evans's examination of architectural knowledge production, this chapter explores the deficiencies and excesses of the intellectual property (IP) system's valuation of architectural knowledge. It shows how the IP system (Figure 23.3) reduces the embodied and affective dimensions of the design process to 'representations' and consequently both devalues the creative labour of architectural formal production processes and

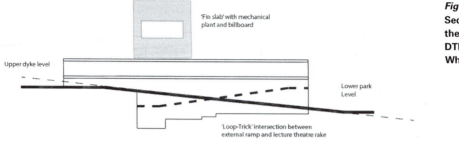

'Fin slab' with mechanical plant and billboard

Upper dyke level

Lower park Level

'Loop-Trick' intersection between external ramp and lecture theatre rake

Schematic section of Rotterdam Kunsthal showing Loop Trick

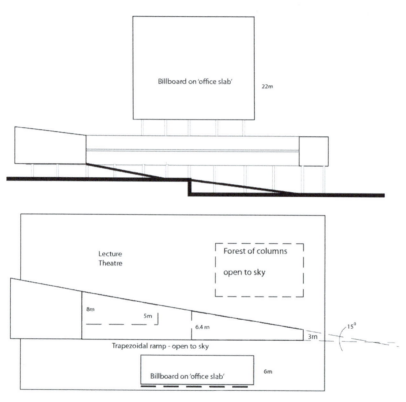

Billboard on 'office slab'

22m

Lecture Theatre

Forest of columns

open to sky

8m

5m

6.4 m

3m

15°

Trapezoidal ramp - open to sky

Billboard on 'office slab'

6m

Plan and section of the Docklands Town Hall reconstructed from Mr Judge Jacobs' description

Figure 23.1
Sectional comparison of the Kunsthal and the DTH. Drawing: Stefan White

overestimates their power to determine formal products. I propose instead an embodied and explicit account of knowledge-making in the architectural design process, outlining a 'projective' mechanism to better account for the role of creative relations and processes in the determination of architectural form.

The Kunsthal case

The Kunsthal case has been used by the UK Design Council to show that 'even strong Intellectual Property law cannot immunise a designer against spurious infringement claims'.[7] However, it has been firmly established since 1774,[8] that the purpose of IP law

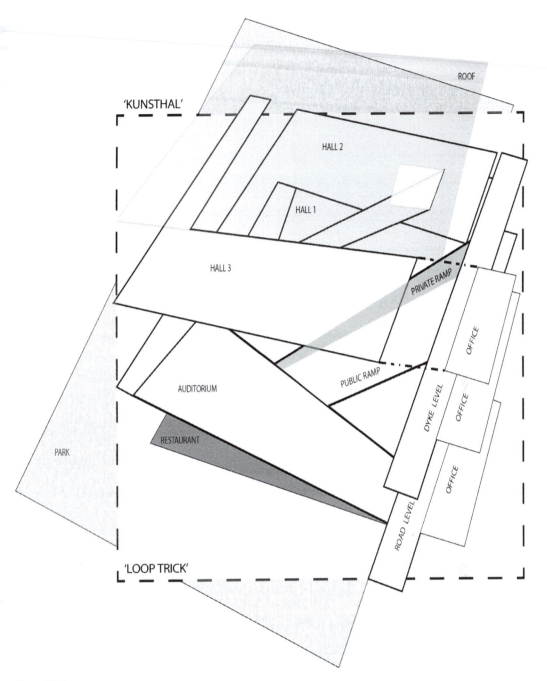

ROOF

'KUNSTHAL'

HALL 2

HALL 1

HALL 3

PRIVATE RAMP

OFFICE

PUBLIC RAMP

DYKE LEVEL

OFFICE

AUDITORIUM

OFFICE

RESTAURANT

PARK

OFFICE

ROAD LEVEL

'LOOP TRICK'

Figure 23.2
Schematic drawing of Kunsthal showing relationship to 'Loop-Trick' patent. Drawing: Stefan White

is precisely to enable a judge to make distinctions between 'intangible assets' in situations where there can be no *natural* right of ownership.[9] Intellectual 'assets' are 'intangible' because I cannot *steal* an idea, depriving you of its benefits, by possessing it *instead* of you. I can only stop you from using one we *share* – by claiming priority access in law. Consequently, IP is administered by the state for the utility of encouraging wealth production and is limited in duration to prevent subsequent generations being restricted in an injurious manner.

The design infringement case 'Pearce v. Koolhaas'[10] was judged against architect Gareth Pearce in November 2001, with the judge remarking that the claims were 'pure and preposterous fantasy'.[11] On the other hand, three expert witnesses all separately concluded that some kind of copying had occurred, evidenced by a large number of graphic similarities – and Pearce has subsequently been granted leave to appeal in the High Court. Pearce was careful not to dispute the 'Distinctive identity' of the Kunsthal in terms of *design protection*, but instead to claim *copyright* infringement of his 'Original expression'. His precise claim concerned 'the copying of his plans *as graphic works*' in a cut-and-paste operation.[12] His argument was not that the buildings are of exactly the same physical form but that there is a genetic commonality in the process of formal production – his actual design drawings being directly used in the production of some stages of the OMA design.

Deleuze's critique of the representational paradigm

For Deleuze, Descartes' faculties of Conception, Perception, Judgement and Imagination each follow an illusory concept of commonality for the purpose of creating 'clear and distinct' identities – illusions which Robin Evans calls 'enabling fictions' when describing their operation in architecture.[13] In Deleuze's account of Descartes, the faculties come to agree a 'common sense' in order to provide a rational and truthful account of the world. However, this *common* sense assumes a *universal* subject who has a '*good* will' – is neither exceptionally clever nor stupid and is not actively evil. In this way, what Deleuze calls *representational thought* is designed to enable differences to be reduced or subordinated to simple recognition, degrees of resemblance, analogies between models or logical negatives.[14] The four faculties each contribute a way of specifying commonality between different embodied instances of sense-making. The process of 'common sense' agreement between faculties starts with the assumption of a direct conformity between thought object and material called intellectual coincidence (the Same – 'conceived identical') which takes priority over any actual perception of different instances of the same material objects (the Similar – 'perceived the same'). It then moves on to cover what is essentially similar between objects of different material form (the Analogous – 'judged the same kind') to account finally for distinctions between different kinds of material and mental objects through a negative process of logical remainder (the Dialectic – 'imagined in opposition'). Each of these consensual judgements requires a fixed, material object and a corresponding mental representation as their metric and each creates a reduction of more dynamic relations in favour of categorisations such as 'Distinctive identity', 'Unique expression' or 'Useful idea'.

Figure 23.3
Intellectual Property categories. Comparison between IP and representational thought. Stefan White

Intellectual Property category	Description of application (Gowers 2006)	Instance of application	Concept of identity	Judgement of Intelligible essence	Judgement of Sensible appearance
Design protection *'Distinctive identity'*	'Non-physical': Logo/identity 'Physical': Design object	**Single**	Form	Distinctive *(not) Same*	Identity *Similar*
Copyright *'Original Expression'*	Literary Graphical Visual Auditory	**Multiple**	Pattern	Original *(not) Similar*	Expression *Analogous*
Patent *'Useful Idea'*	'Simple': chemical compound 'Complex': engineered assemblies	**Possible**	Method	Useful *Analogous*	Idea *Dialectical*
		Focus:	**Origin/Author**	**Physical object**	
		Architectural:	Form	Function	
		(Reduction of):	(Time)	(Space)	
		Structure:	Diachronic	Synchronic	

Common sense judgements

> Mr Pearce's slab is . . . a six-storey office block floating at the end of his building on piloti. The 'slab' of the Kunsthal is much lower and much thinner being just a vertical structure containing lift gear and air conditioning equipment.
>
> (Justice Jacobs, 'Pearce v. Ove Arup' (EWHC: 2001), clause 31)

At the trial, Justice Jacobs untangles Pearce's 'Original expression' by following the *representational* model. He starts from the Kunsthal's 'Distinctive identity' by literally comparing physical models for resemblance asking, what for him, is the simplest question: 'are the buildings the same?' Clearly they are not the *same*: they are not the same mental object; they are conceived differently by the 'common sense'. Deleuze argues that 'common sense' is agreed by men of 'good sense' as evidenced by the perception of similitude, which in this case sees the buildings as dissimilar, thereby failing the resemblance test which forms the first illusion of representational thinking. If they were *the same*, there would be a *conceived* identity between the objects, founded on the good and true sense of the participants, and there would, in effect, be no need for a judgement, since representational truth cannot be contested. As can be seen in Figure 23.4, the buildings do not have exactly the same physical appearance, but while this is the starting point of the IP process, this was not the kind of copying alleged.

The principle of recognition of this epistemological dualism operates through *either* the distinction of intelligible essences *or* of sensible appearances (conception *or* perception) and the judge's attempt to distinguish a 'Distinctive identity' by identifying aspects of drawings with aspects of a building through the representational illusions of

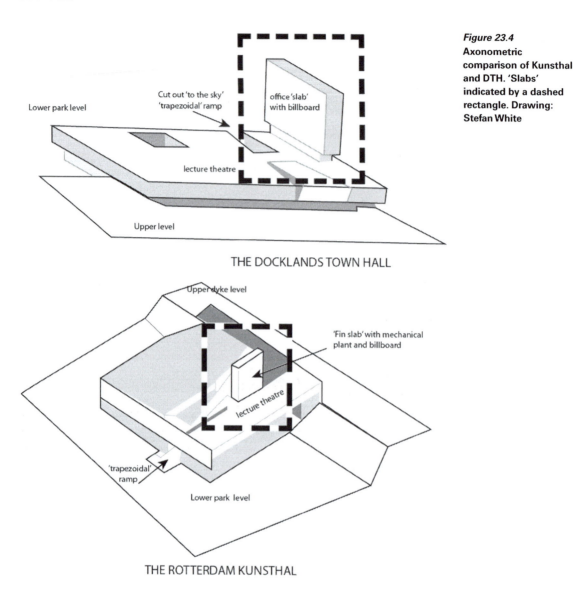

Figure 23.4
**Axonometric
comparison of Kunsthal
and DTH. 'Slabs'
indicated by a dashed
rectangle. Drawing:
Stefan White**

THE DOCKLANDS TOWN HALL

THE ROTTERDAM KUNSTHAL

'the same' and 'the similar' now moves from a discussion of representations of form to representations of function. In this task, one might assume 'function' to be the particular use of a particular space, but in the representational paradigm, it is even simpler: function is literally a label on a drawing which determines the use of a space in the intellect – as a 'picture', not 'in fact' as Robin Evans argues. Consequently, the judge places emphasis on the dissimilarity of the tower 'slabs' in both their visual appearance and their labels of internal function, but fails to recognise their most striking *actual* capability: both serve as advertising 'billboards'.

In following the representational paradigm set up for him by IP law, the judge becomes affronted by the magnitude of divergence between '*common* sense' and the individual sense of the claimant, and declares any perceived similarity to be the erroneous product of a 'fevered imagination'.[15] Deleuze argues that the representational paradigm makes 'all that is not true of identity . . . the subject of error',[16] so it is now the character of the men making these false claims to an indisputable truth that is called into question. It is no surprise that the very first line of the judgement notes, entirely irrelevantly, that Mr Pearce was 'virtually unemployed' whilst Mr Koolhaas 'was regarded as a very considerable figure'.[17] The striking lack of 'common' sense leads the judge to take action against one of Pearce's expert witnesses – setting a shocking legal precedent by referring Mr Wilkey to the Architects' Registration Board (ARB) for disciplinary action on the grounds that his evidence was 'So biased and irrational . . . I conclude that he failed in his duty to the court'.[18] However, three 'good' respected expert witnesses separately held a sense of truth different from the judge's conception of the universal thinking subject who would share his 'common' sense. Mr Wilkey was the second expert[19] to have advised Pearce that he had a case, and in the ARB inquiry prompted by Justice Jacobs's accusations, it was found by a third independent expert that copying had, in all probability, occurred.[20]

By insisting that his claim was focused on the 'graphical' copying of his plans, Pearce requested that a judge in a copyright case understand the 'Original expression' in an architectural production as something created *between* the architect and the architectural drawing *during* the process of composition. While maintaining his focus on the identification of representations of property, the judge then proceeds to explore the possibility of the presence of analogous systems of codification and determination in the drawings. This briefly opens the discussion to address the creative potential of architectural processes, but the judge is unable to understand the mechanism or advantage of Pearce's allegations. How is it that a graphic element can determine one type of thing in one plan and another type of thing on the copied plan (e.g. a DTH balcony indicating a Kunsthal staircase)? He subsequently berates the expert witness Wilkey for never considering 'as an architect, how, supposing use of the DTH plans, the copying could happen'.[21] However, the judge is forced to concede that 'some at OMA (*not Mr Koolhaas*) . . . sometimes would copy . . . an existing building . . . [for] a sort of ranging exercise'.[22]

Exercising range

What then are these ranging exercises copying? OMA are quite capable of drawing a rectangle of the appropriate size on a site plan. Why would they instead overlay the DTH? What range does it give them? Conversely, as they do use ranging exercises, why not use the DTH? It was available[23] and would seem to be at least as useful as Koolhaas *sharing* 'diagrams' with Peter Eisenman (Eisenman and Koolhaas have publicly recognised the similarity between Eisenman's earlier Max Reinhardt tower design and OMA's CCTV tower, noting that they both have the same 'Möbius strip' form).[24] Could use of the DTH provide a quick shortcut to see whether a building with a public route through the middle, which steps up a site and contains similar programmes (such as lecture theatres) would fit? If they wanted to do this, why wouldn't they use the Carpenter Centre by Le Corbusier instead, or as well?[25] To an architect, could the precedent used for the ranging exercise indicate the amount of similar programmes that could be accommodated or do much more?

Whatever has been 'copied', it must be intuitable from a few overlaid and multiply photocopied plans, and enable the architect to begin to apportion form and programme over a site. Here the interpretations or determinations made from drawings which are dissimilar in formal expression (e.g. the Kunsthal and the DTH) but similar in formal content (i.e. containing some of the same lines) require some explicit additional agency. In this case Pearce's design drawings cannot be being used as representations of a final product but as graphical material within a creative process of production. They must therefore be understood to have a value in their own right (as *content*), separate (and additional) to their job as specification devices in a construction process (as *expression*).

In this case Pearce's drawings have *both* an intrinsic form of content understood by architects engaged within the production process (like a musical score) as well as an extrinsic form of expression understood by clients, contractors and judges as representing a specific and particular building (like recorded music). It is also clear that the content of the drawings in a ranging exercise inspires the creative architect in an active and relational composition rather than the discovery and straightforward repetition of an implicit, static organisation. It is thus possible for a simple 'ranging exercise' – when seen as an embodied experiential activity (like a performance) – to result in highly specific – 'new' or 'original' – forms (of expression), *and simultaneously* be derivative in terms of content.

Robin Evans argues that predominant accounts of architectural knowledge operate according to what he calls 'picture theory'.[26] He articulates the inadequacies of a representational dualism in architecture and identifies enduring features of both historic and contemporary epistemology which mirror Deleuze's analysis of representation. Of more interest, however, is that Evans and Deleuze identify positive 'affective' potential in the 'transitions between objects',[27] where an *affect* is a change of state embodied in the architect and their products. Both agree that the dissimilarities or differences between representations and what is represented are central to 'the drawing's power as a medium'.[28] Like Deleuze, Evans proposes the prioritisation of an embodied subject whose imagination and perception are understood as independent attributes of a creative – *projective* – process, which creates both forms of expression *and* forms of content. Evans's 'projection' is thus an intuitive and embodied capability of the architect that enables them to iterate from the content of one formal product (a drawing or model) to a new one through a particular drawing or modelling process.[29] Evans calls this 'projection' because such processes can literally 'project' the content into a new form of expression (e.g when a plan and section are used to create a perspective using lines of projection) but he also applies it less literally (e.g when a sketch model is 'drawn' into an axonometric) and more broadly, to explain how techniques and abilities inform each other over time. In the Kunsthal case, a process of projection appears to occur when cut-and-paste plans of different scales are drawn into a new plan at one particular scale.

Consequently, in the Kunsthal case, we see plans and sections of a precedent used, not for the stealing of an 'intellectual property' but the creation of 'embodied capabilities'. The design team are intuitively aware of some of the potential actual *affect* on a user of the building of the relative elements copied from the ranging exercise ('stairs', 'balconies') with this embodied reading part of 'the form of content' of the drawing. However, they would also see simultaneously the formal expression of those elements (the lines on the page) as another set of potential affects (spaces, scales, diagrams). By selecting (even unconsciously) between different formal contents and expressions (through the act of composing or redrawing) and attempting to maintain their plausible operation amongst new relations of constraint they are *projecting* potential affects into a new 'design'. We can imagine them saying: 'If we want to keep a billboard we can put our mechanical plant in a tower in order to maintain a vertical element rising above the slab.' It is not for the purpose of determining spatial dimensions that a precedent is employed, but for the capacity it creates for a new architectural expression. It does so by offering an existing set of differentials of formal expression *and* their contents (the lines demarking a 'stair' or 'balcony' *and* the environments those inter-pretations and compositions imply), *both* of which require and stimulate the architect to create additional coherences to reintegrate or *project* these challenging expressions into a new system of actual production.

Here the precedent materials create, through the architect's active accept-ance of them, a set of compositional challenges which force the design process to problematise relations *commonly* assumed to be fixed and internal or autonomous. This enables the ranging exercise to *project* forward in time, allowing an immediate affective reaction to a much more developed set of potential arrangements than an initial drawing of a rectangle – providing much more material for the creative imagination to attempt to recompose into a new sensible, coherent arrangement. Consequently, we might expect that there are affective 'similarities' (what Deleuze calls the repetition of differences)[30] in the embodied complexities of constraint that made the DTH a good precedent for a ranging exercise – but the composition of circumstances and potentials makes different sense in different circumstances of sense-making. The affective, differ-ential power of the ranging exercise – the relative affective labour it contains relevant to the new embodied context – is a form of intuitive, projective knowledge, which is actually *created* by being evoked in a new context. It is a repetition of difference for the production of capability. While such design processes (which might be traced in Koolhaas's work to a fascination with surrealism)[31] force assumptions of what is *'common sense'* to be explicitly reiterated and re-embodied[32] and might be referred to as 'critical',[33] it is in fact the redefinition of 'the architect' through this process which holds real socially transformative potential.

Deleuze's analysis suggests that a projective account of the production of knowledge would value the *differences* between the faculties of conception, perception, judgement and imagination which representation instead conspires to reduce to a more easily comprehensible 'common sense'. Projection therefore has the potential to value the architectural design process as a serial production of *embodied* differences between forms of expression *and* their contents *over time* – rather than it being understood as an instantaneous and seamless translation with all errors removed. Valuing the embodied relations which enable the movement from one form of content to another via the

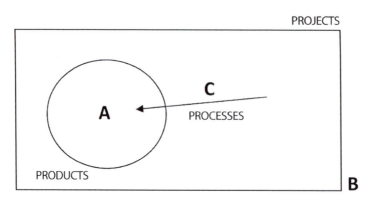

PROJECTS

A

C

PROCESSES

PRODUCTS

B

A = set of existing disciplinary capabilities

B = set of all social capabilities

C = Agency of individual architects

expressive affect of the drawings, models and buildings of the design process (on both
its creators and users) produces a positive role for the architect as the explicit relation
between discipline and society rather than, say, having to resist social pressure to protect
a creative 'autonomy'.

In this embodied account, it is compositions of affective elements placed
in new relations of constraint through the auspices of the architectural agent, which
constitute the distinctive, unique and useful capabilities of the architectural *project*.
The particular expressions of its products or processes – any of its individual drawings
or representations, including the actual building – are valued in terms of the project they
constitute rather than the product they delineate (Figure 23.5). In turn, multitudinous
architectural projects now actively constitute 'the discipline' within and through society.
Representational thought as expressed by the IP system, and by predominant accounts
in architecture, tends to understand the complex world that external engagement
implies, by formally reducing embodied relationships (between architect and user, client,
contractor or drawing) to *either* computational determinisms *or* elitist autonomies.
Positively defining 'the architect' in active embodied terms instead, brings what representational thought places beyond 'architecture' for 'common sense' reasons once
more into our creative territory.

Private potential: the power of projection

The Kunsthal design achieves its singular character by a speculative selection of constraints using the graphical copying of 'precedent', repeatedly personalised through a
series of projective iterations. Each projective instance, regardless of the sources impli-
cated within, creates new contexts and capabilities and generates the unique particularity of the products of 'the project'. The specificities generated during the process of

design which might seem unique and authorial – 'not normally obvious to the expert'[34] – can be seen to be produced through numerous interlocked, embodied and durational relationships both within and outside the processes of commissioning, design, construction and use. Asserting authorship within a representational paradigm deliberately and systematically excises these collaborative activities, although they are central to creativity.

The common sense of IP privatises *potential* that we all share access to by claiming it as proprietorial representations. Representations devalue the creative labour of architecture, either by making creativity an essence of process in which the architect is a genius (suiting only elite processors) or by making it an essence of production in which architecture is a machine (suiting only reductive producers). The manner and extent to which projective relations can be made explicit is shown here to be crucial to the definition of both the value of the architect within society and the exploitation of architectural labour within the discipline. Projection insists that the committed human labour of design is made an explicit part of the epistemological explanation of process and product *in parallel*, with both understood as *serially composed* manifestations of the power and potential of creative, differential relations. It is such compositions of difference (between drawings, disciplines, cultures and individuals) that are themselves composed into *projects*, which exist through and within architecture but always beyond it. Amidst a repressive, dominant representational paradigm, retaining and expanding the potential of architecture as a discipline and as an existence relies on the extent to which creative – projective – relations can continue to be 'made explicit'[35] *both* between the architect and their products *and* the production of architecture and its consumption.

Notes

1   Andrew Gowers, *Gowers Review of Intellectual Property* (HMSO: 2006), p. 13, www.gov.uk/government/publications/gowers-review-of-intellectual-property (accessed 3 March 2015).
2   Rem Koolhaas, *Content* (Koln: Taschen, 2004), p. 76.
3   Rem Koolhaas et al., *S, M, L, XL* (New York: Monacelli Press, 1998), pp. 431–473.
4   This appears to be OMA's competition entry for the Nederlands Institute of Architecture.
5   Koolhaas, *S, M, L, XL*, p. 431.
6   England and Wales High Court, *Pearce v. Ove Arup Partnership Ltd & Ors Ch 455* (EWHC: 2001), clause 30.
7   UK Design Council, *Ten Examples* (2007), www.designcouncil.org.uk/en/About-Design/Business-Essentials/Intellectual-property/Ten-examples/ (accessed 20 June 2007).
8   'In 1774, the House of Lords ruled . . . that copyright was a purely statutory right created for the utilitarian purpose of encouraging literary efforts'. *Gowers Review*, p. 14.
9   Norman S. Kinsella, 'Against Intellectual Property', *Journal of Libertarian Studies* 15(2), 2001: 1–53.
10 *Pearce v. Ove Arup.*
11 Ibid., clause 2
12 Ibid., clause 42.
13 Robin Evans, *Translations Between Drawing and Building and Other Essays* (London: Architectural Association, 1997), p. 154.
14 Gilles Deleuze, *Difference and Repetition* (London: Continuum, 1994), p. 133.
15 *Pearce v. Ove Arup*, clause 41.
16 Deleuze, *Difference and Repetition*, p. 167.
17 *Pearce v. Ove Arup*, clauses 7, 13.
18 Ibid., clause 49.
19 Frederick Hill, *A Claim for Infringement of Design Copyright against Rem Koolhaas by Gareth Pearce, Report* (Middlesex: Landau & Cohen, n.d.), http://issuu.com/stefanwhite/docs/kunsthallcopyrightfrederickhillwitn/1 (accessed 3 March 2015).

20   Ian Salisbury, *In the matter of a charge brought against MR MICHAEL WILKEY* (Mayer, Brown, Rowe & Maw LLP, 2003), pp. 118–119.

21   *Pearce v. Ove Arup*, clause 55.

22   Ibid., clause 19 (emphasis added).

23   It was conceded in court that Pearce had been asked to leave his portfolio after interview at OMA to be shown to 'Mr Koolhaas'.

24   Peter Eisenman and Rem Koolhaas, *Super-Critical* (London: AA Publications, 2009), p. 16.

25   Le Corbusier (1963). The Carpenter Arts Centre has a ramp running through it and is raised on piloti.

26   Robin Evans, *The Projective Cast: Architecture and its Three Geometries* (Cambridge, MA: MIT Press, 1995), pp. 358 and 370.

27   Ibid., p. 367.

28   Evans, *Translations*, p. 154.

29   The 'sense' of the drawing is a form *contained* within the body of the architect as their interpretation of the formal expression.

30   Deleuze, *Difference and Repetition*, ch. 2.

31   Eisenman and Koolhaas, *Super-Critical*, p. 89.

32   Jonathan Hill sees a 'critical' moment in the Kunsthal design, when the introduction of a curtain enables the auditorium to perform as entrance *and* circulation route, breaking the functionalist habit of programmatic discreteness. Jonathan Hill, *Actions of Architecture: Architects and Creative Users* (London: Routledge, 2003), p. 50.

33   For a discussion of the critical in architecture, see Jane Rendell et al. (eds), *Critical Architecture* (London: Routledge, 2007). The status of the procedures outlined here with respect to 'critical architecture' is discussed in detail in: Stefan White, 'Gilles Deleuze and the Project of Architecture: An Expressionist Design-Research Methodology', unpublished Ph.D. thesis, University College London, 2014.

34   Originality criteria for a patent (*Gowers Review*, p. 14).

35   Evans, *Translations*, p. 154.

Part VII

Technologies and techniques

Chapter 24

The electrification of the factory

Or the flexible layout of work(s)

Tilo Amhoff

It is surprising that most discussions of modern industry in architectural history pay more attention to mechanisation than to electrification, even though both have been similarly revolutionary. Electrification brought two main changes to the factory; namely, electrical lighting and heating that enabled the extension of the working day, and electrical drive that made possible the transition to electrical power transmission, which is the primary focus of this chapter. It is generally agreed that electrical power transmission allowed for a new flexibility in the layout of the factory, in the arrangements of the individual machines, and hence also in the organisation of the work process. However there has been less interest in the actual effects of the reorganisation of this process on the spatial division of labour and on the integration of that division in the planning department. To explore its impact on the spatial aspects of the organisation of industrial production this chapter makes use of a remarkable and revealing series of articles on electrification written by Oskar Lasche, the first director of Peter Behrens' AEG turbine factory, and published in trade journals of the time. As the double meaning of my title – the layout of work(s) – suggests, the flexibility of electrification entailed that both workspace and the work process could be simultaneously laid out.

The electrification of the factory transformed the power transmission process from a mechanical system of gears, shafts, and belts to an electrical system of generators, wires, and motors. It happened gradually, from line-shaft drive, then to group drive, and finally to single unit drive.[1] The existing accounts of the electrification of the factory in the USA do recognise the transformative potential of electrical power transmission. For Betsy Hunter Bradley it allowed, 'new freedom in production layouts'.[2] Lindy Biggs argues that, 'electricity's major impact on plant organization lay in the new possibilities for shop-floor layout inherent in the use of the electric motor'.[3] Most importantly the electrification of the factory allowed the flexible layout of work(s), or what historian David E. Nye described as 'flexible factory' in contrast to Biggs's 'rational factory'. According to Nye, 'electrical power made possible entirely new factory forms'.[4]

This desired flexibility had an impact on the possibilities of the design of the factory building and the organisation of the labour process, and especially on the relation between the two. Also, flexibility required *both* organisation and the making of plans. With respect to the factory it is important to distinguish between two kinds of plans: the work-plan for the factory system and the floor-plan for the factory building. The work-plan is concerned with the layout of the system of machines and the cooperation of labourers, while the floor-plan is concerned with the layout of the building. They are, of course, interrelated. This chapter argues that both are plans for the organisation of the production process, and that electricity opened up the possibility for the two plans to merge. They intersect in the spatial organisation of the workplace, which can be distinguished but not separated from the temporal organisation of the labour-time.

Oskar Lasche and the electrification of the AEG factories

Typically, architectural histories of the AEG factories discuss their architect and their structural engineer, and concentrate on the new assembly hall of the AEG turbine factory. They tend to focus either on Behrens' design or on the well-documented dispute between him and the engineer Karl Bernhard over the aesthetics of steel construction and the authorship of the building.[5] Stanford Anderson's monograph on Behrens is largely concerned with the architect's creative process of giving form.[6] He situates Behrens' design of the new turbine hall as part of the shift in German architectural theory from the tectonics of the material structure (Gottfried Semper) to the spatial conception of architecture (August Schmarsow). Anderson states that the architect's concern was with the expression of the factory's symbolic significance for industrial society, as a means to elevate the factory building to the realm of architecture. Furthermore, Frederic J. Schwartz argues that Behrens was only employed as 'artistic adviser' for the 'appearance' of the electrical engineering company, from the factory to its products, and their advertising. He looks at the discourse of the new turbine hall in terms of the shift from labour to culture, whereby the work spirit was elevated through the building's 'beauty'. In his discussion of trademarks as 'magical signs' Schwartz refers to the interpretation of the building as the 'cathedral of work', becoming a 'commodity sign' for the company. He consequently focuses on the role of architecture in the exchange of commodities, giving an image to a product rather than facilitating its manufacture.[7]

In contrast, this chapter builds its argument by taking into account the position of the first director of the AEG turbine factory, the mechanical and electrical engineer Oskar Lasche (1868–1923). Lasche was the head engineer and had been at the drafting office since 1899. From 1902 he became the director of the AEG machine factory in Brunnenstrasse, and in this role he contributed to the company's development of turbines and generators. In 1903 Lasche became the first director of the new established AEG turbine factory in Huttenstrasse, which produced turbines for the generation of electricity in power stations and elsewhere. What follows is my analysis of a series of articles, so far disregarded by other commentators, which Lasche wrote between 1899 and 1911, and in which he discusses, first the electrical power distribution in the factory and, second, the advantages of the electrical single motor drive for machines.

In the first series of articles published in the *Journal of the Association of German Engineers* (1899–1900) Lasche describes the operational and economic characteristics of electrical power distribution in the machine-building workshops of AEG, and highlights the advantages of the use of electrical energy for the rational operation of the factory, which was not only a place of production, but also a test field for development. He uses two examples from his own practice: the ongoing extensions of the appliances factory in Ackerstrasse, designed by Franz Schwechten and Paul Tropp (1888–1895), and the newly built small motors and large machines factory complex in Brunnenstrasse, where Lasche worked on the initial development of turbines, by the same architects (1895–1897). His intent was to outline the influence of electrical power distribution, 'on the layout of the buildings, the arrangement of the workshops and the design of the work processes'.[8] Lasche begins his text with two photographs (Figures 24.1 and 24.2). The first is of the older appliance factory and the second of the newer large machines factory. They show the transition from mechanical to electrical power transmission. We can note the disappearance of the mechanical system and the invisibility of the electrical system.

He goes on to outline the advantages of electrical power distribution in the extension of the AEG appliance factory in Ackerstrasse (1888–1895), one of which was the centralisation of power generation.[9] In fact the most central building of the AEG

Figure 24.1
Photograph (1899) of AEG appliance factory in Ackerstrasse (1888–1895), showing a workshop with mechanical transmission. Oskar Lasche, 'Die Elektrische Kraftverteilung in den Maschine-bauwerkstaetten der Allgemeinen Elektricitaets-Gesellschaft, Berlin', *Z-VDI*, no. 5, 43 (1899), 115 (Textblatt 1)

Figure 24.2
**Photograph (1899)
of AEG large machines
factory in Brunnenstrasse
(1895–1897), showing a
workshop with electrical
single motor drive. Oskar
Lasche, 'Die Elektrische
Kraftverteilung in den
Maschinebauwerkstaetten
der Allgemeinen
Elektricitaets-Gesellschaft,
Berlin', *Z-VDI*, no. 5, 43
(1899), 115 (Textblatt 2)**

turbine factory was the power station, also designed by Behrens and completed prior to the new turbine hall in 1909. According to Lasche, the system of mechanical transmission in the old appliance factory was confusing and unclear. He bemoans the arrangement of workspaces and the positioning of machines. They were not always laid out according to the best route of fabrication. Mostly their location depended only on the most favourable position of the mechanical transmission. But with electrical transmission – in contrast – there would be no great difficulties for the disposition and grouping of buildings, primarily because of its adaptability. Electric cable is, quite literally, flexible. As we can see (or rather, not see) cable is also invisible – hidden either inside walls or behind skirting board. It neither needs much space, nor close supervision and maintenance. However, the main advantages emphasised by Lasche were in the improved organisation that electrical transmission enabled, thereby achieving greater efficiency of the production process. The reduction of installation costs or the saving of power was only a secondary benefit.[10] He illustrates this with the example of a conversion and subsequent reorganisation of an unidentified workshop, before and after electrification (Figure 24.3). Importantly, after electrification and for the first time for the extensions of the appliances factory with electrical power transmission, 'The workshops were distributed only in accordance with the proper route and sequence of operation, following the order of the successive work processes.'[11]

Analogous to the city, the factory was to have a transport system – the industrial railway – and courtyards, streets and sidewalks on the factory site, and inside the factory building a service alley between the machines. Organising the work process according to the route of manufacture entailed the establishment of this route on the shop floor and a transport system to service it. The disappearance of the mechanical

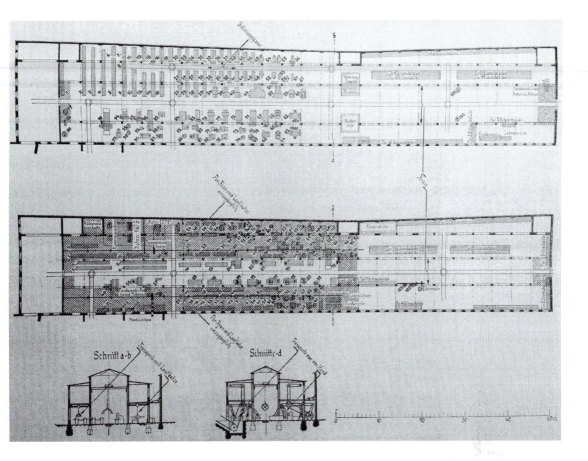

Figure 24.3
Shop-floor plan
(1900) of unidentified
AEG factory with
electrical power
transmission. Oskar
Lasche, 'Elektrischer
Einzelantrieb und seine
Wirtschaftlichkeit',
Z-VDI, no. 36, 44
(1900), 1193

power transmission system allowed for the use of the electrical travelling crane and it made it possible to order the machines according to this new logic. We can also note the hatching, indicating the shadow of the mechanical system, and in that respect the 'daylight factory' probably made more sense when the daylight could actually reach the machine either through the new glass façades, or more importantly the roof lights, which prior to electrification – with all the shafts and belts – would have been more difficult. In that respect electrification also had an agency in the construction of the daylight factory.

The large machines factory (1895) and the small motors factory (1897) in Brunnenstrasse were the first purpose-built AEG factories with electrical power transmission. The new workshops were built according to a uniform plan and based on the experiences of the former machine tool factory in Ackerstrasse. These examples of purpose-built AEG factories – using individual drive with polyphase current – became the 'model factory' informing Lasche's argument. As he states, 'The overall layout of the workshops is no longer the slave of mechanical transmission.'[12] And more importantly, 'The mutual position of workshops and the arrangement of machines within them no longer depend on the supplied power, but on the work to be done.'[13] We see, then, that electrical power distribution allows the whole factory building to be built as a lightweight, single-floor, undivided workshop.

The supervision of work(s)

Moreover, Lasche also recognises that, with the disappearance of the mechanical transmission system, 'almost the entire workshop can be overlooked from a single point'.[14] The 'elevated booths grant the foreman a good overview of all workers, who in turn feel constantly under supervision'.[15] This is, of course, the exact description of the diagram of the mechanism of power in the ideal form of the panopticon plan. Lasche illustrates the point with a photograph showing the overview from one of the elevated glass booths inside the workshop (Figure 24.4). Importantly, he explains that this arrangement allows the shop manager 'to convince himself from the operations of the factory with a single all-encompassing view', without losing time by walking around on the shop-floor.[16] Ultimately, Lasche comes to the conclusion that electrical power drive and electrical power distribution allow for a significant reconfiguration and reorganisation of the production process. We will see, therefore, that with electrification, the emphasis shifts from overseeing the mechanical system of power distribution to overseeing the social system of work distribution, and defines new roles for the director and the engineer.

In the second series of articles published in the *Journal of the Association of German Engineers* and the *AEG Journal* (1907–1911) Lasche discusses the new turbine hall by Behrens and Bernhard, which was built as an addition to the existing turbine hall. He is concerned with the relation between the size and weight of the turbine to be produced, with the travelling crane, and with the size of the workshop, stating, for example, that, 'For these turbines and dynamos the width and height of the existing hall was no longer sufficient, and the carrying capacity of the cranes was too low.'[17] Lasche

Figure 24.4
Photograph (1899) of AEG large machines factory in Brunnenstrasse (1895–1897), showing a workshop with electrical single motor drive. Oskar Lasche, 'Die Elektrische Kraftverteilung in den Maschinebauwerkstaetten der Allgemeinen Elektricitaets-Gesellschaft, Berlin', *Z-VDI*, no. 6, 43 (1899), 143

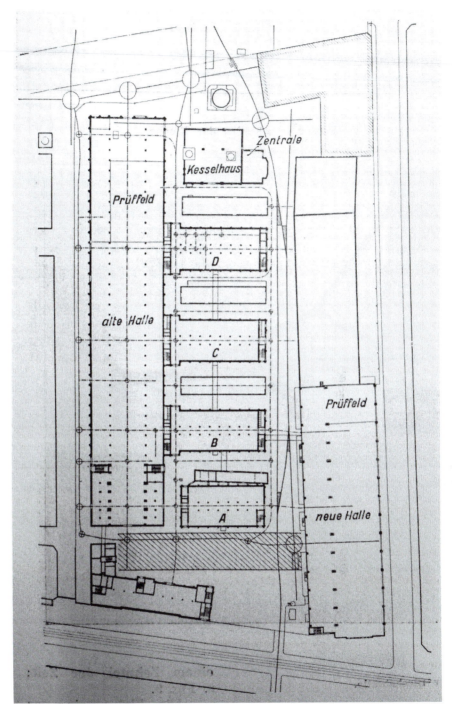

Figure 24.5
Shop-floor plan (1911) of
AEG turbine factory
with old turbine hall
(1896) on the left
and new turbine hall
(1909) on the right.
Oskar Lasche, 'Die
Turbinenfabrikation der
AEG', *Z-VDI*, no. 29, 55
(1911), 1199

explains that the main dimensions of the spaces inevitably determined the fabrication of the turbines – medium-sized for the old hall and large for the new hall.

Giving further detail of the turbine fabrication, he refers to the site-plan of the turbine factory and draws our attention to the four extensions (A–D) of the old turbine hall, which contain four autonomous fabrication departments (Figure 24.5). Here Lasche emphasises that machining, assembling, testing, and shipping are autonomous in the old assembly hall, and also in the new assembly hall, but that they are interconnected through a transport system. The reason for this division, according to him, was to separate every uniform fabrication of different elements (blades, nozzles, controllers, valves, bearings), in order to achieve the clarity and transparency of the production process. According to Lasche, each form of fabrication should therefore be locally self-contained, 'an empire in itself'.[18] In order to materialise his desire for clarity and transparency, a range of inner changes and relocations were necessary. For the director of the turbine factory this could only be achieved through the separation of the whole fabrication process into a number of autonomous individual operations and therefore, individual workspaces.

The desire for clarity and transparency, and to have an overview is, then, another driver for the reorganisation of the production process in the German context. Lasche insists that this is achieved both literally in the construction of the factory building, and figuratively in the organisation of the factory system. For him, clarity and transparency in the arrangement of the actual workspaces and in the organisation of the work processes went hand-in-hand, through functional separation and the subsequent spatial division of the workshops. Unlike Frederick W. Taylor, who was concerned with the separation of the work process into distinct tasks, or the temporal division of labour (scientific management), Lasche was more interested in the spatial separation and order of the individual operations of the production process on the shop-floor, or the spatial division of labour (industrial engineering). For example, in the large machines factory we can see that, despite the possibility of an open floor-plan, the shop-floor was divided into discrete functional units, each served by their own travelling crane, and numbered for identification and possible reconfiguration (Figure 24.6). We can also see the various glass booths for the supervisors of work, and the rays of their potential view.

The rise of the planning department

Through Lasche's writings, then, we begin to understand that the electrification of the factory was one of the material preconditions for spatial planning to occur and to be meaningful in the factory, especially as a part of the planning and supervising of work. At the AEG factories we can observe the relocation of the spatial location of the supervisor of the work process. There were three different locations for three different kinds of supervisors that did not necessarily replace each other, but which were introduced in successive stages. In the first stage the foreman was still on the shop-floor, together with the wage labourers, leading and supervising the group of workers. In this instance the foremen were still 'blue collar' workers, and part of the gangs of workers. In the

Figure 24.6
Shop-floor plan (1900) of AEG large machines factory in Brunnenstrasse (1895–1897), showing a workshop with electrical single motor drive. Oskar Lasche, 'Elektrischer Einzelantrieb und seine Wirtschaftlichkeit', *Z-VDI*, no. 36, 44 (1900), 1194

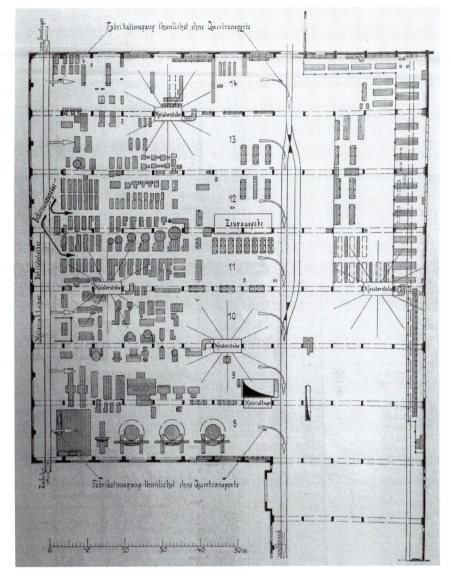

second stage, the supervisor was removed from the shop-floor into a glass booth floating above it from which he could then overlook the production process. In the third stage, the planning department removed the manager from the workshop, the space of 'blue collar' workers, and relocated them to a space of 'white collar' workers, a space of their own. In this separate space the overseeing of the actual shop-floor and the work process was mediated by representations of the work process in a variety of diagrams, charts, tables, models, and other devices. The ongoing separation between conception and execution of work and the removal of the supervision of work from the actual shop-floor was further exemplified in the subsequent separation between production and administration buildings, between factory and office.

In the first-ever German article on the so-called 'Taylor system' under the heading 'A Kind of American Shop Organisation', published in 1907 in the first volume of the new German journal on workshop technology edited by Georg Schlesinger, the author Otto Eichberg discussed the relationship between the technical division of labour in the factory and the subsequent organisation of its cooperation. He argued that 'the precondition for the division of labour, however, is something that tracks the division and the performance, and puts it finally all together at the end, in short: organisation'.[19] For Eichberg, the division of labour and the organisation of work were directly related. According to him there was no division of labour without the organisation of cooperation, and no cooperation without the prior division of labour. They both depended on each other. For Eichberg, following Taylor, cooperation was organised in the planning department or *Arbeitsbüro* in German, which literally translates as 'work-office'. This was the room where the work-plans for the factory were prepared. It was, according to Eichberg, 'the actual head of the workshop in the strict sense: it governs and controls'.[20]

Conclusion

The electrification of the factory enabled a significant transformation of the factory building and of the factory system. Most importantly it allowed for an organisation of industrial production according to the work process. Before electricity the mechanical power distribution system largely determined the layout of the shop-floor. It was only the electrical single motor drive that allowed the independent operation of machines, hence giving the industrial engineer and the scientific manager flexibility in the layout of the shop-floor. In short, while the old factory buildings were to be arranged according to the location and distribution of the power source, the new workshops could be organised according to the work process.

One of the consequences for architects and engineers in the design of the factory was the dominance of materials-handling systems such as the travelling crane and later the continuous moving or conveyor belt, which determined the layout of the shop-floor. From Lasche's point of view, the most important requirement for Behrens and Bernhard's new turbine hall was the type of turbine to be produced, which in turn determined the load-bearing capacity of the travelling crane and its height. According to him, 'the heights of the separate spaces were determined by the positioning of the cranes, and this was determined by the production process'.[21]

When considering the consequences of these changes for the factory workers, one cannot help but see an analogy between the impact of electrical power on the mechanical system of machines in the factory and its impact on labour power. For instance, with the electrical single motor drive there was no more idle time in the running of the machines, as they could just be switched off individually. When one of the machines broke down it would no longer shut down the whole factory, as with the previous mechanical system of interconnected machines. According to the sociologist and labour historian Richard Biernacki, the factory produces labour as a commodity as well as goods. In his book *The Fabrication of Labor*, Biernacki makes a comparative study of work processes in British and German textile factories at the end of the nineteenth and the beginning of the twentieth century. In an attempt to identify the cultural constitution of the production process and the cultural structure of the workplace, he investigates the cultural specifications of labour as a quantifiable, monetised, and marketable commodity in the two countries. The form in which labour was commodified was labour-time or the length of the working day. Interestingly, Biernacki notes in the chapter on 'The Control of Time and Space' that the workplace was organised differently according to the appropriation of labour power. In Britain the working day was defined by the presence of the worker in the factory, while in Germany the working day was defined as the use of the actual labour-time in the production process. According to Biernacki, while in Britain 'space marked the boundaries of employment', in Germany it was time.[22] He proposes that factory-building types concretised these cultural conceptions. In Britain they were fortress-like with only one entrance to the factory. Workspaces were organised around a central courtyard to which all spaces had access (while not connected to each other) and hence circulation was always via the courtyard. In Germany, however, workspaces were grouped and separated from each other and from the ancillary spaces, with multiple entrances. The emphasis was on the supervising of the attendance of the machines, and not on the monitoring of the gateway as in Britain.

With the electrification of the factory the fixed spatial order of mechanical transmission was broken apart and replaced by the continuous reordering process of the now independent, isolated, and mobile machines. At the same time the contracting of gangs of workers led by a foreman was replaced by the employment of individual wage labourers, supervised by a manager. From now on the medium of the plan and the technique of planning were to organise the labour process according to more abstract ordering principles such as the 'sequence of work' or the 'route of manufacture'. In this respect, electrical drive opened up continuing attempts for the ideal layout of the factory work-plan and the factory floor-plan to be considered and designed together.

Notes

1   For more details, see Warren D. Devine, 'From Shafts to Wires: Historical Perspective on Electrification', *The Journal of Economic History*, 2, 43 (1983), 347–372.

2   Betsy Hunter Bradley, *The Works: The Industrial Architecture of the United States* (New York and Oxford: Oxford University Press, 1999), pp. 95–105.

3   Lindy Biggs, *The Rational Factory: Architecture, Technology, and Work in America's Age of Mass Production* (Baltimore, MD: Johns Hopkins University Press, 1996), pp. 85–87.

4   David E. Nye, *Electrifying America: Social Meanings of a New Technology, 1880–1940* (Cambridge, MA: MIT Press, 1990), pp. 185–237.

5   Berthold Hub, 'Architect versus Engineer: Monumentality versus Dematerialization', in Mario Rinke and Joseph Schwartz (eds), *Before Steel: The Introduction of Structural Iron and its Consequences* (Sulgen: Niggli Verlag, 2011), pp. 159–172.

6   For Peter Behrens' design of the AEG factories, see Stanford Anderson, *Peter Behrens and a New Architecture for the Twentieth Century* (Cambridge, MA: MIT Press, 2000), pp. 129–164.

7   Frederic J. Schwartz, *The Werkbund: Design Theory and Mass Culture before the First World War* (New Haven, CT: Yale University Press, 1996), pp. 55–60 and 179–191.

8   All translations from the original German texts are by the author, unless otherwise stated. Oskar Lasche, 'Die Elektrische Kraftverteilung in den Maschinebauwerkstaetten der Allgemeinen Elektricitaets-Gesellschaft, Berlin', *Z-VDI*, no. 5, 43 (1899), 113–121, no. 6, 141–154, no. 7, 178–182 (at p. 115).

9   See Oskar Lasche, 'Das Kraftwerk der AEG-Turbinenfabrik in Berlin', *Z-VDI*, no. 7, 53 (1909), 648–655.

10 Oskar Lasche, 'Elektrischer Einzelantrieb und seine Wirtschaftlichkeit', *Z-VDI*, no. 36, 44 (1900), 1189–1199, no. 37, 1242–1246, no. 38, 1279–1285 (at p. 1189).

11 Ibid., 117.

12 Ibid., 141.

13 Ibid.

14 Ibid., 144.

15 Ibid.

16 Ibid.

17 Oskar Lasche, 'Die neue Turbinenhalle der AEG', *AEG-Zeitung*, no. 7, 12 (1910), 1–4. Oskar Lasche, 'A Tour through the AEG Turbine Works', *AEG Journal*, no. 1, 1 (1911), 1–4, no. 2, 1–4, no. 3, 1–3 (at p. 1).

18 Oskar Lasche, 'Der Dampfturbinenbau der Allgemeinen Elektricitaets-Gesellschaft', *Z-VDI*, no. 10, 51 (1907), 385–388. Oskar Lasche, 'Die Turbinenfabrikation der AEG', *Z-VDI*, no. 29, 55 (1911), 1198–1206 (at p. 1199), no. 30, 1251–1260.

19 Otto Eichberg, 'Über eine Art Amerikanischer Werkstatt-Organisation (Das System Taylor)', *Werkstattstechnik*, no. 8, 1 (1907), 417–419 (at p. 417), no. 9, 459–462, no. 2, 2 (1908), 8–16.

20 Ibid., 418.

21 Peter Behrens, 'Die Turbinenhalle der AEG zu Berlin', *Deutsche Techniker-Zeitung*, no. 6, 27 (1910), 87–90. As reprinted in Tilmann Buddensieg and Henning Rogge, *Industriekultur: Peter Behrens and the AEG, 1907–1914* (Cambridge, MA: MIT Press, 1984), p. 211.

22 Richard Biernacki, *The Fabrication of Labor: Germany and Britain, 1640–1914* (Berkeley, CA: University of California Press, 1995), pp. 93–144 (at p. 125).

Chapter 25

An 'architecture of bureaucracy'

Technocratic planning of government architecture in Belgium in the 1930s

Jens van de Maele

Introduction

In 1936, the Belgian government charged the modernist architect Victor Bourgeois with the design of a new administrative building in the centre of Brussels. The building had to accommodate some departments of the so-called *Compte-Chèques Postaux* (CCP), the rapidly expanding national giro cheque administration. In the years following its establishment in 1913, the CCP had become a key player in the Belgian financial system by providing its customers with a free bank account and swift remittances. During the 1920s the CCP was seen as one of the best performing – or, to use a buzzword of the epoch, one of the most 'efficient' – enterprises of its kind. The internal functioning of the Dutch giro cheque administration, for instance, was modelled after its Belgian counterpart for some years.[1] Later on, the CCP actively promoted the self-image of a perfectly organised corporation at the sixth conference (Warsaw, 1936) of the International Institute of Administrative Sciences, a non-profit organisation that was devoted to the worldwide dissemination of knowledge on administrative management.[2] Yet, the quick growth of the Belgian CCP came at a cost. Already by the late 1920s, the headquarters of the corporation – which were located in a Beaux-Arts office building constructed between 1897 and 1905, close to the nation's Parliament – had become overcrowded, leaving its employees in unpleasant working conditions (Figure 25.1).[3] Hence, the decision to construct a large annex at the opposite side of the existing main office was essential for safeguarding the reputation of the CCP as a 'model' administration.

Figure 25.1
Clerks in the old CCP office building (c.1936). Archives of the Flemish Parliament, Brussels

Victor Bourgeois (1897–1962) was one of Belgium's most eminent modernist architects.[4] In the early 1920s he had designed a couple of state-sponsored social housing projects, including the *Cité Moderne* garden suburb in Brussels, which was quickly taken up by foreign architectural periodicals such as *Bauwelt* and *Das Werk*. From the mid-1920s onwards, Bourgeois had been one of the driving forces behind the Brussels-based *La Cambre* school, which offered an architectural education based on the premises of the international avant-garde. Bourgeois also took a central role within the *Congrès Internationaux d'Architecture Moderne* (CIAM), by co-presiding the first congress in La Sarraz and by organising CIAM III in Brussels (1930).[5] Yet, the CCP project was Bourgeois's first large-scale government commission. By choosing Bourgeois for this economically crucial project, the Belgian government endorsed the 'objective' and 'scientific' planning methods of the Modern Movement.[6] In particular, the internationally renowned socialist theoretician Henri de Man (1885–1953), who served as Public Works Minister (1935–1936) and Finance Minister (1936–1938), provided the decisive backing for the modernist cause. Being a strong proponent of a state-led economy, De Man highly valued technocratic knowledge. In his view, apolitical experts had the task of conducting studies on societal problems, and it was up to politicians to faithfully implement their conclusions.[7] Such a political constellation had always been favoured by prominent modernists like Le Corbusier, who had stated (in a 1933 letter to Siegfried Giedion) that the technical aspect of an architect's job could be equated with the task of 'preparing a plan' – while it was up to those who held political power to enable the 'execution of the plan'.[8] And indeed, as architectural historian Iwan Strauven has shown, Bourgeois – who had little experience with the construction of offices or semi-industrial premises – quickly started planning his task by compiling information on giro cheque administrations in different countries. In March 1936, for example, he wrote a letter to the aforementioned Siegfried Giedion, asking if he could send him information on any recent modernisations of the Swiss postal order system. 'I am studying the issue of giro cheque administration buildings, and I intend to visit all interesting realisations in this domain', Bourgeois announced to his Swiss CIAM colleague.[9]

However, it would turn out that modernists like Bourgeois were not the only ones who claimed to possess knowledge on 'rational' planning methods. From an early stage, the CCP construction project caught the special attention of Louis Camu (1905–1976), a high-ranked civil servant who had been appointed by the Belgian government as 'Royal Commissioner for Administrative Reform' in 1936 – just some months after Bourgeois had been asked to design the CCP building.[10] Like Henri de Man, Camu believed that technocratic expertise had to inform all political and administrative decisions. Up until the outbreak of the Second World War, he would analyse every aspect of the Belgian public service, including the administrations of ministries and state-owned corporations such as the CCP. Camu alleged in numerous official reports that the state administrations could be made more powerful and cost-efficient by implementing 'modern' principles of administrative management, which all revolved strongly around the notion of planning. In the wake of the heralds of Scientific Management (such as the American Frederick Winslow Taylor and his French counterpart Henri Fayol), Camu considered it essential that administrations improved the quality of their output, and got more work done – in a shorter time, with fewer employees. Although his task was, at first, largely consultative, he rose to being one of the most influential actors in Belgian politics by the end of the decade. From 1938 onwards Camu became responsible for the implementation of his reform proposals in the public administrations. This way, his power virtually surpassed that of a minister. Nevertheless, he always kept up the image of a politically neutral 'technocrat', merely concerned with strengthening the power and 'efficiency' of the democratic state.[11] As will become clear, it was almost inevitable that Camu's mission would come to clash with the planning task of Bourgeois and the CCP administration.

Conceiving an efficient government administration

One of the key elements in Camu's programme of administrative reform was the assertion that new office buildings had to be constructed for most of the state-led administrations. The Royal Commissioner considered the existing ministerial offices – which were often located in residential buildings from the eighteenth and nineteenth centuries – maladjusted to modern administrative work.[12] At the beginning of 1937 he requested Jean-Jules Eggericx and Raphaël Verwilghen, two modernist architects (and, as teachers at the La Cambre school, colleagues of Bourgeois), to draw up a plan for a representative, ultramodern office complex, which had to accommodate a large number of ministerial administrations. This so-called *cité administrative* had to provide about 60,000 square metres of office space, on an easily accessible location near the Parliament – and thus, coincidentally, near the existing CCP headquarters. Yet, Camu did not merely want to move administrations from old buildings to a new one. In a special report (1937) on the construction policies of the Belgian state, Camu explained that the removal had to go hand-in-hand with a thorough reorganisation of the departments, aimed at adopting 'rational working methods'.[13] This meant: raising the standards for recruitment and advancement, simplifying the organisation charts, rethinking unproductive routines, making more use of modern office equipment, and improving the workflows. In the same vein, Eggericx and Verwilghen believed that their *cité administrative* had to enable a rigorous work ethic, since the complex was to become 'as efficient as a factory' (Figure 25.2).[14]

Much in the same way as the British architect Leslie Martin conceived a (never-built) governmental office complex for London's Whitehall district during the 1960s,[15] Camu and his team of architects approached the task of designing the (equally never-built) *cité administrative* with an academic state of mind. Like Martin's 1965 report on Whitehall, Camu's second report on the government buildings – which dated from 1940 – resembled a 'scientific research paper', which meticulously attempted to determine the objective needs of the ministerial administrations (Figure 25.3).[16] Camu's report contained detailed studies on topics such as office depths and surfaces, climatisation systems, furniture, and (day)lighting. These studies led to one major conclusion: the majority of the civil servants had to be grouped together in generic 'open offices', ranging in capacity from four to sixteen employees. The internal layout was to be based on a *plan libre*, allowing the placement of flexible, glazed partition walls. Modifying these partitions, which would make the office complex future proof, could theoretically absorb any change in the administrative structure. In this way, Camu sought to override

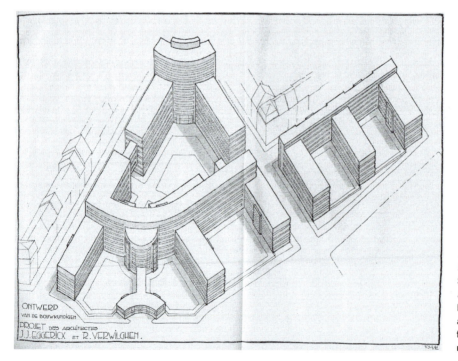

Figure 25.2
Sketch for a *cité administrative* in Brussels (J.-J. Eggericx and R. Verwilghen, 1937) from the 1937 Camu report

Figure 25.3
**Diagram from the 1940
Camu report, showing
the 'ideal' temperature
and humidity levels in
an office. University
Archives, Leuven**

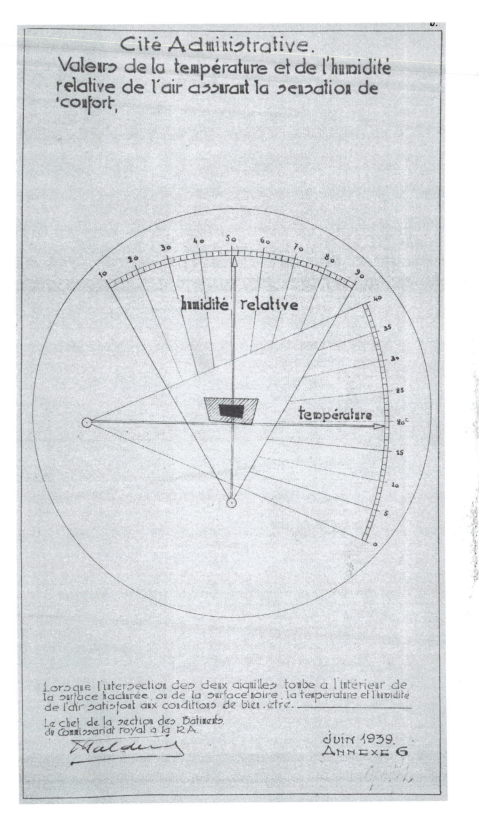

the 'subjective' demands of the civil servants themselves, who generally favoured private office spaces. Administrative experts almost unanimously condemned such private offices, since they were considered obstacles for an efficient workflow and supervision. This stance was probably best summarised by William Henry Leffingwell, one of the American pioneers of modern office management, who already stated in 1925: 'Granting privacy to individuals who do not need it is not only a wasteful practice in office arrangement, but actually lowers the general effectiveness of such individuals.'[17]

Although the Belgian Royal Commissioner eagerly followed the recommendations of his advisory architects Eggericx and Verwilghen, he also took a somewhat sceptical attitude towards architects as a professional group. In his 1937 report, he listed some recent examples of 'faulty' office architecture. In a brand new administrative building of the Ministry of Education, for instance, no 'open offices' had been foreseen, while an internal renovation of the Ministry of Justice headquarters had resulted in the installation of partition walls with opaque (instead of transparent) windows.[18] For these *faux pas*, Camu shifted the responsibility on to the office managers of the ministries involved, who had seemingly given the wrong instructions to their architects. Yet, his criticisms also implied that most architects were incapable of designing 'modern' and 'rational' offices as long as they did not cooperate with administrative experts like him. For Camu, designing buildings was to become, above all, a matter of teamwork – and this was a position most members of the architectural avant-garde would gladly have agreed with. Yet, in Camu's view, the role of the architect was not *superior* to those of other experts. The input of 'administrative scientists' was equally essential, since both types of expertise complemented each other. Again, W.H. Leffingwell had expressed a similar view in his 1925 manual on office management:

> Mistakes in the actual design of a building . . . are almost always entirely avoidable by the owner, if he will but devote a sufficient amount of thought to the problem and insist that his requirements shall be met in the designing of the building . . . It has long been evident that many architects either cannot or will not design a factory building that is efficient, and modern factory buildings are now constructed by architects and engineers working in conjunction . . . In like manner, it is now being gradually recognized that the proper construction of an office building also requires technical knowledge of office procedure and office needs, and architects are either bringing in technical office experts to cooperate with them, or having them thrust upon them by wise executives . . .[19]

In late 1930s Belgium, Camu did not want to rely on contingencies such as the 'wisdom' of executives or the personal initiative of private architects. Instead, he sought to establish a permanent body within the Public Works Department, which would have the sole responsibility for the construction, renovation, and acquisition of all governmental office buildings. This proposed body had to employ a number of specialised architects, as well as 'an expert on administrative organisation, who would be bestowed with authority by the Prime Minister'. Interestingly, this authoritative figure was to impose his managerial views on both the ministerial departments *and* the architects. Lastly, the aesthetic component of future architectural projects would have to be taken under scrutiny by the 'artistic counsellor' of the Public Works Department (who was, at that time, no one less than Henry van de Velde).[20] Within this framework, private architects could still be given specific commissions – but it is clear that the authorship would have to be shared by several contributors. Some ten years before the American architectural critic Henry-Russell Hitchcock made his famous defence for an 'architecture of bureaucracy', Camu thus propagated the establishment of a 'bureaucratic' model for designing buildings, which did not favour any architect's personal expression, but rather the collaborative effort of different experts. While Hitchcock would (no doubt rightfully) claim in his 1947 essay that the Public Works Ministries in most countries were too 'feebly organised' to produce an 'architecture of bureaucracy' (unlike large private corporations, such as Albert Kahn's firm), Camu's pleas for a governmental architecture agency could be seen as an early attempt to overcome this 'feebleness'.[21]

Louis Camu and the CCP project

In December 1937, the CCP administration appointed a contractor for the construction of the annex building designed by Bourgeois. Yet, in February 1938, when the preparation of the building site was already far advanced, Public Works Minister Joseph Merlot urged to halt the construction process immediately. Merlot – whom Camu had probably alarmed – feared that the new CCP building would compromise the planned construction of the *cité administrative,* which was to be located in the same area.[22] As Désiré Bouchery, the Minister of Communications (and responsible for the CCP), was strongly opposed to this sudden intervention,[23] Camu organised a meeting with all parties involved in order to reconcile their differences. At this meeting Camu insisted that all CCP services would have to be located in a single 'ultra-modern building', instead of two separate ones. Furthermore, he requested that Bourgeois would cooperate with the architects Eggericx and Verwilghen, to make sure that the new CCP complex would harmonise well with the future *cité administrative.*[24] Although his power was – at that time – theoretically limited, Camu was able to exert a large degree of (informal) influence, and he managed to impose his proposals on the CCP administration. Already one month later, in March 1938, Bourgeois – who had been assisted by Eggericx and Verwilghen – presented a new master plan for a single CCP headquarters building, which was thereupon approved by Camu, Merlot, and Bouchery.[25]

Despite the fruitful outcome of this meeting, it seems that Camu had developed a certain distrust towards Bourgeois. In July 1938, the Royal Commissioner proposed – in a letter to the Ministry of Communications – that the architect be removed from the job, in favour of Eggericx and Verwilghen.[26] This proposal could, of course, be regarded as a strategy to benefit Camu's own *protégés,* but it seems that Camu was also genuinely concerned that Bourgeois and the CCP administration were unable to design a sufficiently 'rational' office building. In the end, Camu agreed that Bourgeois would stay on the job, although it was decided that all construction drawings had to be reviewed by a specific committee prior to their execution. This committee – which was to be monitored closely by a delegate of Camu – had to make sure that the 'principles for the internal organisation and the functionality of the workspaces' would be identical to those applied in the future *cité administrative*.[27] As such, Camu found himself again in pole position to influence the CCP project. Over the course of the following months, the committee – which, apart from Camu's assistant Marcel Malderez, also included Bourgeois, Eggericx, Verwilghen, and Henry van de Velde – assembled regularly, discussing themes such as the type of stone used for the façade cladding, the position of the building, and the location of stairs, elevators, and toilets.[28] Consequently, substantial aspects of Bourgeois's original plans were turned into a kind of flexible matrix, which could be modified at the discretion of the committee's members. In this new constellation, Bourgeois *de facto* became one of the 'counselling architects' (*architectes-conseils*) of the CCP project, next to Eggericx and Verwilghen.[29] The architectural 'team' – so cherished by administrative experts like Leffingwell and Camu – had become tangible.

Yet, even after the establishment of the aforementioned committee, Camu remained displeased by the fact that the CCP did not draw up any detailed plans on the internal circulation of goods and employees – which made it impossible to adequately judge if the workflows in the future building would be up to the standards of modern administrative science. In June 1939, the Royal Commissioner wrote rather vindictively – and not without pretension – in an official report:

> The methods used to elaborate the building's plan, its technical infrastructure and cost estimation are deplorable. The foundations have been realised, but at the same time no plans have been made regarding the interior, lighting, power supply, transportation, workflows, and furniture. There is no general plan concerning the internal disposition and the organisation of the services that should be provided in the building.[30]

These imputations were countered by Hendrik Marcq, the new Public Works Minister, who stressed that the CCP building would be built according to the principle of the *plan libéré*: a generic floor plan, which – according to Marcq – neutralised the need for detailed preparatory studies on the internal dispositions.[31] Ironically, Camu, who was a strong propagator of the *plan libéré* in the context of his *cité administrative* project, now saw the arguments for this concept turn against him. The Royal Commissioner had always considered the open floor plan as an indispensable means for managerial flexibility, allowing easy and 'rational' rearrangements in office space. Marcq, however, pushed this notion to the extreme. As most parts of the CCP building were basically an assembly of stacked, empty floors, why would it not be possible to start building *before* determining the particulars of the internal arrangement? Here it becomes clear that the concepts of 'flexibility' and 'rationality' could be construed very differently among administrators. Notwithstanding Camu's recurrent criticisms, the CCP administration pursued the construction of the new headquarters building in 1939, and by the end of 1940 it had completed the basic structure. Because of the Second World War, further construction works could only be undertaken after 1945 – without any further interference of Camu, who had left the civil service during the war. The building was finally inaugurated in 1949, and would effectively serve as the CCP headquarters until the mid-1990s (Figure 25.4).[32]

Figure 25.4
The building upon completion (*c.*1950), as shown in *La technique des travaux* (May/June 1950)

Figure 25.5
The rear side of the counters in the new CCP building, equipped with pneumatic dispatch (*c.*1950–1960). Archives of the Flemish Parliament, Brussels

Conclusion

In 1950, the French architecture magazine *La technique des travaux* described the new CCP building in great detail. The editor concluded that the edifice met all architectural and functional standards with great effectiveness, as it was provided with a centrally located 'internal tower', which grouped together most of the building's technical equipment – including goods lifts, a paternoster lift, and a pneumatic dispatch, which assured the connection between the public counters and the processing departments (Figure 25.5).[33] These were all techniques that had been propagated throughout the interwar era by the International Institute of Administrative Sciences, which was actively supported by Louis Camu. Yet, it is unclear to what extent the Royal Commissioner's interferences in the design process of the CCP building have effectively contributed to the exemplary final result. His often biting and impatient interferences, which were indeed aimed at the creation of an 'architecture of bureaucracy' for governmental bureaucracies, do reveal clearly that the aura of the architect as a general expert had become undermined in 1930s Belgium. While so-called 'rational' planning methods and principles of Scientific Management were advocated by many 'administrative scientists', architects, and politicians alike, the notions of these concepts could encompass – together with points of view held in common – crucial aspects revealing individual interpretations.

As Mauro F. Guillén has shown in his historical study on the relationships between modernist architecture and the ideology of Scientific Management during the first half of the twentieth century, modernists believed in 'a vertically stratified organisation of work and decision-making based on the principle of specialisation'.[34] Yet, architects were not the only ones who aspired to take the lead in this nexus of specialisations. The challenges created by a highly technological and administratively complex architectural programme clearly required a multidisciplinary approach, but it was still undecided how authority had to be shared among the different experts. Postulating the need for 'rational' planning methods did not necessarily lead to a consensus – let alone to smooth professional or personal relations between the experts involved. Architecture remained the work of man, after all.

Notes

1   Cita Hartvelt, *Moderne zakelijkheid: Efficiency in wonen en werken in Nederland, 1918–1940* (Amsterdam: Het Spinhuis, 1994), pp. 99–117. All translations by the author throughout.
2   'L'organisation du travail à l'Office Belge des Chèques et Virements Postaux', in *Compte rendu du VI-ième Congrès International des Sciences Administratives* (Warsaw: International Institute of Administrative Sciences, 1936), pp. 513–528.
3   Brussels, National Archives of Belgium (NAB), Records of the Office National pour l'Achèvement de la Jonction Nord-Midi, Box 37, Inv. no. 20/34: Report by Castiau for the Minister of Communications (18 September 1929); NAB, Records of the Commissariat Royal à la Réforme Administrative (CRRA), Inv. no. 25: Report by Houtman (15 July 1939).
4   For a concise overview on Bourgeois' life and work, see Iwan Strauven, *Les frères Bourgeois: Architecture et plastique pure* (Brussels: Archives d'Architecture Moderne, 2005).
5   Ibid., pp. 28–33.
6   On the notion of modernist architects and urban planners as technocratic, 'objective' and 'scientific' experts, see Mauro F. Guillén, *The Taylorized Beauty of the Mechanical: Scientific Management and the Rise of Modernist Architecture* (Princeton, NJ: Princeton University Press, 2006).

7   Hendrik de Man, 'De uitvoering van het Plan van de Arbeid', in *Hendrik de Man: Persoon en ideeën (IV: Planisme)*, ed. by Piet Frantzen (Antwerp and Amsterdam: Standaard Wetenschappelijke Uitgeverij, 1975), pp. 98–99.

8   Cited by Jacques Aron, *La Cambre et l'architecture: Un regard sur le Bauhaus belge* (Brussels: Mardaga, 1982), p. 75.

9   Cited by Iwan Strauven, 'Victor Bourgeois (1897–1962): Radicaliteit en pragmatisme, moderniteit en traditie (part 2)' (unpublished doctoral thesis, Ghent University, 2015), p. 211.

10   On Camu, see Bénédicte Rochet, 'L'impact de la seconde guerre mondiale sur les pratiques administratives', *Pyramides*, 10 (2005), 167–188.

11   See, for instance, Louis Camu, 'La Belgique de demain: La réforme administrative, un des grands problèmes du moment', *Revue Internationale des Sciences Administratives*, 11 (1938), 5–30.

12   Louis Camu, *Rapport sur les bâtiments des administrations centrales de l'État* (Brussels: n. pub., 1937).

13   Ibid., p. 4.

14   Brussels, Archives d'Architecture Moderne (AAM), Records of Jean-Jules Eggericx, Inv. no. 296: *Rapport concernant la construction eventuelle d'immeubles de bureaux pour les administrations de l'État* (internal report by Eggericx and Verwilghen, April 1937).

15   Adam Sharr and Stephen Thornton, *Demolishing Whitehall: Leslie Martin, Harold Wilson and the Architecture of White Heat* (Farnham: Ashgate, 2013).

16   AAM, Eggericx Records, Inv. no. 296: *Mémoire sur les bâtiments administratifs* (unpublished official report by Camu and Malderez, January 1940); Sharr and Thornton, *Demolishing Whitehall*, p. 63.

17   William Henry Leffingwell, *Office Management: Principles and Practice* (Chicago, New York, and London: A.W. Show, 1925), p. 293.

18   Camu, *Rapport sur les bâtiments*, p. 18.

19   Leffingwell, *Office Management*, pp. 281–282.

20   Camu, *Rapport sur les bâtiments*, pp. 22–23 and 45–49.

21   Henry-Russell Hitchcock, 'The Architecture of Bureaucracy and the Architecture of Genius', *Architectural Review*, 101 (1947), 3–6.

22   NAB, CRRA Records, Inv. no. 25: Letter by Merlot to Bouchery (9 February 1938).

23   NAB, CRRA Records, Inv. no. 25: Letter by Bouchery to Janson (9 February 1938).

24   NAB, CRRA Records, Inv. no. 25: Meeting minutes (17 February 1938).

25   NAB, CRRA Records, Inv. no. 25: Meeting minutes (5 March 1938), and report by Camu (23 May 1939).

26   NAB, CRRA Records, Inv. no. 25: Letter by Camu to Rigaux (25 July 1938).

27   NAB, CRRA Records, Inv. no. 25: Letter by Camu to Rigaux (28 July 1938), and memorandum by Camu (28 July 1938).

28   See for instance NAB, CRRA Records, Inv. no. 25: Letters by Camu to Marcq (29 July 1938; 26 September 1938), letter by Marcq to Camu (5 August 1938), meeting minutes (11 October 1938), and letter by Camu to Meunier (22 October 1938).

29   NAB, CRRA Records, Inv. no. 25: Letter by Bourgeois to Malderez (27 March 1939), and letter by the CCP administration to Malderez (28 March 1939).

30   Louis Camu, *Commissariat Royal à la Réforme Administrative: Rapport annuel, 1er juin 1938 – 1er juin 1939* (n.p.: n. pub., 1939), p. 26. Camu made similar remarks in letters to the Minister of Public Works: NAB, CRRA Records, Inv. no. 25: Letters by Camu to Marcq (23 February 1939 and 7 April 1939).

31   NAB, CRRA Records, Inv. no. 25: Letter by Marcq to Camu (12 April 1939).

32   For an architectural analysis of the finished building, see Iwan Strauven, 'The National Giro Bank Building of Victor Bourgeois' (unpublished paper, 2003), http://hdl.handle.net/1854/lu-322638 (accessed 24 March 2015).

33   L. Novgorodsky, 'Le nouvel immeuble des Chèques Postaux à Bruxelles', *La technique des travaux*, 26 (1950), 130–146.

34   Guillén, *The Taylorized Beauty of the Mechanical*, p. 19.

Chapter 26

Laboratory architecture and the deep membrane of science

Sandra Kaji-O'Grady and Chris L. Smith

The word 'laboratory' derives from the Medieval Latin *laboratorium*, a place for labour. What constitutes scientific labour today and where it takes place has become increasingly polarised. Mythologies of serendipitous discovery enabled by increased socialisation have seen the scientist lured from the bench and into conversation on the stair, in the foyer and café. The ensuing division between the laboratory proper and the spaces of chatter is mirrored in the bifurcations of architectural labour between laboratory planners and design architects. These divisions of scientific and architectural labour are spatially configured and coincident with the glass envelopes that secure biological contaminants. This chapter investigates this spatial bifurcation and attends to its aesthetic and theoretical ramifications. The glazed envelope, belonging to both territories, and to neither, is investigated through the discourse of the membrane that extends from Gilbert Simondon's sense that 'interiority and exteriority are everywhere'.[1]

Only in the seventeenth century, with the emergence of the scientific method, does the word 'laboratory' refer to a place set apart for scientific experiments. By the nineteenth century, laboratories are becoming specialised places aligned with industrial cities and scientific markets.[2] As experimental set-ups required more people and more specialised expertise, internal spatial arrangements reflected the hierarchical division of scientific labour: technicians at the bench and scientists supervising from adjacent enclosed offices. From the late nineteenth to the late twentieth century, laboratory buildings largely resembled factories. Scientific ideals of rationality and fitness for purpose intersected with the functionalist strands of architectural modernism. Oswald W. Grube suggests that the laboratories of the post-war period in America were

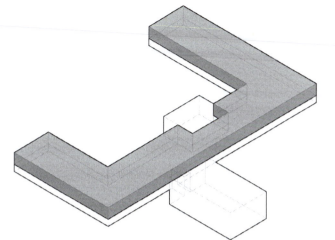

Figure 26.1
Alex P. Morgan, Johnson
& Johnson Laboratory,
configuration of
laboratories within
the building volume.
Illustration: Sandra
Kaji-O'Grady and Chris
L. Smith

lynchpins of modernism in the same way that factories and other industrial buildings were in Europe in the 1930s.[3] He argues that the laboratory shared with industrial buildings, modernist planning principles that yielded open spaces served by separate offices and service zones.[4] Alex P. Morgan's 1952 Johnson & Johnson Research Center, New Jersey, is typical in its distinct division between a large functional laboratory and a small administrative wing (Figure 26.1). This modernist turn was concurrent with discoveries within medical science about the circulation of germs in the late nineteenth century, leading to the transformation of the laboratory into the hygienic space of seamless washable surfaces and impermeable materials that characterised the laboratory throughout the twentieth century.

Louis Kahn's Salk Institute, La Jolla, California, of 1965 is perhaps the first laboratory that successfully departs from a pure functionalist paradigm and deploys architecture as a tool of persuasion and human resource management. The distinct innovation of the contemporary laboratory, which the Salk initiates, is that it serves not only a utilitarian role but that it also operates as a mode of expression: communicating directly to the public, funding bodies and governments, and also to scientists themselves. Architecture now plays an active and self-conscious role in expressing the ideas and ideologies of research activity both to an outside audience and internally. Scientific institutions across the world have been investing heavily in buildings that have as one of their key design ambitions the engineering of internal face-to-face communication. Architects, facility managers and scientists share the belief that buildings might serve to increase socialisation between scientists and thus, quicken the process of discovery. In light of this shift in emphasis, the twenty-first-century laboratory no longer resembles a factory in form, operation or content. Rhetoric around new research facilities suggests that their primary purpose is to urge the scientist into conversation. Pharmacologist Jordi Cami, head of the Parc de Recerca Biomedica de Barcelona, asserts of his purpose-built facility, 'the great purpose of this architecture is to provide spaces for relation and communication'.[5] Professor Kim Nasmyth suggests that the new Biochemistry Building at the University of Oxford, 'allows conversations to happen that wouldn't otherwise take place in a thousand years'.[6] The contemporary laboratory, Nigel Thrift proposes, is 'intended to produce performative, interdisciplinary machines'.[7] It is a 'soft' machine of socialisation in which architecture elicits, regulates and renders visible scientific exchange both to an exterior and interior.

Bifurcations of the profession

The labour of the architectural profession engaged in laboratory design has bifurcated in response to these shifting ambitions. Specialised architectural practices ensure the functionality of the internal wet laboratory proper: they specify its proprietary furnishings, fixtures and finishes in accordance with complex requirements of physical containment and certification; establish and fulfil its equipment and storage needs; organise the flow and containment of services, materials and personnel for experiments in and out of the laboratory; and ensure the laboratory's durability and future flexibility. 'Design' architects shape the surrounding 'rhetorical' spaces of research buildings – expressing in words, images, spaces and surfaces the conversational and convivial aspirations of the scientific organisation. These architects are responsible for the lounges, cafés, courtyards, terraces, atria, auditoria and meeting rooms that now occupy a significant proportion of the volume and capital cost of laboratory buildings; and for the external expression, the façades and public faces of the research facilities.

Invariably, the design of research buildings now requires two different kinds of architects working in association. Will Alsop teamed with Amec on the Blizard Building for Queen Mary University in Whitechapel, London. Gruner AG undertook the planning for the laboratories of Actelion Pharmaceuticals in Basel (2010) for which Herzog & de Meuron are the named architects. For the Novartis Pharma Basel laboratories WSJ-355 by David Chipperfield and WSJ-352 by Tadao Ando, Swiss veterans in the design of laboratory buildings – Burckhardt & Partner – were engaged as collaborators. The British firm of Hopkins Architects designed Princeton University's Frick Chemistry Laboratory (2012) with Payette of Boston and Jacobs Consultancy undertaking the laboratory planning. At Janelia Farm Research Campus in Virginia (2007), Rafael Viñoly worked with San Diego-based Research Facilities Design (RFD). Established in 1984, RFD has worked with Foster & Partners on several projects, including the Sir Alexander Fleming Building in London (1998), the Center for Clinical Science Research at Stanford University (1995) and the MASDAR Institute of Science and Technology (2010). With SOM, RFD undertook the Genome Sciences Building for the University of North Carolina (2012).

The severance of the functional and expressive aspects of architecture in the design of contemporary laboratories led to the founding of several similar specialised laboratory planning consultancies in the 1970s and 1980s, such as RFD and HERA. Simultaneously, several large conglomerate architectural and engineering practices – KlingStubbins (since acquired by Jacobs Engineering Group), Payette, Perkins & Will, and Bohlin Cywinski Jackson, for example – developed significant departments focused on laboratory design. The division between pragmatics and ambience plays out at Janelia Farm, where Rafael Viñoly Architects also worked with Bob McGhee, the in-house architect for the client, the Howard Hughes Medical Institute. Campus director, Gerry Rubin, who describes the project as 'a project of social engineering' recalls that 'Our trustees felt very comfortable hiring a visionary architect because we had Bob McGhee, who is an expert on lab design. He could push back to make sure the building would meet its scientific function.'[8]

Membranes regenerating polarities

This split is at once a division of scientific labour, a division of architectural investment and a spatial division. However, the split is not so simple as the image of a glass envelope might suggest. These envelopes, which secure biological contaminants to an interior and, at the building's exterior, seal spaces of chatter from the outside, also operate as a site of transference: expressing the activities, ideas and ideologies of interiors to exteriors, and vice versa. In many respects the spatial bifurcation between the laboratory proper and its surrounds operates as a complex membrane, a thick membrane or what Simondon might refer to as a 'parcelled haecceity'.[9] Gilles Deleuze would extend Simondon's idea in suggesting that:

> membranes are no less important for they carry potentials and regenerate polarities. They place internal and external spaces into contact without regard to distance. The internal and the external, depth and height, have biological significance only through this topological surface of contact. Thus, even biologically it is necessary to understand that 'the deepest is the skin'.[10]

In order to consider the complex depth of the skin of the laboratory it is necessary to look closely at how architects and laboratory planners demarcate their individual contributions and how such contributions manifest topologically. Cornell University's Weill Hall is typical in its program, funding and institutional context (Figure 26.2). Weill Hall is a central part of Cornell University's Genomics initiative and brings together researchers who had previously occupied twelve separate buildings.[11] It houses 500 staff and cost $162 million, a large part of which was philanthropic funding from Joan and Sanford Weill, who continue to fund its research activities.[12] When completed in 2009 it was one of the largest research facilities in New York State. Its crisp geometry and white aluminium cladding, arranged in a 3 x 3 grid, is consistent with the work of its architect Richard Meier, a Cornell alumnus. Meier lays out his priorities for the building in an interview: 'The labs and the offices are fairly straightforward. What's important to me is how people get together – how they congregate, and how they see one another and interact with one another in the building, and how to create an ambience in which there is an interdisciplinary conversation.'[13] Jacobs Consultancy, a specialised division of Jacobs Engineering, were used to realise the laboratories at Weill Hall. Jacobs Consultancy boast of having 'planned and designed more than 250 laboratory facilities' and '50 million square feet of lab and vivarium space' since they began in 1978. The office has designed laboratories for buildings by numerous architects, including Mitchell/

Giurgola, SOM, ZGF Architects and Polshek Partnership. Their description of the building and its requirements is significantly different to Meier's:

> To achieve the objective of a highly flexible and adaptable facility, the labs floors are designed to accommodate generic and generic/customised units with repetitive, prototypical laboratory modules and adaptable systems and furniture. To promote formal and informal interaction the design includes conference rooms and break rooms, as well as circulation elements to stimulate interaction amongst researchers. [14]

There is unusual consistency at Weill Hall between the aesthetic of the laboratory and other spaces, since Meier's retro-modernism aspires to the hygienic and rational aesthetic associated with spaces of science. Many contemporary laboratory buildings, however, exhibit startling formal and stylistic dissonance between the laboratory proper and the surrounding program. The South Australian Health and Medical Research Institute (SAHMRI) designed by Woods Bagot and opened in 2013 would be a case in point (Figure 26.3). This formal dissonance occurs regardless of whether the division of labour is between two practices or within a single firm. While at the scale of the building, new research buildings exhibit heterogeneity, the laboratory itself has solidified into a generic form with proprietary furniture and fixtures. In countless examples, the laboratory proper is enclosed by frameless, non-reflective, floor-to-ceiling plate glass. This tactic achieves a symbolic disintegration of the laboratory envelope and, like a museum vitrine, puts the scientist on display but out of reach (Figure 26.4). The glazed envelope is a compromise between the need for physical containment and the desire for visual transparency, motivated by institutional aversion to secrecy and public interest in informational transparency, albeit metaphoric. And this would seem to be the point: to 'regenerate polarities'.

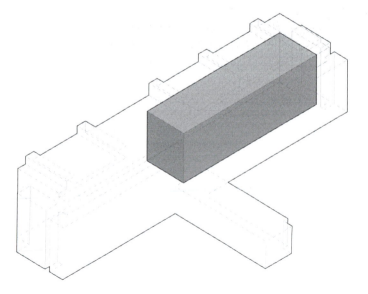

Figure 26.2
Weill Hall, configuration of laboratories within the building volume. Illustration: Sandra Kaji-O'Grady and Chris L. Smith

Figure 26.3
SAHMRI exterior.
Photograph: Sandra
Kaji-O'Grady

Figure 26.4
View of the PC2 bridge
between laboratories at
SAHMRI, showing the
stretched membranes of
glazed walls internally.
Photograph: Sandra
Kaji-O'Grady

The envelope of the laboratory is thus defended, its openings secured, and the difference between its internal atmosphere and neighbouring atmospheres is tightly regulated. These controls and regulations concern the negotiation of noxious risks that different microorganisms present to other organisms, research personnel and the public. The World Health Organization classifies microorganisms into four risk levels, and the Biosafety level and physical containment certification of laboratory buildings, classified as PC1 through PC4, correspond to these risk levels. The highest level of containment, PC4, houses diseases that presently have no known cure, such as the Marburg and Ebola viruses. PC3 is for pathogens that usually cause serious human, plant or animal disease and could present a risk if spread in the community or environment. HIV is considered risk group three. For PC2 to PC4,

> The facility to be certified must be a fully enclosable space bounded by walls, doors, windows, floors and ceilings . . . This barrier protects all spaces outside the facility, including internal spaces of buildings in which a certified facility is located, and the environment.[15]

What seems to become important in the guidelines for certification of a Physical Containment Laboratory is the 'viability' of the contaminants that might transgress the membrane.[16] That is, the ability of the contaminant to spread, self-reproduce or propagate. The limits of this space are programmatically secured by swipe card access, along with protocols of scientific dress and behaviour. They are atmospherically managed to eliminate the flow of air out of the laboratory and to prevent any seepage.

Membranes carrying potentials

These membranes that 'regenerate polarities' also 'carry potentials'. That is, on closer examination the envelopes are all about transmission and are particularly porous. If we depart from the idea that the laboratory proper is sealed then we must consider what is actually 'contained' within that laboratory. Strangely, the only real thing that is contained in a laboratory is a contaminant; whether biological or chemical. If this is the case, then everything else that comes to occupy a laboratory negotiates the membrane. People, personal protective equipment, furniture, fittings, biological material, waste, water pipes and sinks, electricity cables and conduits, air, ductwork, specialised equipment, machines and all sorts of biological and chemical material negotiate the membrane between the laboratory proper and exterior spaces. This may be why so much space in guidelines is dedicated to describing the importing, transportation and disposal of that which might carry contaminants into and out of a laboratory. These same guidelines tend to concentrate not on the laboratory itself but on the practices and procedures of the management of the laboratory, the potential for contamination and the ease of decontamination in the worst-case scenarios. Air locks, barrier seals, HEPA filters, fumigation chambers, dunk tanks, drainage traps, backflow prevention mechanisms, barrier seal autoclaves and observation windows, as well as inner and outer change rooms, are all

Figure 26.5
SAHMRI, configuration
of laboratories within
the building volume.
Illustration: Sandra
Kaji-O'Grady and Chris
L. Smith

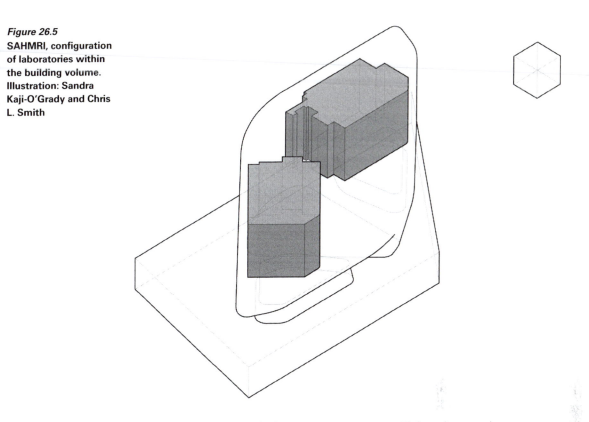

about negotiating the barrier in a very porous manner. All these items and areas occupy the membrane. That is, they are not of the inside or outside but very much part of the complex depth of the membrane. The membrane is thus a particularly deep, complex and managed porosity.

The membrane is also topologically dynamic in the sense that it is extended in all the sealed containers that move in and out of the laboratory. This complex relation of interior and exterior milieu in the contemporary laboratory building is an odd inversion of the functioning of the membrane of the living organism where, for Simondon, even that which might be thought of as interior and in need of containment becomes 'annexed exteriority':

> According to the topology of the living organism, the interior of the intestine is in fact exterior to the organism, even though it accomplishes in this space a certain number of transformations conditioned and controlled by organic functions; this space is an annexed exteriority; thus if the contents of the stomach or intestine are noxious for the organism, the coordinated movements that direct the expulsion finish by emptying these cavities and rejecting into the completely (independently) exterior space the noxious substances which were previously in the exterior space annexed to the interiority.[17]

The *raison d'être* of the laboratory lies in the management of variables – vibration, moisture, noise, dust, light, heat, bacteria, unauthorised people – that are not a defined part of the experimental set-up; along with the containment of all materials and waste products that pertain to the experiment. The laboratory is, or has been, a single-program space with a tightly managed envelope that brings together the materials, subjects, funds and equipment of the experimental apparatus with the scientists and laboratory assistants that generate, implement and analyse the experimental process. As the meeting point between the pragmatic responsibilities of the laboratory planner and the theatrical ambitions assigned to the design architect, the glazed envelope operates as a frontier. However, 'Even the frontier is not a serration but rather the element of an articulation' as Deleuze suggests.[18] The self-effacing quality of its materiality, its transparency and continuity, sets out to visually discount the physical border that it, in fact, enacts *between* two very different modalities of scientific labour. It denies its own existence, yet in doing so the opposed interior qualities of adjacent spaces are made more apparent; as we see them together without a visual pause. On the laboratory side, washable, chemically resistant hard surfaces in neutral tones, task lighting and regularly placed laboratory benches, establish an atmosphere of clinical efficiency. On the other side can be seen the architects' efforts to make convivial workspaces with bright colours and soft furniture arranged for conversation, carpeting, unpainted timber and softer lighting. Instead of a *Gesumtkunstwerk*, the research building presents as a 'parcelled haecceity'.

The drive for laboratories to present a 'public face', an engagement with exteriors means that a large part of the transmissions that a laboratory membrane must negotiate are also representational – about communication and expression. Though we might consider the laboratory as biologically secured, the complex membranes that operate between wet laboratories, the spaces of chatter and building envelopes are ideologically infected, 'carrying potentials' for the driving home of messages related to the bio-medical endeavour either quietly, as in Weill Hall, or with a shout, like SAHMRI. Such messages are conveyed to those who operate on the inside, and to the exterior that sustains the interior with public and private investment funds, public support, talent and knowledge.

Conclusions

Scientific labour has slid into the physical manipulation of experimental materials and generation of data (the wet lab), the dissemination and analysis of results (the dry lab), and the work done in constructing the scaffolding of experimentation – writing grants, attracting sponsorship and philanthropy, recruiting students and staff, delivering public lectures, staffing open days and other events. Threaded between the conceptualisation of a scientific question and the translation of findings is the less precise, but heavily emphasised, activity of talking, of expressing ideas. The research building surrounds the laboratory within spaces for chatter – conversation nooks, 'break out' spaces, meeting rooms, foyers, cafés and auditoria. The divisions of labour enacted by scientists and their architects that are mirrored and intertwined as solitude and socialising, interior and exterior, are folded together.

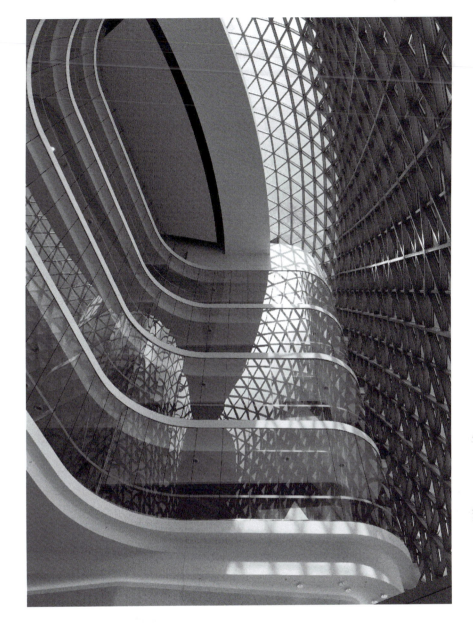

Figure 26.6
Interstitial spaces between successive exterior and interior glazed membranes at SAHMRI. Photograph: Sandra Kaji-O'Grady

Like the Möbius strip or the Klein bottle, the laboratory research building comprises successive folds of containment and transmission. The deepening of the membrane between the laboratory enclosure and the building's exterior surface suggests a deepening of the zone between expression and content. Hence, the surfaces of the contemporary laboratory building have become the site of intense manipulation. We find it dressed in patterns intended to resemble chromosome mapping or the periodic table and wallpapered with images of cells and organs and other literal diagrams of science. Between this surface and that of the wet laboratories are the spaces in which the public is admitted as an audience for the performance of science, the glazed wall of the laboratory framing experimentation like a proscenium arch. The scientist herself occupies the interstitial space as a player, liberated from the stage to devise impromptu scenes with other scientists. In these pre-scripted spaces, 'Two scientists working on two pieces of research could bump into each other in the corridor and have a eureka moment, and say, my God, there's the possibility of some really interesting scientific breakthrough here' as Sainsbury Laboratory architect Alan Stanton claims.[19] For him, 'The building is there to try to ambush scientists into meeting and talking.'[20]

The so-called public interface is, then, a space of rhetoric and social management. In turn, the architect of this realm is an image-maker who renders science palatable for consumption and an inventor of lures that tempt the scientist away from the bench. The laboratory planner, by contrast, is set up as a logistician, a sort of arch-scientist who gathers together the machinery of experimentation. Between the two lies the deep membrane of the laboratory vitrine, a slippery surface that is both inside and outside and neither. The scientist may have escaped her bench and be outside the laboratory proper but she remains at work regenerating polarities and carrying potentials, all the while, still within the annexed exterior of the laboratory.

Notes

1   Gilbert Simondon, *L'Individu et sa genèse physico-biologique* (Grenoble: Jérome Millon, 1995), p. 159.
2   Bruno Latour, 'The Costly Ghastly Kitchen', in *The Laboratory Revolution in Medicine*, ed. by Andrew Cunningham and Perry Williams (Cambridge: Cambridge University Press, 1992), p. 299.
3   Oswald Grube, 'The Birth of the Modern Research Building in the USA', in *Principles of Research and Technology Buildings*, ed. by Hardo Braun and Dieter Grömling (Basel: Birkhauser, 2005), p. 21.
4   Mellon Hall of Science at Duquesne University in Pittsburgh, designed by Mies van der Rohe and awarded the 'Laboratory of the Year' in 1969 by *Industrial Research Magazine*, exemplifies the fit between a late modernist architecture of rational organisation and industrial construction. It deftly conveys the scientific ideal of neutral inquiry pursued dispassionately by experts using logical methods. Like most laboratories of the era, Mellon Hall was constructed and owned by a single entity, in this case a university, was located outside the city, was inaccessible to the public and was used by a single discipline. The twentieth-century laboratory exhibited a dry functional character, visual impermeability and a complete absence of facilities for public engagement.
5   Jordi Cami, 'Introduction', in *Parc de Recerca Biomedica de Barcelona*, ed. by Manuel Brullet, Albert de Pineda and Alfonso de Luna (Barcelona: Edicions de l'Eixample, 2007), p. 12.
6   Kim Nasmyth quoted in 'New Biochemistry Building Opens', www.ox.ac.uk/media/news_stories/2008/081212_1.html (accessed 27 March 2012).
7   Nigel Thrift, 'Re-inventing Invention: New Tendencies in Capitalist Commodification', *Economy and Society* 2, 35 (2006), 279–306 (at p. 293).
8   Stephen Zacks, 'The DNA of Science Labs', *Metropolis Magazine*, February 2007, www.metropolismag.com/February-2007/The-DNA-of-Science-Labs/ (accessed 3 September 2014).
9   Gilbert Simondon, *L'individu et sa genèse physico-biologique* (Paris: Presses Universitaires de France, 1964), p. 52.
10 Gilles Deleuze, *Logic of Sense* (New York: Columbia University Press, 1990), p. 103.
11 PhotoSynthesis Productions, 'Weill Hall Dedication', 15 December 2008, www.youtube.com/watch?v=J3uwNFtblxs (accessed 24 August 2014).
12 'Major Private Gifts to Higher Education', *The Chronicle of Higher Education*, 25 August 2014. http://chronicle.com/article/Major-Private-Gifts-to-Higher/128264/ (accessed 24 August 2014). Since 1998, Mr Weill and his wife, Joan, and the Weill Family Foundation, have given more than $600 million to Weill Cornell Medical College and Cornell University to promote new medical discoveries, research and cures. (They have also made large contributions to Carnegie Hall and the Alvin Ailey American Dance Theatre.)
13 'Architect Meier speaks about creating a space where people are happy working together', *Cornell Chronicle*, 10 October 2008, www.news.cornell.edu/stories/2008/10/architect-richard-meier-speaks-about-weill-hall (accessed 26 August 2014).
14 Jacobs Consultancy: Project Portfolio, Cornell University Weill Hall and Weill Hall Institute, www.jacobsconsultancy.com/consultancy.asp?id=7082 (accessed 26 August 2014).

15   The Australian guidelines for certification have been referred to because there is no global regulator, despite significant consistency between national regulators. *Guidelines for Certification of a Physical Containment Level 2 Laboratory*, Version 3.1, effective 1 July 2007, Office of the Gene Technology Regulator Australia, www.ogtr.gov.au/internet/ogtr/publishing.nsf/content/PC2-4/$FILE/PC2LABv3-1-1.pdf (accessed 24 February 2013).

16   Reference is to the Australian Government Department of Health, Office of the Gene Technology Regulator, 'Guidelines for Certification of a Physical Contaminant Facility'. Refer to www.ogtr.gov.au/internet/ogtr/publishing.nsf/content/certifications-1 (accessed 8 March 2015).

17   Simondon, *L'individu et sa genèse physico-biologique*, p. 223

18   Deleuze, *Logic of Sense*, p. 125.

19   Ian Youngs, 'Sainsbury Laboratory wins Stirling architecture prize', *BBC News,* 13 October 2012. www.bbc.co.uk/news/entertainment-arts-19923820 (accessed 18 October 2013).

20   Ibid.

Chapter 27

Performativity and paranoia

Or how to do the 'Internet of Things' with words

Claudia Dutson

> The beauty of what [Nest] is doing, is that it's not necessarily defining a new look, but it's defining a new performance.
>
> (Rem Koolhaas, in conversation with Tony Fadell, Nest CEO)[1]

The performative and the paranoid

The floor, the wall, the ceiling, the roof, the door, the window, the façade, the balcony, the corridor, the fireplace, the toilet, the stair, the escalator, the elevator, the ramp: these constituted the *Elements of Architecture*, an exhibition curated by Rem Koolhaas for the 2014 Architecture Biennale in Venice. Each single element had a room dedicated to it in the Central Pavilion, and was investigated through 'objects, data, images and film clips from across time and place', that were 'presented in a collectively compiled non-hierarchical assemblage'.[2] *Elements* tended to be perceived by the exhibition's critics as an encyclopaedia or a product catalogue, or (symptomatic of the digital regime that Koolhaas and his researchers identified as starting to merge with architectural objects) as an 'obsessive series of retweets', where it was unclear if 'quotations from others equal endorsements'.[3]

Koolhaas's thesis is that after thirty-five years of a neoliberal market-driven economy that started with Ronald Reagan's election to president, architects have been left behind. They are no longer relevant to the production of the built environment except as 'so-called form-givers' – an 'increasingly precarious and hollow role'.[4]

Their former position of working as extensions of the state in a civic capacity has shifted to one where the architect works for the market and whichever private enterprise is setting the agenda.

Koolhaas's second premise is that the ubiquitous elements that architects deploy 'anytime, anywhere'[5] have evolved (independently of an architectural theory) from their archetypal form through a technological revolution of mass production and regulatory requirements and into a new digital paradigm. For example, the fireplace became central heating controlled by an off-the-shelf household thermostat. In the gap vacated by architects uninterested in such banal technologies, commercial interests have moved in, reforming traditionally 'deaf and mute' elements into ones that are 'listening, thinking, and talking back, collecting information and performing accordingly',[6] and communicating via the internet with data-centres and other objects.

Silicon Valley-style tech companies, bringing their own ideas of the future home, office and city, have recast inhabitants as customers, whose data is collected to serve both commercial interests and the new dogma of 'comfort, security and sustainability'.[7] They are eager to promote the 'Internet of Things' – the term given to consumer products with sensors, software and connectivity – as being the solution to a modernity that they themselves produce. Technological innovators such as Tony Fadell, the CEO of Nest Labs, who Koolhaas says 'prove their worth by identifying a multiplicity of disasters that can now be averted by the application of digital technology',[8] are also operating with a performative (and paranoid) attitude. The city and home are presented as being in a state of imminent threat; from water shortages or running out of milk, urban flooding or kitchen fires, rolling blackouts or rising household bills. This attitude raises questions of accountability and ethics. 'Entrepreneurs', writes philosopher Isabelle Stengers, are 'persons of opportunity, deaf and blind to the question of the world that their efforts contribute towards making'.[9]

Elements – described as becoming 'weirdly self-affirming, like a methodological echo-chamber'[10] – could be seen as owing much to the 'paranoid critical method' (PCM) that Koolhaas deployed in *Delirious New York*. The PCM is a surrealist activity drawn from Salvador Dalí and 'a fabrication of evidence for unprovable speculations' with a 'rich harvest of unsuspected correspondences, analogies and patterns', which are presented alongside 'real' facts in order to, 'absolutely confirm and reinforce' a thesis.[11] The PCM is performative in so far as it does more than merely describe a current condition, it produces the reality it sets out to investigate.

In linguistics, performativity is the potential for utterances to do more than merely describe the world as it is. Spoken language is also used to create changes in the world. In J.L. Austin's speech-act theory, to say something *is* to do something.[12] He gives examples, such as 'I name this ship the Queen Elizabeth' and 'I bet you sixpence it will rain tomorrow', neither of which are a report or description about the action taking place. Rather the action takes place *in* the performance of the sentence. Austin's primary examples are limited to ceremonial cases, where acts are performed by people with the judiciary or legislative power to name ships, wed two individuals, sentence a criminal, or who are circumstantially in the position to make a bet, promise a favour, or order a subordinate to do something.

Throughout his book *How To Do Things With Words*, Austin describes the different types of act an utterance can perform, depending on whether the action is stated explicitly or whether the utterance leads to actions as a consequence of what is said. A speech act where the action is the utterance, such as 'I name this ship . . .', differs from those where the action is performed through the utterance, such as 'I warn' or 'I inform'. Further, both are different from an utterance that performs its action as an effect of what is said, where by saying something the speaker can 'convince', 'surprise' or 'deter'. Speech-act theory is a pragmatic discourse on the use of language, with some very particular conditions that render it useful for interrogating the actions of objects, such as those exhibited at *Elements*, and in particular, those objects such as the Nest Thermostat that are operating increasingly autonomously and intelligently.

The recurring criticism of *Elements* was that there was nothing holding its parts together. It only 'fetishised building bits [that] don't actually yield an applicable synthesis'.[13] Even a techno-enthusiast like Reyner Banham didn't survive intact: eviscerated, tracheotomised, his standard-of-living package dissected and displayed as a Sankey diagram – and located in at least three different exhibition rooms: the Toilet, the Ceiling and the Fireplace. For many critics, the mere accumulation of material about each element resisted any attempt to derive a system. Instead, they sought a method, a pattern language, a 'compositionist rulebook with which to creatively reconfigure [the] elements', as if some reassurance from the nihilism Koolhaas was presenting could be found.[14] As Peter Eisenman put it, 'for me, what's . . . purposely missing, is the grammatic',[15] a sentiment echoed in other reviews: 'If architecture is a language, all that is given here is the vocab, not the grammar'.[16]

It is true that 'the door', for example, seems lacking in grammatical function, and when spoken on its own – 'the door' – merely a pointless signifier. But if I were approaching you and carrying a stack of books and then say to you 'The door', you might understand this as a *request* to hold the door open for me. Or if on leaving an office, your manager were to call after you, 'The door!' you might understand her as *ordering* you to shut the door. Such utterances belong to a class of speech acts, and suggest that *Elements* is not to be read as a text. This chapter argues that where objects such as smoke alarms, thermostats, cars and washing machines are bestowed with digital intelligence and networked together via the internet, algorithms and banks of data,[17] the configurations will not resemble anything remotely like a grammar. They will, instead, produce a new performance, and politics.

The internet of 'thoughtful things'[18]

The Nest smart thermostat, exhibited in the Fireplace room at *Elements*, is one of the first mainstream 'Internet of Things' products. The Nest senses occupancy and, by learning from users' activity and temperature preferences, it re-programmes itself with a bias towards saving energy. Koolhaas approaches the Nest from the paranoid-critical position, and invokes facts and fictions in his speculations. He asks, for example, whether:

> At some point after ten o'clock you could have a device that tells you that, to be responsible to mankind you should go to bed. Because otherwise you consume energy beyond your allotted quantity. Unless you pay of course.[19]

In suggesting here that the machine is 'telling you what to do' Koolhaas is not necessarily making the mistake of anthropomorphism. Objects such as Nest are not (yet) literally speaking or listening, but they are picking up, tracking and recording human activity. Nor do they have the requisite faculties to produce original speech.[20] Any sound they make is prerecorded or predetermined. It is not a problem of confusing the unique characteristics of human speech with synthetic machine 'speech'. Applying speech-act theory, an alarm, a voice message or even a visual icon appearing on a screen can all qualify as 'actions' when they are subject to some equivalent contextual conditions to those of human speakers.

We might also object to Koolhaas's attribution of purpose to the Nest because its programming does not produce a condition of sincerity. But in speech-act theory there is a lack of necessity to 'mean it'. For example, if two people are in the right circumstance and conditions to be married (neither of them are married to other people, they are both humans, and they are in the presence of somebody with the authority to wed them), yet say, 'I do' without really meaning it (for instance, one or both are secretly in love with others), it doesn't automatically nullify the marriage. The actions of speech acts are not entirely dependent on the intentional state in the speaker. It is neither artificiality, nor the lack of sophistication of the programme that are at stake. Rather it is contextual. When the 'speaking' Nest smoke detector loses authority, it is not because it cannot 'speak' in the truest sense. Whether or not the machine announces 'Heads up! There's smoke in the kitchen',[21] or emits a high-pitched alarm, it certainly falls foul if there is a false alarm.

In an early prototype of the Nest, designers discovered that the algorithm performed all too well, with 'beta' users reporting the kind of authoritarianism that Koolhaas invokes in his statement above (and that Nest CEO, Tony Fadell is also eager to distance himself from). Once the thermostat sensed that occupants had left the room it would immediately switch off the boiler if it was winter, in journalist Stephen Levy's words, 'greedily lower[ing] temperatures in winter and rais[ing] them in summer'. Users reported that the thermostat was *forcing* them to change their behavior; 'It was like Al Gore himself was in the room, barking at you to put on a sweater'.[22]

Actions and scripts

From self-closing taps to thermostats that indicate when an occupant should be saving energy, we might see these objects as standing in for disciplinary notices such as DON'T LEAVE THE TAPS RUNNING and TURN OFF THE HEATING WHEN YOU ARE NOT IN. Bruno Latour describes such mundane artefacts as a seatbelt alarm in a car, a door-closer mechanism, and a hotel key designed to 'constrain or shape the actions of humans', as standing in for utterances such as FASTEN YOUR SEAT BELT![23] He suggests that they contain a mechanical riposte to human transgressive actions; to the driver who does not want to wear a seatbelt, to visitors to the School of Mines who leave the door open to the cold Parisian wind, or to hotel guests who wander off with the room key.[24]

In Latour's account these objects seem endowed with a deterministic force that can condition the behaviour of the user. He writes that prescriptions of behaviour 'encoded in the mechanism' can be replaced by 'strings of sentences . . . that are uttered (silently and continuously) by the mechanisms for the benefit of those who are mechanised: do this, do that, behave this way, don't go that way, you may do so, be allowed to go there', and that such sentences, 'often in the imperative' look very much like a programming language.[25] So the hotel manager's verbal request to the guests, 'Please bring back your keys' is replaced at first by a written notice 'LEAVE YOUR KEYS, PLEASE', and finally by the attachment of a clumsy weight to the key to ensure compliance by the guests. Crucially, Latour suggests that the weight produces a new action in the guests. It is not that the heavy weight on the hotel key 'disciplines' the guest. Rather, the wish of the hotel manager becomes the internalised wish of the guests themselves – they are only too willing get rid of such an irritating and heavy object.

The work of Keller Easterling, an architect and writer who also has a background of theatrical training, might help us trace how the hotel manager's order ('PLEASE BRING BACK YOUR KEYS!') changes into a request performed by the guest ('Is there anywhere to leave these heavy keys please?'). Easterling describes the relationship between script and action in the theatre:

> While performing, actors rarely deal with states of being that can be named. Actions are the currency or the carrier of information. An actor would not play 'being a mother' but rather 'smothering a child'.[26]

A story is not told to the audience by the characters on stage – rather it is revealed through what they say and do. It is their *actions* that are central to drama. For each line of spoken dialogue in a script, actors attempt to figure out what the characters are doing, moment by moment. Breaking the drama into units of action, each identified unit is annotated with a verb to describe what one character is trying to do to another.[27] Easterling describes action as operating beyond what is explicit in the script:

> An actor adheres to [a] script, but the scripted words are considered only to be traces or artifacts that provide hints of an underlying action . . . The character saying, 'I am pleased to meet you' may actually be expelling someone from society. The character saying, 'I don't love you' may actually be straining to connect. Action . . . can be decoupled from declaration.[28]

Easterling proposes that this separation of narrative from action is how advanced infrastructures and technologies operate politically: 'the powers that be . . . are usually offering persuasive stories that are decoupled from what their organisations are actually doing'.[29] In much the same way, the objects produced by companies such as Nest, start to tell a different story as the actions change.

In the case of the Nest Thermostat, the algorithms were changed, 'shifting [its] personality to more of a gentle coach than a noodge with a climate-change slide show'.[30] The device's reprogramming displaced the formalised speech acts of imperatives and requests, 'PUT ON A SWEATER!', 'TURN DOWN THE THERMOSTAT!' with 'You're doing really well today' and 'Compared to your neighbours, you maybe wanna improve'.[31] Fadell uses the analogy of the diet coach to describe how the Nest 'helps you to do things *you* want to do', giving suggestions such as, 'Hey, here's a better way to save'.[32]

By appealing to the emotional values of the user – in Nest's case to their concern for the environment, and for their families[33] – rather than solely to financial reward or moral discipline, Fadell implies that the smart thermostat is merely facilitating a pre-existing action desired by the user. But Latour warns that it is never clear where or in whom the action originates:

> The question of who is carrying out the action has become unfathomable . . . the very word actor directs our attention to a complete dislocation of the action . . . Action is borrowed, distributed, suggested, influenced, dominated, betrayed, translated.[34]

Just as the weight of the hotel key transforms the wishes of the hotel manager into a counter-performance by the guest, the reprogrammed Nest enlists the user into a new performance of wilful competition with themselves, and their neighbours. This is a form of what is termed 'normative control' and can be better understood through the context of the management culture typical of the companies creating the technology.

Normative control and performative trouble

The Silicon Valley management style operates on the motivations and values of the employee by, 'controlling the underlying experiences, thoughts, and feelings that guide their actions. [Employees] are driven by internal commitment, strong identification with company goals, and intrinsic satisfaction from work'.[35] It was developed by technology companies such as Varian and Hewlett Packard in the 1940s and 1950s, and went against the traditional model of top-down authoritarian management by originating ideas such as open-door policies and what is known as 'management by wandering around'. Employees were offered the chance to buy into the company through being given stock options. Leadership and innovative working practices were encouraged, along with a focus on the individual, risk-taking and an entrepreneurial spirit. The result was employees who were highly motivated and, because of their stake in the company's success, shared its goals and values.

In Silicon Valley-style management, 'internalised standards for performance' replace financial incentives, and the sense of reward comes from the employees' own desires to make a difference and do worthwhile work. The behavioural rules for such performance are expressed in vague terms such as 'be creative, take initiative, take risks', 'push at the system' and, ultimately, 'do what's right'.[36] Discipline is not exerted on employees directly by the management, but comes from within themselves. This kind of company culture is endemic in technology companies who see as their mission not only the solving of existing problems, but also the identification of new ones in order to create new markets in a process of 'disruptive innovation'. In the face of the power politics of security and surveillance associated with the 'Internet of Things', Koolhaas has been encouraging architects to collaborate with Silicon Valley, to move from their marginal role as form-makers and take up positions where they can influence the profound changes taking place. He clearly knows the language of his techno-enthusiast counterparts. When on a visit to d.school (a 'hub for innovators'[37] at Stanford University in California), he greets the journalist accompanying him with a wry 'So, what are *you* disrupting?'[38]

But calls to architects to innovate and become more entrepreneurial with the implication that this is the only way in which the profession will have a stake in any discussions are worrying. The idea that they can do so 'knowingly' or somewhat 'ironically' – that subversive practices could be enacted through the performance of the system under critique – is also problematic, since as I have argued, the force of the performative is not drawn from intent, or equal to the degree to which you 'mean it'. As Austin states:

> Precisely because a promise is made in being said: declaring later that you didn't mean it, that you didn't enact it inwardly, that you never intended to keep it, will not relieve you of the . . . pragmatic implications of your utterance . . . A false promise is still a promise.[39]

As Judith Butler emphasises in her writing on speech-acts, performatives draw their force from conventions and conditions already in existence,[40] and thus, are highly normative. One needs only to be in the right place at the right time, and satisfy certain conditions to render any performative successful (and chances are, in the discipline of architecture, that enough of the conditions will be satisfied by virtue of gender, class, race, education, and so on). Further, Butler resists giving explicit methods for using the performative subversively, precisely because of 'the risk [of them] becoming deadening clichés through their repetition and, most importantly, through their repetition within commodity culture where "subversion" carries market value'.[41]

In fact I would suggest that attempting to produce new subversive tactics is a strategy too similar to 'disruptive innovation' and all too readily co-opted by precisely the system that they were intended to critique. I propose instead an attentive accountability in a practice whose convergence with the digital seems rather inevitable. As these technologies and their working practices approach architecture, we must train ourselves, not so much to be fluent in the language, processes and protocols in use, but adept at tracking the actions that are transferred through their performance.

Notes

1   Tony Fadell, Rem Koolhaas, 'Design in the Digital Age', *Vanity Fair*, 24 October 2014, http://video. vanityfair.com/watch/tony-fadell-and-rem-koolhaas-on-design-in-the-digital-age (accessed 3 February 2015).

2   Barbara Penner, 'Rem Koolhaas Needs to Get Back to the Fundamentals', *The Architectural Review*, 236, 1410 (2014), p. 31.
3   Kieran Long, 'Elements Makes You Unutterably Sad for Koolhaas and What He Thinks Architecture Is', *Dezeen*, 12 June 2014, www.dezeen.com/2014/06/12/kieran-long-venice-biennale-rem-koolhaas-opinion (accessed 23 March 2015).
4   Rem Koolhaas, 'The Smart Landscape: Intelligent Architecture', *ArtForum*, April 2015, pp. 212–217.
5   Rem Koolhaas, *Fundamentals*, 14 International Architecture Exhibition. La Biennale Di Venezia (New York: Marsilio, 2014), p. 193.
6   Koolhaas, 'The Smart Landscape', p. 215.
7   Ibid., p. 216.
8   Ibid.
9   Isabelle Stengers, 'The Cosmopolitical Proposal', in *Making Things Public*, ed. Bruno Latour and Peter Weibel (Cambridge, MA: MIT Press, 2005), pp. 994–1003.
10 Penner, 'Rem Koolhaas Needs to Get Back to the Fundamentals', p. 31.
11 Rem Koolhaas, *Delirious New York: A Retroactive Manifesto for Manhattan* (New York: Monacelli Press, 1994), pp. 238–241.
12 John Langshaw Austin, *How to Do Things With Words* (Oxford: Oxford University Press, 1962). This chapter uses J.L. Austin's work on Speech Acts, but not John Searle's later formalisation.
13 Samuel Medina, 'Rem's Kit of Parts', *Metropolis Magazine*, September (2014), p. 112.
14 Ibid.
15 Peter Eisenman, 'Rem Koolhaas is stating "the end" of his career, says Peter Eisenman', *Dezeen*, 9 June 2014, www.dezeen.com/2014/06/09/rem-koolhaas-at-the-end-of-career-says-peter-eisenman (accessed 11 April 2015).
16 Rob Wilson, Sophie Lovell, Florian Heilmeyer, 'Rem-Membering and Dismembering Architecture at the Biennale', *Uncube Blog*, 12 June 2014, www.uncubemagazine.com/blog/13420199 (accessed 9 April 2015).
17 Nest Labs, acquired by Google in 2014 for $3.2 billion, announced partnerships with Mercedes Benz, Whirlpool, Jawbone and Dropcam to develop a standard platform for interaction between different products.
18 'Thoughtful Things' is the tagline for Nest products.
19 Rem Koolhaas, Tony Fadell, *Elements of Architecture: 5000 years of architecture . . . and now what? architecture and technology?* 5 June 2014, www.labiennale.org/en/mediacenter/video/fundamentals 29.html (accessed 2 March 2015).
20 Nest's other product, a 'talking' smoke detector, utters the phrase 'Heads up! There's smoke in the [kitchen]', in the USA, and 'Please be aware . . . There's smoke in the [hallway]' in the UK version.
21 Oliver Wainwright, 'Nest, Google and beyond: How much technology do we really want in our homes?' in the *Guardian*, Friday 27 June 2014, www.theguardian.com/artanddesign/2014/jun/27/-sp-the-nest-google-technology-future-homes (accessed 18 March 2015).
22 Steven Levy, 'Brave New Thermostat: How the iPod's Creator Is Making Home Heating Sexy', *Wired Magazine*, October 2011, www.wired.com/2011/10/nest_thermostat (accessed 15 January 2013).
23 Bruno Latour, 'Where Are the Missing Masses? The Sociology of a Few Mundane Artefacts', in Wiebe Bijker and John Law (eds), *Shaping Technology/Building Society: Studies in Sociotechnical Change* (Cambridge, MA: MIT Press, 1992), pp. 225–259.
24 Ibid., also in Bruno Latour, 'Technology is Society Made Durable', *Sociological Review* (1990), 103–132.
25 They also look a lot like speech acts.
26 Keller Easterling, *The Action Is the Form: Victor Hugo's TED Talk* (Moscow: Strelka Press, 2014), pp. 16–17.
27 Mike Alfreds, *Different Every Night: Freeing the Actor* (London: Nick Hern Books, 2007), pp. 125–140.
28 Easterling, *The Action Is the Form*, p. 16.
29 Keller Easterling, *Extrastatecraft: The Power of Infrastructure Space* (London: Verso, 2014), p. 91.
30 The etymology of the word 'noodge' is Yiddish, meaning to pester, or nag. Levy, 'Brave New Thermostat'.
31 Ibid.
32 The Nest thermostat does not actually 'speak' but these phrases were given by Fadell as examples of what a Nest thermostat 'coach' might say. Wainwright, 'Nest, Google and beyond: How much technology do we really want in our homes?'
33 'We're all concerned about the same things. We're concerned about the Environment, we're concerned about cost, we're concerned about our children.' Tony Fadell in Koolhaas and Fadell, *Elements of Architecture: 5000 years of architecture . . . and now what?*
34 Ibid.
35 Gideon Kunda, *Engineering Culture: Control and Commitment in a High-Tech Corporation* (Philadelphia: Temple University Press, 2006), p. 11.

36   Ibid., p. 90.
37   d.school is described on the Stanford homepage as being a 'deliberate mash-up of industry, academia and the big world beyond campus', http://dschool.stanford.edu/about (accessed 26 April 2015).
38   Pooja Bhatia, 'Rem Koolhaas Takes Silicon Valley' in *OZY,* 28 December 2014, www.ozy.com/rising-stars-and-provocateurs/rem-koolhaas-takes-silicon-valley/36643 (accessed 2 April 2015).
39   James Loxley, *Performativity* (Oxford: Routledge, 2007), p. 36.
40   'The . . . performative derives its forcefulness or efficacy through recourse to established conventions'. Judith Butler, *Excitable Speech: A Politics of the Performative* (London: Routledge, 1997), p. 146.
41   Judith Butler, *Gender Trouble* (New York: Routledge, 1999), p. xxi.

Part VIII

Contemporary questions

Chapter 28

On site

Nick Beech, Linda Clarke and Christine Wall

Contemporary debates on the transformation of building methods, the structure of the building industry, and the introduction of new technologies (informational, material and structural) in professional literature and in the architectural humanities tend to ignore the realities of work on construction sites. This follows a long history of failure to recognise the importance of workers' experience and knowledge of building as a process by the key professions in the industry. The absence of the working process in accounts of historical development is exacerbated by abstract reflection on building know-how, categories of expertise, and the structure of the industry, when these are not supported by direct observation and engagement with building work and workers. Key assumptions about the relation between structural and technological changes in the industry and the knowledge, skills, composition, and requirements of the workforce can be challenged by paying attention to day-to-day activities and conditions of site work.

The site visit – once common in programmes of architectural education – is increasingly restricted to construction and site management education. To provide humanities researchers with an experience of what might be learned from a site visit, a workshop was organised at the 'Industries of Architecture' conference.[1] The site visit was hosted and organised by the Mechanical and Electrical (ME) arm of a family-based firm, with a £700m turnover. ME has a turnover of about £170m, £8m of which is attributable to prefabrication. The site visited, a hotel, is part of a £50m project, with ME responsible for about £7m, whose main contractor was recently taken over and which is financed by a group of investors, including a city council. There are about one hundred and forty working on the site. ME employs forty to sixty on site, including twelve 'sub-trades' (ductwork, electrical, and so on), and those present for the workshop included: the contracts manager, two project managers (for mechanical work and electrical work), a former electrician and trainee planner, and an architect (CEO of the architectural practice). At the time of our visit, the project was in the process of finishing and fitting out of services – major service ducts and key services were already in place, tiling had begun in a basement-level swimming pool.

The architect made much of this being a 'BIM building'. We understood too that BIM was now a verb, 'to BIM'. We were shown computer-generated BIM drawings available on iPads, which seemed to override any need for paper. Nevertheless, all BIM-generated drawings had also been reproduced in standard job drawings, available in racks at the site office. The utility of BIM was illustrated by a hole in a wall. It was explained that in the past, the hole would have been cut out of the blockwork, rather than being already built in following the drawings. It was argued that this allowed for a faster transition between structural and fitting-out work and the elimination of errors resulting from misreading of instructions, faulty measuring out on site or poor construction skills. It also allowed for a compression of the project programming; numerous fitting and fixing operations were programmed to occur at the same time, rather than a traditional succession of works.

However, it was clear that the hole we were shown did not account for block size, resulting in cutting of blocks to conform to the BIM model. Indeed, it remained unclear whether the resulting hole had been produced any faster, or more accurately, than a standard construction procedure. Further BIM misalignments were in evidence throughout the site, as one would expect on a large project. But it remained unclear whether these were the result of 'BIM clash' (faults generated in the original model due to miscalculation between different professional teams) or due to 'human error' on site.

A further product of the concertinaed works programming was increased pressure between sub-trades on site. This resulted when different teams, programmed to conduct work at the same time – in the swimming pool for example, installing lighting, fitting tiles, plastering, wiring, and so on – nevertheless could not complete their different tasks outside of a strict sequence. Tensions between teams were resolved through onsite negotiations – pressure of time and money trumping other concerns. The design teams working on a BIM model experienced the same intensification of processing. This resulted in positive and negative reflections – better understanding, greater co-operation or increased pressure, further competition.

Problems resulting from the compression of the works programme were further highlighted with the larger prefabricated elements of the scheme. Corridors of the upper storeys were largely in shell form, yet a small number of rooms already had completely finished bathroom units.[2] These 'pods' – delivered prior to finishing of the exterior concrete face of the building – were prefabricated, delivered and crane-lifted into position. Failure of the firm making bathroom pods (due to bankruptcy) meant that only twenty of the two hundred and fifty bathroom pods had been delivered. Had the contractor awaited the identification of a suitable manufacturer to draw up, process, manufacture and deliver the remaining pods the project would have been brought to a catastrophic halt. Instead, the exterior of the building was completed and traditional bathroom fitting and fixing commenced. As the bathrooms had to be produced to the same dimensions as the original pods, an experimental fitting-out room – including a prototype metal frame to hold the washbasin – had been welded and hand made to the right dimensions. This all resulted in an extra 6,000 man-hours.

Other parts of the project simply could not be produced to modular dimensions in the first place. An enquiry was made about a workbench in a corridor with a metal vice and tube cutter. This was for cutting modular components that did not fit together because, in certain tight situations, it was too expensive to install modular piping. The fitters measured the space and cut and fixed the pipe to fit – neither a result of 'BIM clash' nor 'human error' – indicative of the processes of production on a construction site that cannot be resolved through offsite planning and conception, but only through the construction process itself.

There was evidence too of the highly skilled individuals required to fit and fix standardised components. Every member of an entire complex of interlocking copper service pipes in the main basement control room was labelled with felt-tip initials. All fitters are required to initial these joints, prior to lagging, so that if any subsequent fault or error were identified – by regular inspection on the job or subsequently in use – that fault could be traced to the worker responsible. And, whilst much was made of a possible future in which operatives would walk about with tablets containing the BIM model, evidence on this project was of an already existing network of communication: text, dimensions and sketches were evident in handwriting across walls, floors, and formwork (Figure 28.1). These included a range of languages – English, East European and possibly Punjabi. The evidence indicates that contemporary advances in information technology and the new structures of prefabrication and site contracting relied upon – and in crisis situations depended upon – the traditional skills and communication of the building operatives.

There were no apprentices on this site, though ME do have apprentices, who also go to a college of building. Apprentices tend to be referred by the local authority and allocated via Section 106 'local labour' clauses, and include those who have already studied full-time in Further Education and need the necessary work experience to complete. This appears as a solution to the problem of employer disengagement with apprenticeships and vocational education and training in general, though the training lasts altogether four to five years. These young local people are given site experience with a qualified tradesperson acting as mentor, though there is no in-firm training of mentors.

The main contractor does not have an operative workforce at all but is essentially a contract manager responsible for the building workforce subcontractors, whose workforce is in turn composed of approximately 60 per cent East European migrants. One of the noticeable developments identified in discussion with ME is that it is composed increasingly of a supervisory team, the majority of whom have come through 'the tools' rather than through 'education'. Their workforce is with the trade union Unite.

Queries as to how cost was estimated for the project revealed the current distribution of risk. This had been almost entirely transferred from the client to the contractor, a key feature of the 'Design and Build' contract under which the project was operated. The architect described how their workforce of one hundred people all use BIM

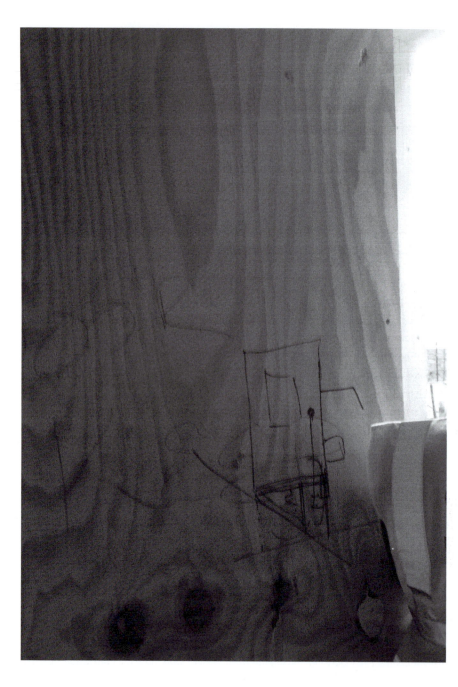

Figure 28.1
Onsite sketch.
Photograph: Nick Beech

after three months of training. No traditional drafting is done by the practice. They have been using BIM for eight years and have found it to be extremely cost-efficient for the firm – 1,200 hours were saved with an eight-storey building.

The result is a massive 'front loading' of projects. The RIBA Plan of Work 'Stages' 2, 3, and 4 (from concept design, through developed design, to technical design) are, in essence, treated as a single stage. But this single stage is significantly increased in time, as the architectural team attempt to 'build' a virtual model by BIMing. The intention is that Stage 5 (construction) is shortened. All of this is intimately bound to the issue of risk allocation. As the contractor takes on all the risk, the identification and elaboration of costs and the elimination of costly errors – prior to production – are imperative.

There are a large number of questions that arise from this brief site visit. We adumbrate only a few here. A project such as this raises serious questions about the impact of new forms of financing and investment in building. The structure of the developer (a mix of private and public investment) retains some benefits – such as the inclusion of Section 106 in the contract – but it increases the allocation of risk to the contractor. That in turn increases the desirability of generating as much information as possible prior to the construction project itself. This would seem natural to the professions, but it raises necessarily awkward questions for the status and function of the architect (the ethical position of the disinterested professional seems very distant). It also has the effect of further distancing the design process from the construction process (the office from the site) and therefore the very knowledge that is needed to produce a production programme that will work to expectation.

BIMing itself appears to hold the most fascination and the most contradictory conditions in all of this. Although it is a design tool specifically generated to bring about increased collaboration and cooperation between professions, it also appears to increase the fragmentation of knowledge. As a result, BIMing is, it seems, supposed to *be* 'knowledge' – the wish image is of a large team of discrete professionals working in an empty room, wearing Google glasses and working *directly* on the virtual model. The further utopian image is of workers on site doing the same – simply lifting and fitting into place 'matter', with the location in space and time given to their vision by the same Google glasses. Wild fantasies and fears need not concern us – it seems highly unlikely that BIM will be able to transcend the need to 'put something on paper' (or bench, or floor, or sheet material, or wall) so that people can then translate this, through their understanding and skills, into practice on the construction site. Nevertheless, those design practitioners imagining that the increase in digital design and manufacturing will magically bring them into 'craft' relation with building activity, may need to think carefully about what BIMing actually allows the designer to do, know, or even perceive.

The contract manager ended by saying – highly sympathetically – that 'we're proud of what we do', emphasising the 'creativity' involved in building work, but that people 'don't understand' this because 'we get such bad press'. It is not only the bad press. There is continued pressure – from finance, from professional institutions, and from broader social and material transformations – to 'erase' the worker from the process whilst increasingly resting on his or her skills and abilities.

Notes

1   The workshop organisers thank Ian Fitzgerald (Northumbria University) for all his support and the construction team who provided access, time and thoughtful responses to all our questions.
2   An interior view of one of the bedrooms, facing out towards a window opening, is provided as the cover image of this volume.

Chapter 29

BIM

The pain and the gain

John Gelder

Culture and information technology

Improving the construction sector's efficiency (in terms of time, cost, quality, risk and impact) is seen as a major gain. The ambition to achieve it has resulted in pressure over the years to move to more collaborative procurement. It has led to other changes in the industry, each with a cultural dimension, including other changes in procurement (e.g. design-build, fast-track, and build-own-operate-transfer), the ongoing push for prefabrication, the increasing importance of sustainability, and project management (to integrate all these approaches).

Meanwhile, construction-sector information technology (IT) has been spreading and developing inexorably, as computers become more powerful and ubiquitous. Building information modelling (BIM), which is still developing, integrates geometric and non-geometric data across disciplines and along the timeline, and has its own momentum and appeal. Being computer-based, BIM facilitates any tasks that are calculable – and a surprising number of design tasks are calculable.

These two trends intersect. In order to collaborate we need to share managed digital project data of the kind supported by BIM. To use BIM data we must collaborate. BIM has the potential to support the other changes mentioned, too – procurement, prefabrication, sustainability, and project management.

Understandably, some in the industry still equate BIM with software (21 per cent of respondents to the UK *NBS National BIM Report 2015*, for example).[1] But most (57 per cent in that report) have a more rounded view of BIM as being 'all about real time collaboration'.[2] They have seen the intersection. If we want to achieve collaboration in construction, we have to promote the enabling software. We have to teach both the end and the means.

Collaborative working

If all participants are to work from the one dataset, the fundamental change that must be embraced is collaborative working. Use of one dataset simply doesn't work in adversarial procurement. The model must be available to everyone along the timeline – sending paper or PDF drawings and specifications to any participant, including authorities, would break the model development chain. This requires trust and openness, which is not a characteristic of adversarial procurement. Users such as the contractor have to be able to interrogate the model (read), but must also be able to change it (write), to bring incomplete designs to the point where they can be built, or to replace a generic product object with a branded one. This free access to the 'documentation' is new for contractors and for many other participants, as is a hands-on attitude to the 'documentation', but it is essential if the full benefits of BIM are to be realised. Making construction industry silos very porous is a huge cultural change – many have been with us for centuries. It will be painful.

Nevertheless, collaboration has been on the construction industry's wish list in the UK (and elsewhere) for a long time. The report for the UK government by Sir Michael Latham – *Constructing the Team* (1994) – recommended integrated design among designers and 'specialists', collaboration between consulting engineers and specialists, research into integration of design and construction, and experimentation with partnering.[3] A subsequent report by Sir John Egan – *Rethinking Construction* (1998) – advocated integrated and collaborative working.[4] Interestingly, both reports foresaw that computer modelling would be a part of collaborative working. Now we see that BIM is both forcing us into collaboration, and enabling it.

Technical and cultural change

The impact of BIM, even in its immature state, has already been profound:

- Quantity take-off is fully automated.
- Perspectives are generated on the fly for any view selected.
- Beams and columns can be sized automatically.
- Spaces can pack themselves in 3D in the most efficient way automatically.
- Clash checking is fully automated.
- Specifications can be accessed from within the geometry, and vice versa.
- Team members automatically use the same project information as each other.
- If one wants to query any bit of the model, the software will tell you automatically who was responsible for that bit, and provide a timeline for its development.

- Fabricators can make directly from the model.
- Construction timelines can be generated automatically from the model and viewed geometrically.
- Team members can run all kinds of queries from the model, e.g. show me all the proposals I am required to submit, or everything about acoustics, or all the unresolved physical clashes.
- The model can be interrogated live at any time, from any place.
- Surveyors can set out the structure directly from the model.
- Non-expert users can understand the proposals they are shown.
- Use of resources such as the NBS BIM Toolkit will define communications and coordination across the various disciplines.[5]

This does not mean that the various disciplines have nothing to do. Rather, some old skill sets can be discarded (such as hand drawing a perspective), and new skill sets must be learned. For instance, for automated space-planning we need to be able to program the space proximity rules we have hitherto held in our heads and, if the computer generates several space packing solutions for us, we need to be able to recognise the best one.

Once over the learning curve, older workers in the industry familiar with traditional ways of working welcome these changes – they know from experience how problematic the old ways have been. For younger workers, using BIM and collaboration will be just the way things are. To do anything else is unimaginable. Why go backwards?

As BIM matures and evolves we can expect further technical changes. This may mean that some current disciplines cease to exist. Once industry-supported national cost datasets serving the whole timeline become available and are embedded in BIM software, for example, many traditional cost-management services will disappear. Likewise, conventional design services will disappear, at least at the 'low end' of the market. Clients will be able to generate and procure fully documented designs them-selves. Websites have been offering (non-BIM) services along these lines for some time:

- B&Q Projects (www.diy.com);
- Kitchen Planner (www.kitchenplanneronline.com);
- IKEA 2008 Office planner (www.ikea.com/ms/en_US/rooms_ideas/office/download1.html);
- ISIS 3D Spacer (http://isis.3dspacer.com);
- PlanningWiz (www.planningwiz.com).

BIM goes the architect. Eventually. Maybe.

Demonstrable benefits

Is the gain really worth the pain? The benefits of using BIM have been demonstrated in built projects time and again. In the UK, the thirty or so projects under the Avanti umbrella were an early demonstrator of the benefits of collaboration using advanced IT (Avanti started in 2002, was taken over by Constructing Excellence in 2006, and fed directly into the activities of the BIM Task Group – now Digital Built Britain).[6] Following on from this, the BIM Task Group ran several BIM pilot projects, such as the Houseblock and Education Building at the Young Offenders' Institute Cookham Wood.[7]

In the USA, the General Services Administration's BIM Pilot Program in 2005 included nine building projects, such as office buildings and courthouses.[8]

In Finland, Senaatti carried out over a dozen BIM pilot projects from 2001 to 2008.[9] The Norwegian Defence Estates Agency ran three pilot projects from 2007 to 2009.[10] In Sweden, Trafikverket had four large BIM pilot projects underway in 2012: the West Link rail tunnel in Gothenburg, the Hallandsås rail tunnel, the Stockholm bypass, and the Mälaren railway line expansion.[11]

In Germany, the Reformkommission Großprojekte has four BIM pilot projects underway at the time of writing: Rastatter Tunnel, Petersdorfer Lake Bridge, Chemnitz ring road south link, and Filstal railway overpass – again, all transport infrastructure.[12]

As a consequence of running these pilot projects, government clients in these and other countries have been sufficiently convinced of the benefits to them of BIM that they have (or will have) mandated BIM in all the projects they commission.

Scepticism

In spite of the readily available evidence, the idea that the use of BIM means that construction projects will be quicker, cheaper, safer, and better meets with scepticism from some. But evidence suggests that most sceptics are those who have not used BIM. BIM users are very positive about the new technology and culture.

This was illustrated in a small way through the 'BIM goes the architect' workshop panel at the Industries of Architecture conference.[13] All the panellists were BIM users, and all would rather use it than not, and all believed that BIM is here to stay. It has been demonstrated more robustly in the *NBS National BIM Report 2015*, and more widely in the *NBS International BIM Report 2013* (covering the UK, Canada, Finland, and New Zealand).[14] The former report noted that, 'Those who have adopted BIM are more likely to be positive about it (in terms of visualisation, productivity, cost efficiency, speed of delivery, and profitability) than those who have yet to.'[15]

The latter report showed that the number of users who wished they hadn't adopted BIM ranged from just 4 to 9 per cent, whereas the number of non-users who would rather not adopt BIM ranged from 21 to 26 per cent. Non-users – a shrinking number (fallen in the UK from 88 to 53 per cent from 2010 to 2014, according to the *NBS National BIM Report 2015*) – are much more sceptical. Users know better.

Carrots

The enthusiasm of design and construction teams for using BIM arises because they have found that using BIM brings benefits to them – there are carrots as well as sticks.

Figure 30.1
Manor Crescent, before refurbishment by ECD Architects. The energy-inefficient house meant that occupants had unaffordable energy bills, were thermally uncomfortable and had health problems. Image copyright ECD Architects. Photograph: Jake Fitzjones

Figure 30.2
Manor Crescent, after retrofit by ECD Architects in 2011, including addition of 220mm externally rendered wall insulation, roof insulation and solar panels on the roof, significantly reducing energy bills (by about 65%) and environmental impact while increasing occupant thermal comfort and health. Image copyright ECD Architects Photograph: Jake Fitzjones

high performance, standards in retrofit do not have to be contradictions (Figure 30.3). There is, however, much room for growth and improvement in that area. An opportunity for humanities research would be to provide professionals with clearer guidelines and theoretical foundations for sustainable retrofit and architectural heritage.

Figure 30.3
Section of Princedale Road house, owned by social landlords Octavia in a conservation area in West London. This section illustrates that the fabric was upgraded from the inside with little change to the external façade, as stipulated by local conservation requirements. Image copyright Paul Davis & Partners

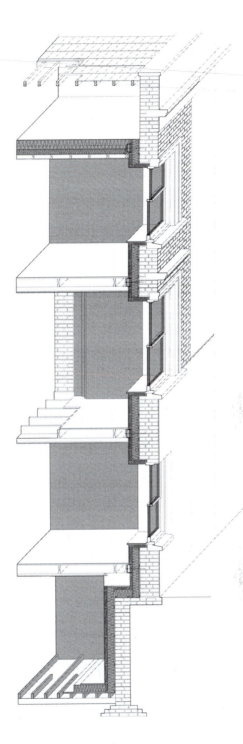

Figure 30.5
Ferrier Point after its energy-efficient upgrade with new windows, externally insulated metal rain screens and 370m² vertical PV panels, all installed while residents remained *in situ*. Image copyright ECD Architects. Photograph: Jake Fitzjones

Not just a technical problem?

The scale of the challenge raises a number of important political, economic and technical problems to be overcome – concerning funding, regulatory frameworks, skills (in both

design and cons
evaluation. The n
questions that de
to redefine our nc
the traditional di
conservation. A la
and adaptation o
heritage and its p
and updating of pa

need for sustainable retrofit requires us to critically re-examine some dearly held architectural ideas, and this debate should include questions such as:

- Does retrofit involve only adding or changing? Or can it also mean taking away? Or any of these combined?
- Can we use the need for sustainable retrofit as an opportunity to enhance the architectural quality of our buildings?
- How does retrofit relate to conservation and heritage? Where is the value in historic buildings we are trying to protect? Is it the entire building or a specific aspect or part of it?
- Should a listed building be altered at all? Or is wrapping the building in a new protective, 'conserving' layer part of conservation, as it increases the durability of the building and retains and protects its structure and purpose? In particular, which parts can we alter and which do we need to leave untouched? Should we make a clear distinction between old and added or should the added match the existing?
- Could qualitative building characteristics, such as heritage and building character, be quantified in assessment tools and road maps to clarify where and how much retrofit is possible?
- What constitutes our built heritage? Are we only concerned about the retrofit of listed buildings, most of which are pre-1900, or also about more recent architecture (Figures 30.4 and 30.5)? If non-listed buildings are also valued, how can and should those be upgraded?

The role of architectural professionals, critics, teachers and researchers

Considering the magnitude of the task and resulting commercial opportunities, this topic needs to be given a more central position in academia and practice. Appropriate energy-efficient upgrades reduce reliance on the burning of fossil fuels for building operation and reduce the need for new building construction, minimising the use of finite resources. However, given the sheer scale and urgency to increase occupant thermal comfort and to reduce building energy use, we need innovations, new solutions and creative approaches, alongside evidence-based reviews and critiques to support this real, pressing and large-scale upgrade of our built environment.

Architects and designers are well placed to help deliver such an ambitious retrofit plan by 'making efficient and holistic decisions on any scale of project, while understanding the broader conservation issues'.[14] Architects and other experts are instrumental in achieving ambitious building upgrades and appropriate standards, technically and architecturally. However, heritage, conservation and building refurbishment are generally not considered to be a core part of architectural practice by the architectural community, and these subjects are still often excluded from architecture schools' curricula.[15] To take the required scale of retrofit seriously, the architectural profession will need to adjust its self-image from one creating the new, to one that is also responsible for updating the old. Architectural critics and theorists are well placed to challenge and review current and proposed approaches to building conservation and our built environment legacy, both through the education of the next generation of architects and by challenging practitioners about their retrofit approaches and design strategies.

Retrofitting at the scale required brings with it a whole host of challenges, but it also provides opportunities to establish a new 'retrofit poetic' and for architecture to remain relevant to society. The need for sustainable retrofit of the existing building stock will be an area of significant growth in the construction industry over the next few decades. Architectural professionals, humanities researchers and educators have a unique opportunity to be involved in this transformation of our built environment. We should seize it.

Notes

1   Committee on Climate Change, *Fourth Carbon Budget Review Technical Report*, ch. 3: 'Reducing emissions from buildings' (Committee on Climate Change, 2013).
2   Anne Power, 'Housing and Sustainability: Demolition or Refurbishment?', *Proceedings of the ICE, Urban Design and Planning*, 163 (2010), pp. 205–216.
3   'Dukes: Domestic Energy Consumption in the UK 2011', ed. DECC (London: 2011).
4   IPCC, *Climate Change 2007: The Physical Science Basis: Contribution of Working Group I to the Fourth Assessment Report of the Intergovernmental Panel on Climate Change* (Cambridge: Cambridge University Press, 2007).
5   DECC, *The Energy-Efficiency Strategy: The Energy-Efficiency Opportunity in the UK* (London: 2012).
6   Brenda Boardman, 'Examining the Carbon Agenda Via the 40% House Scenario', *Building Research & Information*, 35 (2007), 363–378.
7   Ibid.
8   Anne Power, 'Does Demolition or Refurbishment of Old and Inefficient Homes Help to Increase Our Environmental, Social and Economic Viability?', *Energy Policy*, 36 (2008), 4487–4501.
9   Anne Power, M. Zulauf, 'Cutting Carbon Costs: Learning from Germany's Energy Saving Program', (LSE Housing & Communities, London School of Economics, 2011).
10   Ian Hamilton et al., 'The Impact of Housing Energy-Efficiency Improvements on Reduced Exposure to Cold: The "Temperature Take Back Factor"', *Building Services Engineering Research and Technology*, 32 (2011), 85–98.
11   Power, 'Does Demolition or Refurbishment of Old and Inefficient Homes Help to Increase Our Environmental, Social and Economic Viability?'
12   Ibid.
13   Historic Scotland, 'Scotland's Listed Buildings' (Historic Scotland, 2014) and The National Heritage List for England, www.historicengland.org.uk/listing/the-list/ (accessed 30 April 2015).
14   Terry Farrell, 'Our Future in Place: The Farrell Review of Architecture and the Built Environment' (London: Farrells, 2014).
15   Ibid.

Chapter 31

Risk and reflexivity

Architecture and the industries of risk distribution

Liam Ross

If we follow the Risk Society analytic proposed by Ulrich Beck, Anthony Giddens and colleagues,[1] the problems and conflicts of highly industrialised societies can be understood to arise, not principally as a result of the unequal distribution of *wealth*, but rather the unequal distribution of *risk*. Once a society succeeds in overcoming genuine material scarcity, its concerns turn to the unintended consequences of industrial production. In this so-called 'reflexive' period of our modernity – when our processes of industrial development, rationalisation and growth become limited by their own manufactured side-effects – the assessment, mitigation and redistribution of socially constructed risk becomes a dominant rationale for both industry and government.

Risk is, of course, a familiar concept within the language and practice of contemporary building design and construction. As building industry professionals and academics, we are well versed in the design of corporate entities through which to limit our exposure to *financial* risk. We have developed processes of professional self-regulation through which we legitimate our capability to *assume* specific risks. We have well-established forms of documentation to clearly define the opportunities for profit and loss within any construction project. And we are used to thinking about the design of our built environment – its spatial arrangement, its material or constructional specification – as something which exposes us to, or militates against, a wide range of hazards; accidental injury, threats to health and well-being, health, crime, terrorism or climate-change. Indeed practices such as 'risk assessment' have become so embedded in our everyday life as to have become banal, and even counterproductive. But if we can estrange ourselves from this familiarity, to what extent could we say that architecture and building construction have offered an important site through which the risks of indus- trial production have made themselves known? To what degree has our understanding of building design been transformed through the analytic construct of 'risk'? How have the industries of architecture, in attempting to mitigate or design-out specified risks, come to act as governmental technologies? And what kinds of reflexive effects, what 'moral- hazards', might lurk within, complicate and create internal limits for such governmental ambitions?

At the Industries of Architecture conference (Newcastle, 2014) four figures – a politician, a policy-maker, a designer and a historian – were brought together to workshop these questions and their responses follow.

Daniel Moylan is a Conservative Councillor for the Royal Borough of Kensington and Chelsea, Non-Executive Director of Crossrail and – amongst other things – he chairs Urban Design London, and is an honorary fellow of RIBA in recognition of his association with streetscape improvements. Moylan argues that, in the arena of building procurement and public policy, 'risk management' is not usually focused on reducing the prevalence of concrete *hazards*, but rather the reduction of *litigation* risk. Its main function is to pre- manage corporate exposure to financial or reputational damage. Risk management practices, he suggests, rarely make recourse to empirical data on the effectiveness of proposed mitigation measures, being based on compliance with 'best practice'. Lacking such an evidence base, they are susceptible to a dependence on often-unexamined historical norms, and to being 'captured' by the self-interests of those involved in their design. Best-practice guidelines and legislative frameworks are often written in con- sultation with industry representatives – manufacturers, consultants and associations of experts – and so offer a means to create a niche demand for products and services. An initiative such as 'Secure by Design' serves as an example here: there is a nexus of interest connecting the police, and a security industry populated by retired police staff, with a regulatory framework that drives the demand for security products and services. Such schemes and frameworks, which architects and builders participate in wittingly or otherwise, lack evidential justification.

While we might think such practices simply produce a distracting clutter of well-intentioned, ineffective technologies – unwatched CCTV cameras, irritatingly positioned barriers, unnecessary paperwork – Moylan argues that they can also be actively counterproductive. Taking conventional technologies of road-safety engineering as an example, he suggests that speed limits, traffic lights, and pedestrian crossings often have detrimental road-safety outcomes. These structures – physical and temporal inscriptions of legal rights – create a sense of entitlement which can stimulate aggressive and dangerous driving. By contrast, streetscape de-cluttering and 'shared-space' projects such as Exhibition Road, or Poynton Town Centre, have been shown to counterintuitively improve both traffic flow and road-safety. Echoing the views of Hans Monderman, the renowned Dutch road traffic engineer, he suggests that an awareness of *danger* in the environment is healthy, and creates its own self-governing effect, leading us to act more carefully and responsibly. However, there are practical and political difficulties in developing policies based upon such insight, and in challenging counterproductive regulation – the totemic value of getting legislation into the statute book, the politically difficult task of inviting 'risk' on to the public, and an unwarranted, but apparently ingrained fear of litigation – but he encouraged architects to use their position to highlight and question such instances of institutionalised ignorance.

Paul Stollard is an architect, a lecturer and a civil servant. He was responsible for the reform of building standards in Scotland, for drafting the Building (Scotland) Act of 2003, and served as the first Chief Executive of the Scottish Building Standards Agency. He was subsequently regional director for the Health and Safety Executive in Scotland, and is the author of a number of books on design and safety, including *Fire from First Principles: A Design Guide to Building Fire Safety*, and *Crime Prevention through Housing Design*. While recognising its susceptibility to political hubris, Stollard offered a defence of current practices of risk-assessment regulation, and of governmental regulation more broadly. He suggested that the discipline of considering the severity and likelihood of a hazard, putting mitigation measures in place, and promoting an awareness of residual risks, was precisely the means by which society established a collective concept of *safety*, agreeing on the level of risk we deem it socially acceptable to bear as individuals. He agreed, however, that the way in which risk-assessment practices have been popularly adopted is fraught with problems: they have been over-zealously applied – feeding on or stoking a fear of litigation – at the same time as providing a straw-man for our mistrust of government (think Digby Jones and *The Times* claiming, 'Safety Goggles Required When Playing Conkers', etc.).

Offering an overview of the mechanisms of building regulation, he identified where opportunities for misunderstanding and contradiction can occur. In Scotland, the building codes establish mandatory *functional* standards that define the governmental outcome required of building. These are given further specificity through *performance* requirements that begin to specify what the building must do to satisfy this outcome. Finally, a *prescriptive* guideline recommends construction arrangements that are deemed to satisfy this performance specification. Stollard suggested that, rather than going straight to the prescriptive guidelines, architects should rather rely on the functional standard; prescriptive guides only represent one means of satisfying the actual goal, and when blindly adhered to, they not only stifle design possibilities, but can also lead to counterproductive results. He suggested, for instance, that a drive to ensure equal opportunity of *access* for wheelchair-bound building occupants did nothing to ensure their equal capacity to *escape*, and that a focus on security in airports was leading to contraventions of escape principles. He enjoined architects, and architectural educators, not to simply apply rules and regulations, but to return to their first principles, which he suggested could be seen as design generators.

Luke Bisby is Arup's Professor of Fire and Structures at the University of Edinburgh, where he directs the BRE Centre for Fire Safety Engineering, as well as being a member of the University's project, 'Integrating Technical and Sociological Expertise in Fire Safety Engineering'. Bisby offered a further critique of prescriptive regulations, demonstrating their susceptibility to commercial interests, and their dependence on (sometimes nonsensical) historical norms: the recent mandatory requirement for sprinklers in Wales, he argued, was a result of industrial lobbying as opposed to scientific evidence, and taking Scotland's key regulation on fire escape as an example, he observed that the limitation on travel distance within buildings in the UK was based on the assumption that people can exit a building safely in the duration of the British National Anthem.[2] But he also went further, arguing that prescriptive standardisation poses fundamental limits both to the efficacy of design consultancy, but also to the ambitions of scientific enquiry: the 'black-boxing' of ignorance that such 'magic numbers' create can limit safety outcomes at both a professional and an academic level. Since such unexamined standards are so embedded within processes of fire-growth and evacuation modelling, they thwart attempts to develop a genuinely knowledge-based discipline of fire-safety engineering. He made a case for developing a rigorous empirical basis for the definition of 'safety' – recognising that this was a slippery term whose meaning had to be open to debate and must be carefully defined – such that it could be incorporated as another 'load case' in structural engineering.

Jonathan Massey is an architect and a historian, director of architecture at the California College of the Arts, and member of the Aggregate group of architectural historians. His numerous publications have often addressed the close relation between design practices and financial instruments. Jonathan's contribution offered a critique, even an inversion, of some of the assumptions of the discussion so far. Drawing on his own work and that of other researchers,[3] he tried to demonstrate that the risks associated with construction were not always construed as negative, offering compelling examples of ways in which policy-makers, building commissioners and architects have sought to define risks precisely as a means to mobilise, dramatise and profit from them. Considering the importance of mortgage-financed home-ownership for American architecture, urbanism, economics and governance, he began by discussing how the liberalisation of financial regulation had played an important role in constructing America's 'property-owning democracy', transforming the home into something we think of as an investment opportunity, but also creating new markets for design and construction in practices, such as 'house-flipping' and tear-down redevelopment. He noted how new kinds of spatial products – the internet café, or co-working suite – played a part in romanticising the increasingly casual and precarious nature of contemporary employment. Referring to research concerning the politics of US social housing, he discussed governmental projects to intentionally cut off centrally supplied heat – requiring social tenants to assume the 'risk' of meeting their own utilities bills – as an active policy of 'responsibili-sation'. And analysing Foster's Swiss RE project in terms of its claims to mitigate financial, political and environmental risk, he suggested that this project should be understood principally as a means to *dramatise* the perception of these risks – and architecture's capacity to manage them – as a means to meta-engineer markets for insurance products and design services.

If a point of consensus emerged between the differing viewpoints, it was an antipathy to prescriptive standards, and a call for a critical return to 'first principles'.

Liam Ross

Raising questions for future practice, research and pedagogy, the speakers demonstrated that – despite an intention to make visible the unaccounted costs of industrial production – our technologies of risk-management can create their own opportunities for obfuscation, and their own niches for profit, effects that any science of risk must remain attendant to.

Notes

1   See Ulrich Beck, *Risk Society: Towards a New Modernity* (London: Sage, 1992); Ulrich Beck, Anthony Giddens and Scott Lash, *Reflexive Modernization: Politics, Tradition and Aesthetics in the Modern Social Order* (Cambridge: Polity Press, 1994); and Bruno Latour, 'Is Re-Modernization Occurring – And If So, How to Prove It?', *Theory, Culture and Society*, 20 (2003), 35–48.
2   The convener's contribution to this volume, 'Chapter 22 Regulatory spaces, physical and metaphorical: On the legal and spatial occupation of fire-safety legislation', offers a further analysis of this specific regulatory requirement.
3   See Jonathan Massey, 'Risk and Regulation in the Financial Architecture of American Homes', in *Governing by Design* (Pittsburgh: University of Pittsburgh Press, 2012): Jonathan Massey, 'Risk Design', *Grey Room*, 54 (2014), 6–33; and Catherine Fennell '"Project Heat" and Sensory Politics in Redeveloping Chicago Public Housing', *Ethnography*, 12 (2015), 40–64.

Chapter 32

Unapproved Document, Part O: Design for Ageing

Sarah Wigglesworth

Contrary to many people's preconceptions, building regulations are written not so much as prescriptive rules (although there are some rules) but rather, as performance specifications. This is to say that many of their provisions state the standards to be achieved but leave it to the design team, and budget, in the manner and demonstration of how to achieve them. The 'deemed-to-satisfy' provisions, therefore, are simply the default solution. Given time, money and an enlightened Building Control Officer, or even better, an Approved Inspector collaborating with the design team, inventive solutions are available. In reality, a constructive and intelligent dialogue on aims and methods with skilled people negotiating towards a satisfactory solution can be a rewarding aspect of the designer's role.

According to Richard Harrall, an architect working for the Department for Communities and Local Government, who is responsible for drafting building regulations, they are at their heart about people and their behaviour, rather than simply the mute fabric of the buildings. Addressing the 'Creative Potential of Regulations' workshop that Rob Imrie, Emma Street and I organised at the Industries of Architecture conference (Newcastle University, 2014), Harrall explored why and how regulation has come about and the mechanisms through which new regulation is introduced and enacted. Insights included the degree of scrutiny that is demanded in the process of bringing new regulation forward. Currently, every outcome in this process is monetised to ensure it will provide value (note the 'cost of a life' is reckoned at £1.37 million) and each proposed piece of legislation is subject to the 'one in, two out' rule. This states that for every pound spent on enacting a new item of regulation, two pounds of savings must be found.

It should be remembered that the recent backdrop to this has been the coalition government's interest in deregulation. Furthermore, Harrall posited to the architects and academics present that, while there are committees of experts scrutinising and making recommendations on proposed new regulations, to the extent that we elect the governments that are responsible for those laws, it is ultimately a democratic process in which we are all involved.

In my introduction to the participatory exercise which followed his talk I raised the idea that recent regulation has begun to respond to the interests of specific groups of users such as the disabled, and that the general drift of regulation is shifting from being about the basic tenets of avoiding endangering or killing people to more aspirational and affirmative aspects that include wellbeing and quality of life. With the removal of the Code for Sustainable Homes,[1] for example, it is possible that the building regulations will pick up some of the requirements around areas such as day-lighting – aspects of building design that incorporate an element of comfort and quality. There would be social gains too: by addressing areas of design that promote wellbeing, health and independence in the older population, we stand a chance of their living longer and better lives, and living more economically with less strain on increasingly expensive resources.

We asked workshop participants to explore the possibility of a regulation that would address the needs of the ageing population and to consider the following:

- How might design professionals respond to the needs of older people?
- What role does regulation have in responding to those needs?
- What form could a regulation covering the needs of older people take, and what issues might it cover?
- How might it be created?
- Should such a regulation be applicable to all environments or only selected ones?

The workshop touched on many aspects of growing older, and, surprisingly, perhaps, focused mainly on how to configure society to overcome its limitations. Discussion included how to organise communities to promote health and wellbeing and avoid isolation, and the difficulty of addressing the range of issues encountered across a wide age spectrum.

Following the workshop, and taking a different tack, I produced an 'Unapproved Document' which builds on the work of the DWELL project.[2] It addresses the workshop theme directly by making a speculative exploration of the contents of what a building regulation dealing with ageing could comprise (Figure 32.1). Taking its format and language from the official Approved Documents, the 'guidance' that introduces the document explains it as a provocation that nevertheless offers a set of new require-ments to be met – more as guidelines than as prescriptive solutions, and open in terms of compliance:

> This speculative document is the first in what may become a series of provocations intended to explore potential scenarios for future Building Regulations. It has not been approved by the Secretary of State, and it does

Figure 32.1
**Unapproved Document
O: Design for Ageing:
front and rear covers.
Copyright Sarah
Wigglesworth. Graphics
by Fran Williams at
Sarah Wigglesworth
Architects**

not yet form part of the current Building Regulations' Approved Documents. However it is intended to provide guidance for some of the most common building situations encountered by older people. There may be many ways of achieving compliance with the requirements. Thus there is no obligation to adopt any particular solution contained in an Unapproved Document if you prefer to meet the relevant requirement in some other way.

The DWELL team framed its requirements in terms of performance criteria, and attempted to define older people's wellbeing as the key outcome that should be met:

In the research team's view, the requirements will be met by making reasonable provision to ensure that buildings are healthy, pleasurable, suitable and manageable by older people.

People, regardless of age, gender, ethnicity, status, ability or wealth should be able to:
(a)   live in buildings that promote their independence, happiness, conviviality, security and safety;
(b)   engage with the external world easily and economically.

The provisions are expected to enable older people to cope better on their own and live well, as active participants in their communities, assisting independence and connectivity. The provisions are not necessarily expected to facilitate fully independent living for all older people, especially the very old or those with disabilities.

The first requirement is aspirational and states clearly that 'wellbeing' for older people would involve the right to quality of life, and mobility and connectivity with the outside world:

Access and Use
Wellbeing in housing for older people
O1. Reasonable provision shall be made for older people to:
(a) live a happy, healthy, independent and secure life; and
(b) move about in and make connections with all aspects of the outside world.

Yet it is left to the agreement between client, user, Building Control Officer (or Approved Inspector) and the designer to define what is an appropriate solution for any given circumstance. Addressing this requirement means referring to the Definitions on page 8 of the document, which offer interpretations of concepts such as happiness, independence and wellbeing (see Figure 32.2).

Reproduced below (Figures 32.2, 32.3, 32.4 and 32.5) are pages 8–11 of the 'Unapproved Document'. These extracts illustrate the principles behind the speculative regulation. By proposing a regulation as a way of meeting the aspirations of a growing section of the population, we hope it raises questions not just about how we make better and more economical provision for ageing in the built environment and the role of regulation within that, but also about what constitutes quality of life and design's contribution towards it.

Notes

1   The Planning and Energy Act 2008 gave power to Local Authorities to set Code for Sustainable Homes requirements through the planning consent process. This power has now been removed through the Deregulation Act 2015, which received Royal Assent on 26 March 2015. The new edition of the Building Regulations (anticipated to come into effect in 2016) will in future become the mechanism for picking up increased energy-efficiency in dwellings. This will also cover water use, access and space standards, and they will be optional.
2   DWELL is 'Designing for Wellbeing in Environments for Later Life', a three-year interdisciplinary research project led by Professor Sarah Wigglesworth and based at the University of Sheffield. The project uses participatory and co-design to develop exemplary designs for housing and neighbourhoods and explores the mechanisms for the delivery and management of these. It is funded jointly by the EPSRC, the ESRC and the AHRC.

The Building Regulations 2016

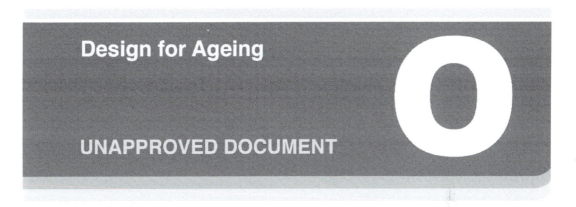

O1   General Guidance
O2   Dwellings

2016 edition - for use in England*

Figure 32.2
Unapproved Document O: Design for Ageing: front cover. Copyright Sarah Wigglesworth. Graphics by Fran Williams at Sarah Wigglesworth Architects

 **Design for Ageing**

Definitions

The following are key terms used in this document:

Accessible
In relation to buildings or parts of buildings, means that people are able to gain access regardless of age, gender, ethnicity, status, ability or wealth.

Amenity
An outdoor place for peaceful personal fulfilment and leisure.

Suitable
Means appropriate, responsive to and relating specifically to the needs of the older occupant.

Connectivity
Means the capacity for engaging with other people, places, concepts and events.

Dwelling
Means a house or flat ("flat" is defined in regulation 2(1)).

Engage
Means actively take part or participate in.

Happiness
Means being in a state of fulfilment and contentment.

Independent
Means being capable of making choices and take action by and for oneself without the need for assistance from others.

Manageable
Means the ability of the occupant to live life independently and operate a building's systems without assistance both internally and externally.

Mobility
Means the ability to move around internally and externally, and make meaningful connections with places, people, nature, or events.

Wellbeing
Means a state of good physical and mental health, autonomy, sufficient resources to get by, and the ability to connect to people, places and events in a meaningful way.

Figure 32.3
Extract from Unapproved Document O: Design for Ageing: p. 8. Copyright Sarah Wigglesworth. Graphics by Fran Williams at Sarah Wigglesworth Architects

Design for Ageing

Section 1: Dwellings

Objectives

1.1 The aim of this new document is to provide for the wellbeing of older people as they age. It adds to, and must be read in conjunction with, the existing body of Regulations; this requires the designer to exercise judgment in their application and prioritisation.

1.2 The Regulations aim to secure Wellbeing for older people in dwellings, but it is recognised that what applies to older people is applicable to all people. It is expected that AD_O will become the adopted standard for all types of dwelling.

Approach to the dwelling

1.3 All thresholds should be level to permit wheeled vehicles to pass easily into the dwelling. Follow the guidance given in AD_M.

1.4 External entrance thresholds to dwellings shall provide sufficient space to allow for personalisation. They shall be generous enough to provide a place to rest, to chat to neighbours, shelter from the weather and grow plants. If possible they should provide sufficient space to store and charge a mobility vehicle.

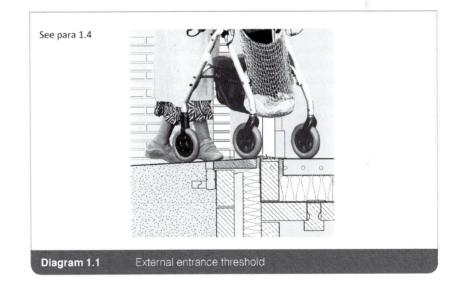

See para 1.4

Diagram 1.1   External entrance threshold

Figure 32.4
Extract from Unapproved Document O: Design for Ageing: p. 9. Copyright Sarah Wigglesworth. Illustration by Adam Park, copyright DWELL project and the University of Sheffield. Graphics by Fran Williams at Sarah Wigglesworth Architects

Design for Ageing

Space Standards

1.5 Space standards for older people need to be larger than a normal house if it is to remain resilient to life changes. Dwellings also need to be capable of accommodating changes such as rails and hoists as and when they may be required, and should be designed accordingly. Dwelling sizes should follow Lifetime Homes guidance as a minimum to allow for a future of limited mobility (www.lifetimehomes.org). Where possible larger accommodation should be provided which accommodates wheelchair users (GWDG).

1.6 Within the provisions of AD_B, dwellings should be designed to be open plan so that those people confined to bed can participate in the social life around them. There should be sufficient openings to enable this, such as sliding doors between rooms, which shall be minimum 1500mm wide measured between door stops.

1.7 An area of 2.5 width x 2.5 depth in plan shall be provided for storage of a lifetime's possessions. This may be within a dwelling or external but if it is external it shall be easily accessible, subject to the same provisions of accessibility as the dwelling itself.

1.8 Sufficient space shall be provided to allow a carer or relative to live with the occupant. Where it is not possible to provide this in a separate room, provision shall be made for a temporary bedspace that can accommodate a carer staying for up to a month, such as a fold-down or sofa bed or a guest apartment provided as part of the dwelling complex.

See para 1.10

Diagram 1.2   Connections with relatives and the outside world

Figure 32.5
Extract from Unapproved Document O: Design for Ageing: p. 10. Copyright Sarah Wigglesworth. Illustration by Adam Park, copyright DWELL project and the University of Sheffield. Graphics by Fran Williams at Sarah Wigglesworth Architects

Design for Ageing

1.9 Sufficient space shall be provided to allow for hobbies, pets and for the accommodation of a special piece of furniture, for example, a dresser, dressing table, wardrobe or dining table.

Steps
1.10 Any steps used shall be shallow and shall have handrails provided in accordance with public buildings requirements of AD_M and AD_K.

Outdoor space
1.11 Private outdoor amenity space shall be provided which is minimum 1.5 deep x 2.5m wide and accessible by level threshold from the interior of the dwelling.

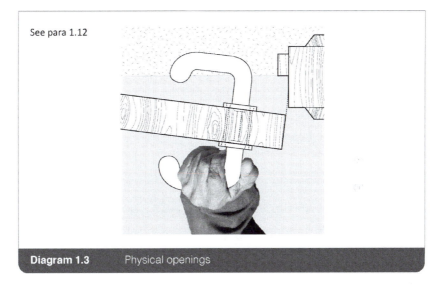

See para 1.12

Diagram 1.3   Physical openings

Security
1.12 All dwellings shall have appropriate security devices to provide the ability for an older person to monitor who is visiting both in the street and outside their door from a chair in their living room or their bed.

1.13 Every dwelling shall have appropriate security devices to ensure reasonable peace of mind. Nothing herein shall however contravene the provisions for means of escape set out in AD_B.

Figure 32.6
Extract from Unapproved Document O: Design for Ageing: p. 11. Copyright Sarah Wigglesworth. Illustration by Adam Park, copyright DWELL project and the University of Sheffield. Graphics by Fran Williams at Sarah Wigglesworth Architects

Index